My Journey with the United Nations and Quest for the Horn of Africa's Unity and Justice for Ethiopia

By
Kidane Alemayehu

RoseDog Books
PITTSBURGH, PENNSYLVANIA 15238

RoseDog Books
585 Alpha Drive
Suite 103
Pittsburgh, PA 15238
Visit our website at www.rosedogbookstore.com

ISBN: 978-1-4809-7048-9
eISBN: 978-1-4809-7071-7

This book is dedicated to:

- The United Nations organization, the Kingdom of Lesotho, and Dubai Municipality, true partners in development;
- Ethiopian Patriots, including my forefathers who immensely contributed to Ethiopia's continued independence;
- *Qegnazmach* Abba Nada (nom de guerre; actual: *Qegnazmach* Dilnessahu Tenfu), one of those heroes who saved Harar, Ethiopia's eastern province, from being grabbed by colonialists, and for his patriotic service in the diplomatic effort which resulted in the successful Ethiopian victory against the Italian aggression at Adowa;
- My grandfather, *Grazmach* Gessesse Fanta who was martyred at the Italo-Ethiopian war in the Ogaden, Eastern Ethiopia;
- And my father, Mr. Alemayehu Gebremichael, who also fought against the Italian occupation in the same Italo-Ethiopian war in the Ogaden, Eastern Ethiopia, alongside my grandfather;
- The Global Alliance for Justice – The Ethiopian Cause (www.global-allianceforethiopia.org) under the leadership of HH Prince Ermias Sahle Selassie, Dr. Aklilu Habte, Dr. Getatchew Haile, Dr. Girma Abebe, Dr. Astair Gebremariam, Dr. Jon Levy, Dr. Mikael Wosen, Mr. Nicola DeMarco, and Dr. Steve Delamarter as well as supporters throughout the world who, despite all odds, continue with their relentless struggle for justice on behalf of Ethiopia.

Contents

Part 4

INTRODUCTION

This book comprises three phases of my life's major activities, namely, my service with the United Nations, the initiative aimed at achieving peace and development in the Horn of Africa (Djibouti, Eritrea, Ethiopia, and Somalia), and the struggle for justice owed to the Ethiopian people as a result of the huge Fascist war crimes committed with the complicit support of The Vatican.

Part I, dealing with the United Nations, is the result of 28 years of service with the organization in ten countries in Africa and the Middle East. The other parts (Parts II and III) deal with my 14 years struggle for peace and unity in the Horn of Africa as well as for the justice denied to Ethiopia for the Fascist Italian crimes committed during 1935-41.

The countries and the UN agencies where I served as a UN Team Leader/Expert/Consultant were, in chronological order, as follows:

1. Lesotho/UN International Telecommunications Union:
    a. Director of Posts, Telecommunications, and Civil Aviation;
    b. Permanent Secretary for the Ministry of Public Works;
2. Tanzania/UN Department of Technical Cooperation and Development, later taken over by the UN Center for Human Settlements (UN-Habitat):
3. Senior Management Expert and Chief Technical Advisor(CTA) to the then Ministry of Capital Development; and, later, Consultant to the Tanzanian Ministry of Planning.
4. UN Center of Human Settlements (UN Habitat), Nairobi, Kenya: Inter-Regional Advisor including short-term consultancy missions at:
    a. Botswana;

> b. Swaziland;
> c. Malawi;
> d. Uganda;
> e. Nigeria; and
> f. The Gambia;

5. United Arab Emirates (UAE)/UN Center for Human Settlements (UN-Habitat):
   > a. Consultant and, later, Senior Management Expert/CTA at the Ministry of Works and Housing;
   > b. Consultant at UAE University;

6. Qatar/UN Center for Human Settlements (UN-Habitat):
   > a. Institutional Development Consultant for Doha Municipality;

7. United Arab Emirates (UAE)/UN Center for Human Settlements (UN-Habitat);
   > a. Senior Management Expert/CTA at Dubai Municipality;
   > b. Consultant to the UAE University;
   > c. " " UAE Development Board;
   > d. " " Dubai Emirate's Central Government Garage;
   > e. " " Dubai Emirate's Transport corporation;
   > f. " " UAE Ministry of Public Works and Housing;
   > g. " " UAE Federal Environmental Agency.

My work assignments varied from an operational assistance in a substantive post, termed OPAS (Operational Assistance) Expert, in the case of Lesotho; to a UN expert and a project team leader service in Tanzania, and the United Arab Emirates; and to UN consultancy services in various countries.

Part II deals with the struggle for peace and unity among the countries of the Horn of Africa, where nearly 115 million people live, mostly, in abject poverty, and lack of democracy as well as prevalence of instability despite the abundance of natural resources including the Nile river which provides 86% of the water that cascades to Egypt as well as the rich agricultural and mineral potential. Lack of democracy, and appropriate development policy have contributed to the prevalence of instability where people have not been able to capitalize on the rich agricultural and mineral potential. An attempt is made to provide a glimpse of the region's historic background and to relate the current challenges as well as the opportunities for overcoming them for the achievement of peace, unity, and development in the region with the support of and the mutual benefit of the international community. It highlights the important prospect of achieving an unprecedented collaboration for peace and development among the countries surrounding the Red Sea.

Part III is concerned with the effort to achieve justice with regard to the Fascist war crimes perpetrated in Ethiopia, with the Vatican's complicit support during 1935-41. As a result of the use of various war materials including the internationally forbidden poison gas that was sprayed in many parts of Ethiopia with numerous Fascist war planes, one million Ethiopians were massacred including my grandfather, *Grazmach* Gessesse Fanta. 2,000 churches and 525,000 homes were destroyed. The outcome was catastrophic causing a huge environmental disaster resulting in the loss of an estimated 14 million animals. In addition, numerous Ethiopian properties were looted and still remain in the custody of the Vatican and the Italian Government. For all the war crimes, Ethiopia has never been adequately compensated nor has the Vatican apologized to the Ethiopian people.

This book also attempts to present, concisely, some of the main roles, outputs, and tangible impacts achieved by the UN projects in which I was involved as a UN expert/consultant and team leader at the request of the concerned member countries. Many of the methodologies applied in the various projects as well as the concrete outputs achieved were of practical benefit to the concerned institutions including those engaged in municipal administration and local government, public works, human resources development and management as well as those who provide consultancy/expert services in institutional development and human settlements activities. It underlines the important management systems that are critical to the achievement of the required effectiveness and efficiency in human settlements services including the formulation of strategies, policies, plans and work programs, performance indicators and appraisal/monitoring systems, delegation of authority, regulatory frameworks, operational systems, customer-oriented services...etc.

The United Nations is typically known as an international organization that is focused on global political issues of peace, human rights, conflict prevention and resolution. The typical general awareness about the United Nations revolves around its General Assembly meetings, the UN Security Council, and, to a lesser extent, on some of its vital agencies such as WHO (UN World Health Organization), UNHCR (UN High Commissioner for Refugees), FAO (UN Food and Agricultural Organization), IAEA (UN International Atomic Energy Agency), etc. Very little is known about numerous other UN agencies and services without which the world would be chaotic. These include ITU (International Telecommunications Union) which facilitates and coordinates international telecommunications services; UNCHS (UN Center for Human Settlements also known as UN-Habitat) which has the mandate on global urban and rural settlements including the required land, housing, environmental and infrastructural services; and UNDP (UN Development Program) that has the mandate of funding and monitoring development projects implemented in various countries by UN executing agencies such as ITU and UNCHS with which I was associated in my 28 years of service with the United Nations.

For the purpose of writing this book, I travelled to Lesotho, Tanzania, Kenya, and the United Arab Emirates during November, 2011 to January, 2012 and was able to collect, wherever possible, the available background information and data from concerned organizations and former counterparts. Due to resources and time constraints, it was not possible to undertake travels to the other countries where I had worked as an expert and/or consultant. The update process was, by itself, quite interesting as some counterparts who were on mid- to junior staff management levels had, in the years since I left the particular country, shot up to much more prominent posts. A few examples of these include H.E. Mr. Tim Thahane who was Director of Planning of Lesotho during my assignment there as an expert, became his nation's Minister of Finance; Mr. Percy Mangoaela who took over from me as Lesotho's Director of Posts, Telecommunications and Civil Aviation eventually retired after a distinguished service with the United Nations; Mr. P. Phofoolo who initially took over as Assistant Director of Posts subsequently rose to the post of Senior Permanent Secretary of Lesotho as head of the Kingdom's entire civil service as well as being secretary to the Cabinet and the Prime Minister; and Mr. Mohammed Abdelkarim Julfar who was my counterpart as head of the Administrative Development Office rose to the important post of Assistant Director General for the Corporate Support Sector which comprised the financial, human resources, information technology, contracts and purchasing departments of Dubai Municipality. Another example was Mr. Faisal al Gurg who was Director of Planning in the Ministry of Works and Housing in the United Arab Emirates was later elevated to the post of Director-General of the Sheikh Zaid Housing Program in the United Arab Emirates until he retired following a distinguished service. It is important to note that these counterparts as well as many others including other project staff have, in their own rights, made significant contributions to the development of the respective countries. That is the true meaning of sustainability.

There were, unfortunately, other cases of counterparts who had passed away including the Hon. Minister of Works of Lesotho, H.E. Mr. K.

Maphathe, and Mr. Peter Ndosi, Director of Planning at the then Ministry of Capital Development in Tanzania. I would like to express my heartfelt condolences to members of their families as well as my appreciation in memory of their services.

ACKNOWLEDGMENT

I wish to acknowledge, with the utmost appreciation and thanks, the very extensive support provided by the numerous organizations and individuals I consulted including, especially, Dr. Daniel Biau, former Director of the Regional and Technical Cooperation Department of UNCHS – HABITAT; H.E. Mr. Tim Thahane, former Minister of Finance of the Lesotho Government; H.E. Mr. Qassim Sultan, former Director General of Dubai Municipality; H.E. Mr. Faisal Al-Gurg, former Director of Planning at the Ministry of Public Works and Housing of the United Arab Emirates and, later, Director General of the Sheikh Zaid Housing Programme; and H.E. Mr. Paanya Monyane Phoofolo, Lesotho's former Senior Permanent Secretary, for their respective contributions, included in this book, as statements of their recollections regarding my participation in the various UN projects. My appreciation is also due to Mr. Kitila, Director General of Tanzania's Capital Development Authority; Mr. Mohamed el Sioufi of UN-Habitat; Mr. Mohammed Abdelkarim Julfar, Dubai Municipality's Assistant Director General for the Corporate Support Sector; and Mrs. Sabina Fernandes, Secretary at Dubai Municipality and former member of the project's support staff.

All the United Nations experts, consultants, associate experts, specialists, and local counterpart staff deserve the highest appreciation for their dedicated services for the achievement of the respective projects' objectives.

My thanks are also due to Prof. Bahru Zewde, for his review, incisive remarks and suggestions regarding my presentation concerning the Horn of Africa.

My sincere thanks are also owed to my friends, Mr. Betru Gebregziabher and Mr. Teferawork Assefa for their encouragement in the writing of this book.

I would also like to express my gratitude to Dr. Yacob Hailemariam, Prof. Theodore Vestal and Mr. Semere Habtemariam for their meticulous review of this book's manuscript.

A special word of appreciation and gratitude is due to my wife, Amsale Hailu, without whose unstinting support this book would have not been possible.

Medal of honor granted to me during the reign of Haile Selassie I

PART 1

MY JOURNEY WITH THE UNITED NATIONS

With Dr. Joan Clos, Executive Director of the UN Center for the Human Settlements

Chapter 1: United Nations Assignment in Lesotho (1972-78)

Director of Posts, Telecommunications, and Civil Aviation (1972-76) (UN OPAS Expert)

It was in February, 1972 when the then General Manager of the Imperial Board of Telecommunications of Ethiopia (IBTE), Mr. Betru Admassie, called one morning and informed me that the United Nations (UN) International Telecommunications Union (ITU) had asked for a nominee from Ethiopia for the post of Director of Posts, Telecommunications (PT) and Civil Aviation in the Kingdom of Lesotho. Furthermore he had decided to nominate me for the post for a contract period of two years. I was rather surprised by the offer since I had not expressed any intention or desire to join the UN; in fact, a few years earlier, I had declined a similar offer by UNESCO to work at its headquarters in Paris, France. I, therefore, requested the General Manager to give me some time to think about it.

Two weeks after the nomination, I was informed that both the ITU and the Lesotho Government had accepted my nomination and that I had to proceed to Geneva, Switzerland for a briefing and travel thereafter to Lesotho immediately. The briefing was conducted in Geneva at the ITU headquarters in March, 1972. I arrived at Maseru, Lesotho at the beginning of April, 1972.

When I look back and think about the possible reasons for being selected by the United Nations, the Ethiopian Government, and the Lesotho Government to serve in Lesotho, I believe it was due to my experience, primarily, as the head of the Administration Division of the Imperial Board of Telecommunications of Ethiopia (IBTE) with special responsibilities for Organization and Methods, Human Resources, Legal Services, and the Telecommunications Institute. My 15-year experience by that time, also included service, in IBTE, as a Public Relations Officer, and Assistant Head of Purchasing. During my tenure as IBTE's Administration Division Manager I had, at ITU's invitation, served as one of the instructors in its Management Seminar in Tananarivo, Madagascar. Previously I had served as an Administrator at the Commercial School in Addis Ababa as well as a short stint at Ethiopia's Ministry of Interior. Here, I recall, with appreciation, the scholarship I had been granted by USAID to study Business Administration at the American University of Beirut in Lebanon.

Emperor Haile Selassie I delivering a short speech at the inauguration ceremony of the IBTE headquarters building. I was taking notes of his speech.

Department of Posts, Telecommunications, and Civil Aviation in 1972-76

In April 1972 I took over as the Director of the Department, from a British colonial expatriate, while simultaneously serving as a UN OPAS (Operational Assistance) Expert. This arrangement meant that I was working as a civil servant—being paid the salary due to a Department Director and subject to

Lesotho's civil service regulations; while the UN made up the difference according to its payment scale for an Expert.

It was only six years after Lesotho's independence from British colonialism that I arrived at its capital city, Maseru. Lesotho was headed by its monarch, His Majesty King Moshoeshoe II, and the Prime Minister, The Honourable Mr. Leabua Jonathan. The ruling party was the Basotho National Party (BNP) while the main opposition party in parliament was the Basotho Congress Party (BCP).

The Department of Posts, Telecommunications and Civil Aviation was operating under the auspices of the Ministry of Works which had a mandate over a variety of activities including works, transportation, water, electricity, posts, telecommunications, and civil aviation.

Despite its independence, Lesotho was still highly dependent on its colonial civil servants. For instance, key posts such as the Chief of Police, the Permanent Secretary for Finance, and several other important Government offices were manned by remnants of the British rule. In the Department of Posts, Telecommunications and Civil Aviation, the situation was dire as the posts from the Assistant Director to the Foreman levels, as well as, virtually all technical and administrative posts were held by former expatriate colonial civil servants. Lesotho's postal, telecommunications, and civil aviation services were, to a major extent, dependent or linked to the South African services. South Africa was under an apartheid regime!

For a detailed presentation on the conditions that prevailed in Lesotho during the early 70's and the process through which the UN project was initiated as well as its impact, please see, at the end of this chapter, Recollection No. 1 by H.E. Mr. Tim Thahane, Lesotho's former Minister of Finance, and Membeer of Parliament as well as Recollection No. 2 by H.E. Mr. Paanya Phoofolo, Lesotho's former ambassador and Senior Permanent Secretary.

Major Constraints

The Department had no plan. In the case of telecommunications, it was remarkable to note that, for instance, there was no record of the telecommunications line networks and, therefore, workers were digging in various directions to find and repair a faulty cable. I found this out when I conducted a field visit to check on a telephone repair that had taken over a month to deal with!

The telecommunications service was very limited and mostly available in Maseru and a few other urban areas. The rural areas were not serviced. Lesotho's international telecommunications services had to go through apartheid South Africa's network.

His Majesty King Moshoeshoe II, 4th from left, Queen Moshoeshoe, 3rd left, myself, first from right.

The number of post offices in the country was very small concentrated in the main urban areas and virtually excluding the rural, especially the mountain regions. Here again, there was a heavy reliance on the South African postal service for international mail.

The Civil Aviation sector was operating Lesotho Airways and a minor flight control station adjacent to a golf course that also served as an airport accommodating only small aircraft such as Cessna. Lesotho did not even have a single local pilot!

Unique Challenges:

In addition to the huge, fundamental challenges that Lesotho faced: lack of plans, adequate financing, and trained human resources, as well as the constraints faced by the country as a whole due to the poor infrastructure network; there were, also, unique problems that had to be dealt with.

One such problem was the highly racist attitude of the expatriate senior staff who continued to serve in the Department after Lesotho's independence. One example of this predicament was the Assistant Director for Telecommunications, Dr. Kiderlen, a South African. About a month after my arrival in Lesotho, I invited him to discuss ideas for formulating the Department's strategy and action plan as well as commencing the training of local staff (Basotho) in order to hand over the work to them in due course.

His response astounded me! He told me that Lesotho, being a tiny country, did not need any plan and that as regards the training of the Basotho, he stated:

> "Do you want me to train Mothibi? He is no better than a monkey!"

Mr. Mothibi was among the better qualified Basotho staff with some telecommunications network skills, however limited they might have been. Dr. Kiderlen's response made it obvious that he was not suited to Lesotho's particular needs: the planning and development of its telecommunications services in the urban and rural areas as well as enhancing its self-reliance for international services, and human resources for a sustainable development. Under the circumstances, Dr. Kiderlen was replaced by an expert from the Netherlands with the core competencies for planning, development and training.[1]

Another example of the expatriates' negative attitude was the one by the then Assistant Director for Civil Aviation, Mr. Higginson, who had no hesitation in telling me that there were no Basotho with adequate mathematics and science capabilities to be trained as pilots and that there was no land in Lesotho which was suitable to be used for an airport. As we will see hereunder, he was found wrong on both counts.

It is fair to mention that not all the expatriate colonial staff had a negative attitude towards the local, Basotho staff. Although few in number, some were positively inclined in responding to the new management system of assigning local counterparts to each expatriate for training and eventual handing over of the respective posts. An example of such a positive outcome was Mr. Van der Merve who was a telegraph technician and was able to train his counterpart thoroughly within the stipulated time and departed from Lesotho at the end of his contract period. I recall that I was the one who made the glowing speech about him at his farewell party. He finally came over to me to tell me that he could not believe that I was talking about him!

Resource Constraints

The other major constraints were the lack of financial and human resources. The department had to fight for its share of the meager national resources as well as utilizing all the means at its disposal for raising its own revenue. The department's revenues had to be transferred to the Ministry of Finance, which was the main organ for allocating the budgetary provisions to the various ministries and departments, after approval by the cabinet of ministers.

An additional weakness that had a significant financial consequence was the fact that most procurements for the department such as telecommunications equipment, order of new postage stamps…etc. were conducted from the United Kingdom, without any competition, through the British Crown Agents, a British Government purchasing agency.

Need for Educated Local Human Resources

The most serious challenge was, however, the very limited availability of local trained human resources in all the Department's sections. There was no national of Lesotho (Mosotho: singular; Basotho: plural) with a university degree in the department at that time; and no technician with the necessary skills. Therefore, the prospect for a sustainable development was in serious jeopardy.

In view of the above mentioned constraints, it became evident that a comprehensive and an integrated development strategy had to be formulated and the process itself generated yet another amazing challenge! This concerned the formulation of a telecommunication strategy which was to be arranged, with my naïve trust, through a technical assistance offered by the United Kingdom. When the huge proposal document finally arrived following a field visit by a British expert, its main objective turned out to be to eliminate the new Director of PT and Civil Aviation, i.e. myself! I was asked for comments by the Lesotho Government's Planning Department as well as the United Nations Development Program (UNDP). I suggested that the best course of action would be to bring in another telecommunications consultant to evaluate the document as well as the actual situation in the Department. A German consultant arrived soon and delivered his professional verdict which resulted in the rejection of the British consultant's report.

Main Achievements in Lesotho
Formulation of a Comprehensive Development Strategy and Action Plan
A development strategy and action plan was formulated for the telecommunications, postal, and civil aviation services with technical assistance by the Swedish Government, the British Commonwealth, and the UN International Civil Aviation Organization respectively. The action plan anticipated the provision of postal and telecommunications services in both urban and rural areas progressively as well as the establishment of a radio communication station that would enable Lesotho to have its own independent international telecommunications service. It was also recommended that the telecommunications service be operated as an independent entity so that it would generate and utilize its own revenues.

The most important initiative in the civil aviation sector was the identification of a suitable area for the construction of an appropriate airport for Lesotho, which is operational today as well as the production of Basotho pilots with assistance by the UN and the British Commonwealth.

Human Resources Development and Self-Reliance
There is no doubt that the most critical contribution by the United Nations to Lesotho's development in the postal, telecommunications and civil aviation sectors was the action taken, with the approval of the Lesotho Government, in assigning local nationals (Basotho) to key posts in the various sections. Among the early recruits were the young Basotho with relevant university education. They were given some practical and on-the-job training at home as well as in some other countries.

Some of the early recruits included Mr. Percy Mangoaela, who initially took over as the Assistant Department Director for Civil Aviation, eventually becoming, in 1976, my counterpart as the Department's Director Mr. Paanya Phoofolo subsequently took over as the Assistant Department Director for Postal Services, and Mr. Matsobane Putsoa became the head of the Accounts Section.

Some of the unprecedented historic achievements in the human resources sector included the training of Basotho in Zaria, Nigeria as well as in Scotland to become pilots. This achievement was considered so phenomenal in the context of the prevailing apartheid system in neighboring South Africa that the event of the new Basotho pilot graduates had become a major news item in the region!

Training sessions were arranged for lower category staff in the postal, telecommunications and civil aviation sections so that they would achieve at least the minimum skills and attitude to work including the prevalence of an outlook that was oriented towards an appropriate customer care. Attention to staff services through field visits at various locations greatly enhanced employee morale and productivity.

The young Basotho graduates who joined the Department used their opportunities for leadership with great success thereby making it possible for the United Nations project to achieve its fundamental objective of facilitating Lesotho's self-reliance and sustainability.

One other success story related to human resources development was the establishment of a regional training center in Malawi to serve the needs of the countries in southern Africa including Lesotho.

Expansion of Services

As stated above, the initial focus was on the formulation of a development strategy and action plan as well as the recruitment and training of local Basotho staff. This was followed by the improvement of existing services after which developmental activities ensued in all the three services of the telecommunications, postal, and civil aviation.

For instance, the new Chief Engineer for the telecommunications services was able to train the local staff that facilitated a more efficient service. At the same time he was working on the implementation of the telecommunications development plan which had been prepared with the assistance of the Swedish Government utilizing the expertise from Swedtel. The plan included the establishment of a telecommunications radio station to facilitate Lesotho's independence in international service. Lesotho was actively engaged as a member of the International Telecommunications Union (ITU). I recall, for instance, that I led the Lesotho delegation to the international ITU conference at Malaga-Torremolinos, Spain in 1973 where, among other things, Lesotho's interests were adequately represented. By coincidence, it was at that conference that apartheid South Africa was suspended from the organization with the fundamental reason that the apartheid system did not facilitate communication among human beings.

Lesotho's postal service was extended to the rural areas. In addition, Lesotho became an active member of the Universal Postal Union with its own international postal services.

The department's acquisition system for the supply of required materials, equipment, postage stamps, services, etc. was changed completely to a self-reliant system. Work on the preliminary study of the new airport project commenced. The ICAO consultant's study revealed that there were three alternative sites in Lesotho that could be used as airports one of which was eventually approved and constructed by the Government.

For more information on the challenges and impact achieved in the postal, telecommunications, and civil aviation services, please see Recollection No. 2 by H.E. Mr. Paanya Monyane Phoofolo at the end of this chapter.

Handing Over To The Counterpart
By early 1976, that is four years after my arrival in Lesotho, the basic elements for self-reliance were in place. These included, in particular, the timely assignment and training of my counterpart, at my request, of Mr. Percy Mangoaela who proved capable to take on the post of Director of Posts, Telecommunications and Civil Aviation.

Upon completion of my assignment, I was ready to depart Lesotho for Ethiopia when, however, the Lesotho Government and the UN came up with another idea!

Permanent Secretary for the Ministry of Works (UN OPAS Expert) (1976-78)
After the successful handing over of the post of Director of PT and Civil Aviation to the counterpart, Mr. Percy Mangoaela, I was offered another assignment by the Lesotho Government and the UN to work as Permanent Secretary for the Ministry of Works. I commenced this assignment in April 1976.

The Ministry of Works was responsible for the design, construction and maintenance of government buildings, roads and bridges; water and sewerage affairs; electrical services; Government furniture; hydrology and mete-orology; as well as a plant and mechanical workshop. The Ministry was headed by a cabinet Minister under whom served a Permanent Secretary and a Deputy Permanent Secretary. There were two general sectors, namely, Works (Architecture, Water and Sewerage, Meteorology and Hydrology, and Roads Sections); and the Plant Pool & Mechanical Workshop (Plant Pool, Workshops, Transport, and Finance services). There was also a Principal Assistant Secretary who was responsible for administrative, personnel, and accounting services. In addition, the Lesotho Electricity Corporation was operating under the auspices of the Ministry of Works as a parastatal (semi-government) organization.

Main Constraints Faced by the Ministry of Public Works
In 1976, the Ministry was facing numerous internal and external challenges some of which made it extremely difficult to perform even its routine tasks[2]. The most serious constraints were the following:

1. The Ministry was operating under a severe understaffing as 45% approved posts were vacant.
2. The approved budget for 1976/77 was obtained four months after the beginning of the year.
3. The flow of funds for approved projects was even worse. For instance, of the 50 approved building projects for 1976/77, funds were obtained for only four of the projects four months after the beginning of the fiscal year. A similar predicament was being faced with regard to other operations. Internal control and decision making processes left a lot to be desired. Employee morale was low. My preliminary report had indicated, among other things:
4. The Ministry's management system including its planning, implementation, and monitoring operations left a lot to be desired. According to my report at the time[3]:
    "4.4.1 Very serious problems adversely affecting implementation of projects are (a) an inefficient budget process, (b) lack of timely preparedness on the part of Ministries, and (c) over-centralization of the civil service procedures and (d) delays and complex terms and conditions imposed by donors.
    4.4.2 It is essential to rationalize the administrative processes so that by reorganization, decentralization and streamlining procedures it

would be possible to cut down on red tape and get on with the job of project implementation. In particular, every effort should be made so that by the beginning of the fiscal year everything is ready for implementation unlike the present situation whereby the budget process is still incomplete and then the various inputs are not forthcoming until a good part of the fiscal year is already over!"

The Ministry's organization that was prevalent at the time can be seen in Fig. 1. My proposed organization charts for the Ministry as well as a recommended Transport Authority are presented as Figs. 2 and 3.

5. The lack of adequate local human resources and training was one of the major causes militating against self-reliance and efficiency. There were 42 expatriates, mostly ex-colonial staff, at the Ministry. The number of local engineers in the Ministry was only four!

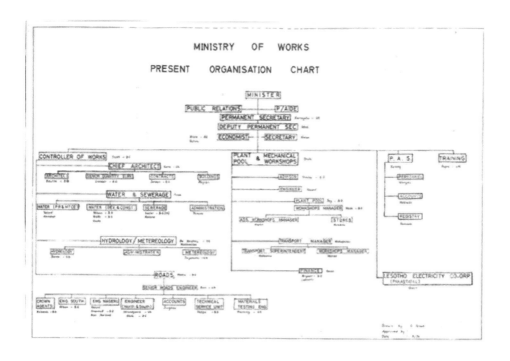

Fig 1

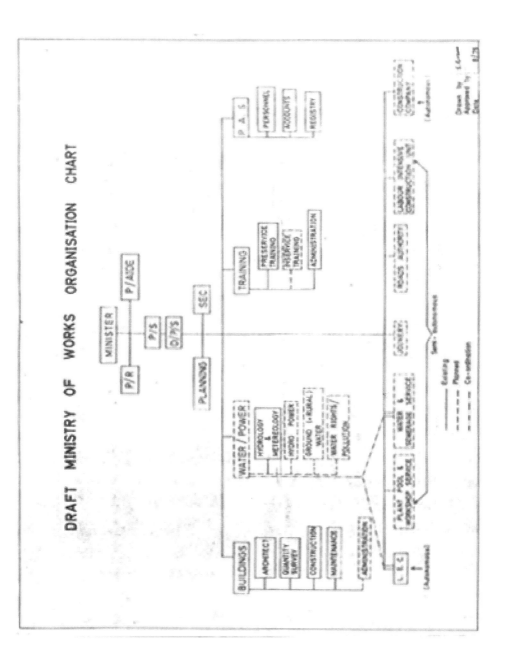

Fig 2

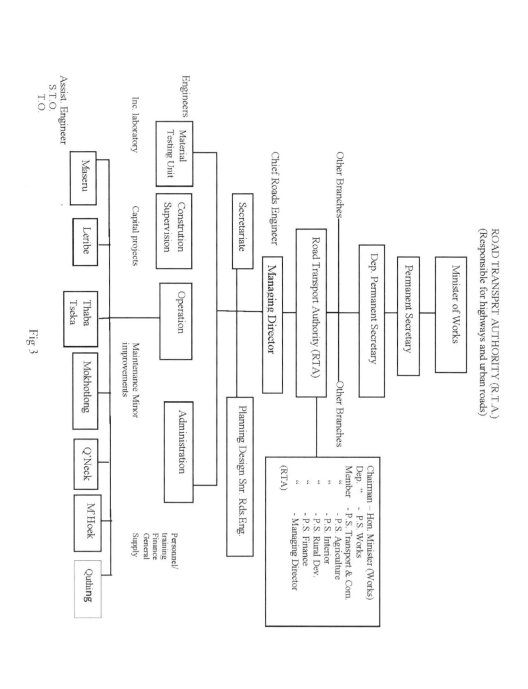

ROAD TRANSPRT AUTHORITY (R.T.A.)
(Responsible for highways and urban roads)

Fig 3

6. The Ministry was not focusing on some of the most important natural resources in the country, especially, its rich water and hydro-power potential.

7. There was a poor coordination among the concerned departments within the Ministry as well as between the Ministry and other Ministries.

8. Lesotho's private construction capacity was not only limited but also largely operating under the leadership of foreigners.

9. The University of Botswana, Lesotho, and Swaziland did not have an engineering faculty.

10. Due to limited resources and capacity, the Ministry's performance in implementing projects was extremely weak. Therefore, the Ministry was perceived as a drag in development efforts by other concerned Ministries.

11. Need to improve the Ministry's organization.

12. Lesotho's poor road network, which made it essential to use the roads within South Africa to travel from, for instance, the capital city, Maseru, to Mokhotlong in eastern Lesotho.

Main Achievements At The Ministry of Works

The following were the main achievements during the 1976-78 UN assignment at the Ministry:

1. Planning, Organization and Management Systems

One of the foremost areas of focus at the Ministry was the formulation of a strategic plan and the establishment of an institutional capacity that would facilitate a timely implementation. Therefore, a preliminary plan was recommended with regard to core areas of the Ministry's responsibilities. These included the need for enhancing the Ministry's building and roads construction and maintenance capacity, recommendations for the development of a road network that would facilitate transportation within Lesotho, especially from/to the lowlands and the rural and mountainous areas, the utilization of Lesotho's main natural resources i.e. its water and hydropower potential, the improvement of the Ministry's mechanical, workshop, and other services.

The introduction of a streamlined institutional framework was another important area of focus. As can be seen on Fig. 2, on page 13 new essential elements were recommended including a planning capacity as well as the establishment of semi-autonomous entities for certain operations such as a Roads

Authority, a Water & Sewerage Service, a Joinery unit, a Plant Pool & Workshop Service, and a Labor-Intensive Construction Unit. It was also recommended to establish an autonomous, efficient and competitive Construction Company in order to enhance Lesotho's development capacity and employment opportunities. It was further proposed that the Lesotho Electricity Corporation be elevated from being semi-autonomous to an autonomous company status so that it would operate in a fully transparent, accountable and cost-effective manner.

Among the most important achievements was the establishment of a streamlined hierarchy with clear lines of authority and responsibility. Efficient means of coordination and consultation were established with a result that employee morale within the Ministry was enhanced. For instance, the weekly management meetings of the key officials of the Ministry under the chairmanship of the Permanent Secretary were instrumental to a continuous exchange of information and decisions that facilitated expeditious action and implementation.

The Ministry's internal control system was also strengthened resulting in improved accountability and transparency as well as, in some cases, the dismissal of certain staff who were engaging in unacceptable practices. As a result the Ministry's performance was enhanced significantly.

Human Resources Development
As indicated above, one of the most serious constraints facing the Ministry in 1976 was the lack of trained local human resources. There were only four Basotho engineers available in the whole Ministry of Works. The Ministry was completely dependent on 42 mostly ex-colonial, expatriate staff who manned virtually all the key management/supervisory and professional and sub-professional posts. Therefore, it became essential to take drastic steps in order to achieve the fundamental objective of self-reliance and sustainability. This included the arrangement of engineering scholarships for 16 qualified Basotho to study civil engineering at the University of Puna in India, and training locally and abroad for the few available local staff.

Arrangements were made for the training of available local staff including Mr. Peter Ntholi, the Deputy Permanent Secretary and my counterpart who eventually took over as the Ministry's Permanent Secretary in 1978. Similar to the Department of Posts, Telecommunications, and Civil Aviation, available local (Basotho) counterparts were assigned to expatriate staff whenever possible. Unfortunately, in those days, this possibility was very limited as the number of qualified local staff was very few.

Desperate Need for Rural Roads

The huge predicament confronted by Lesotho, in those days, due to lack of suitable roads connecting the low-lying urban centers such as the capital city, Maseru, to the other settlements in the rural areas e.g. Mokhotlong was felt dramatically when the apartheid regime in South Africa suddenly closed its boarders against Lesotho. This was apparently in reaction to Lesotho's stand at the Organization of African Unity (now the African Union) and the United Nations against the apartheid system. In any case, the use of South African roads to travel from one city to another in Lesotho was suddenly made unavailable.

Therefore, Lesotho had to develop its own internal road network as a matter of urgency. In view of its limited resources, a delegation including the Minister of Transport, the Lesotho Ambassador to the United Kingdom, and myself had to travel to London, Brussels, Stockholm, and Ottawa in order to seek funding from the British Government, the European Union, the Swedish Government, and the Canadian Government for the construction of the rural roads.

Gravel roads were eventually constructed thereby liberating Lesotho from being a dependent on South Africa for its internal road transportation. It was a great pleasure for me to witness those gravel roads improved to a proper highway standard when I visited Lesotho in 2011!

Lesotho's Huge Water and Hydro-Power Potential and the Government's Exemplary Action

One of the natural resources with which Lesotho is blessed is its rich water and hydro-power potential. However, in 1976, the country was not making much use of it. An important issue concerning Lesotho's water resources was the fact that South Africa was interested in benefiting from it. However, Lesotho's rivers, including the Organge River, were not flowing to regions in South Africa where there was a need for the water. Therefore, there was a requirement for redirecting the river flow to other parts of Lesotho and South Africa by establishing new dams and channels.

The South African government was fully aware of the great benefit it could achieve from Lesotho's water potential. However, it was attempting to get it at minimal cost.

Lesotho's electricity supply was imported from South Africa although Lesotho had huge hydro-power resources.

It was pleasing to note that my recommendation concerning the need for a serious focus on the utilization of its water resources was accepted by the Lesotho Government. This resulted in a Lesotho-South African negotiation about water development and utilization. It was a source of great honor and privilege for me to lead the Lesotho delegation comprising representatives from the Ministries of Foreign Affairs, and Planning as well as the World Bank for the negotiation that took place in Cape Town, South Africa. It was at that negotiation that the South African Government took the Lesotho stand seriously and got down to dealing with the issue in a mutually satisfactory manner. One of the important members of the Lesotho delegation to that important meeting was Mr. Tim Thahane (later Lesotho's Minister of Finance) then working as Executive Director for Lesotho at the World Bank. For more details, please see his recollection (Recollection No. 1 on page 25) in which he states, among other things:

Mr. Alemayehu leads Lesotho Delegation To Cape Town To Resume Water Negotiations.

9.1 In July/August 1977 the Two Governments (Lesotho and South Africa) decided to resume the discussion on Water transfer at the Official level. Mr. Kidane Alemayehu, who was the Permanent Secretary for the Ministry of Public Works and Transport, led the Lesotho delegation to Cape Town which included among others Mr. A. M. Monyake, Permanent Secretary for Planning, Mr. .J.R. L. Kotsokoane from the Ministry of Foreign Affairs. I was asked to join the delegation as Executive Director for Lesotho at the World Bank which was expected to play an important role as technical adviser to Lesotho eventually a financier. I was also expected to defend the project in the Board should there be reservations in view of the increasing political criticism and demands to isolate South Africa.

9.2 The Mandate that was given to Lesotho delegation was:
(a) to agree to sell water to South Africa provided that water was also used to generate electricity before it leaves Lesotho.
(b) South Africa should contribute financially to the costs of any feasibility studies to demonstrate its commitment to the project. South Africa had not paid for the feasibility study of the Oxbow scheme and could, therefore, walk away from the table without losing anything.

9.3 Mr. Alemayehu, as leader of delegation did an excellent job. The project was resumed under the leadership of the technical Ministries, which is still the case today.

"The Rest Is History!"

Once I realized that the Lesotho Government was fully on board regarding the need for a strategic and accelerated focus on water issues, I recommended that a Ministry of Water and Natural Resources be established to fully develop and make use of its significant natural resources. The Government approved my recommendation and invited me to be the first Permanent Secretary for the new Ministry. Unfortunately, by then, I had already accepted to move to Tanzania to work for the UN Center for Human Settlements as Project Manager/CTA at Dodoma, the new capital city project.

A Dream Come True! Lesotho's Highland Water Project, Roads, Airport, Etc.
I returned on a visit and search for materials for this book to Lesotho in November, 2011. Words cannot express adequately the deep sense of joy I felt to see, on the ground, the projects I had recommended as ideas on paper many years ago. I landed at the very airport the idea of which was initiated in 1973. Instead of the rough gravel mountain roads, I travelled luxuriously on tarred roads in the mountainous areas. What was particularly gratifying was to see the water dams and some parts of the long tunnel for which over $3 billion was invested with a result that both Lesotho and South Africa were benefiting from the highly successful project.

The Lesotho Highlands Water Project was developed in two phases.[4] The basic objectives of the project were (a) to transport Lesotho's water to South Africa thereby earning export revenue for Lesotho and supplying the "lowest cost alternatives for supply of water to the Gauteng Region"; and (b) to maximize "the local development spin-offs of the project in Lesotho".

The first phase (Khatsie Dam) required an investment of $2.5 billion financed by a "consortium of lenders including the United Nations Development Program, African Development Bank, European Union, European Investment Bank, Development Bank of Southern Africa, Commonwealth Development Corporation, commercial banks, and export credits". IBRD's planned contribution was $110 million. The second phase (Mohale Dam) involved $858 million planned financing of which $629 million was actual by 2010 utilizing various sources: IBRD, Development Bank of South Africa, European Investment Bank, Government of Lesotho, and Commercial loans as well as money markets. A third phase (Polihali Dam) is planned near Mokhotlong.

Lesotho's supply of water to South Africa has been over 700 million cubic meters per annum for which it has received an average $40 million per year.

With regard to electricity, Lesotho has reduced its dependence on South Africa by producing its own hydropower (70 mw/annum initially) as well as by importing 40 mw from Mozambique. There is a plan to produce 1,000 mw from the Katsie Dam. Thus, Lesotho has elevated itself from being a totally dependent nation to a mutually dependent relationship with South Africa.

Among the benefits of Lesotho's highland water project is the employment opportunity it has generated for hundreds of Basotho as well as the 30,000 tourists visiting the dam area annually. A further important direct benefit obtained from the water project is the development of the road infrastructure in the previously inaccessible mountainous regions of Lesotho. The travel from eastern to western Lesotho that used to take 12 hours is currently a maximum 2-hour comfortable drive.

It is anticipated that the goal of "water-for-all" will be achieved by the year 2020.

One continuing concern that required a special attention by the Government of Lesotho was the need for a systematic and sustainable rural development. In fact, during the formulation of the highland water project, one of the fundamental objectives had been specifically stated to be rural development. However, this objective has not been achieved. The World Bank's "Project Performance Assessment Report" (April 6, 2010) (p.8) stated:

> "From Government letters, workshops and actions such as the establishment of the LFCD (Lesotho Fund for Community Development) before Board approval of CDSP (Community Development support Project), there appeared to be good government commitment to the participatory community driven approach to be used under the project. However, this was not to be the case in practice. Almost immediately, the project went seriously off track due to the influence of political vested interests."

The report further refers to the occurrence of corruption and mismanagement that negatively affected the project's core objective of community development.

Nevertheless, the Lesotho highland water project has important lessons for other countries sharing rivers similar to Lesotho and South Africa. The above report states:

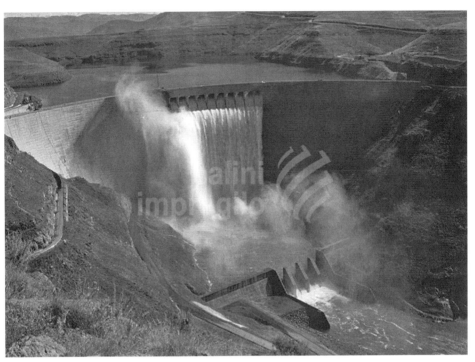

Picture of Katsie Dam in Lesotho

"Lesotho and South Africa's "Good Practice" Water Treaty has features that may be relevant elsewhere". The following features have contributed to success: (i) clarity and detail in the treaty document, including procedures for adjusting to changing circumstances; (ii) appropriate institutions – a bridging institution has worked well in coordinating actions between the two countries; (iii) focused objectives; and (iv) independent dispute resolution mechanisms within the institutions themselves. The Bank's 20 year engagement providing technical and policy support, and as a motivator for the financial involvement of other lender, also contributed to the treaty's success."

Building Construction Capacity

As stated above, one of the major constraints faced by Lesotho in those days was the very weak building construction capacity. Whatever limited capacity existed within the Ministry of Works and the private sector was largely dominated by expatriate, ex-colonial staff. Therefore, it was absolutely essential to initiate measures that would enhance Lesotho's local building construction capacity, with a special focus on providing opportunities for self-reliance and sustainability to the Basotho in their newly independent nation.

In addition to initiating the human resources development referred to above, one of the practical measures applied was to afford opportunities to small scale Basotho building contractors by enabling them to execute Government projects on their level. This was achieved, for instance, by sharing a 30-unit housing project to 15 Basotho contractors by providing them with some technical support especially a Quantity Surveyor paid by the Ministry of Works. The Quantity Surveyor assessed the materials needed by all the contractors and helped in obtaining them, at their cost, at competitive prices from South Africa. It was hoped that at least some of the contractors would gain sufficient experience in eventually dealing with larger building projects. The Ministry's enhanced system of internal control, accountability and transparency enabled an adequate control over the Quantity Surveyor's services.

Conclusion: Mission to Lesotho

Thanks to the active and decisive participation and support of the Lesotho Government and the fullest backing of the United Nations, especially the

United Nations Development Program and the International Telecommunications Union, it can be stated that the objectives of the project were achieved. Through the active recruitment, training, and affording of opportunities to local (Basotho) counterparts, it was possible to create an important momentum of sustainability and self-reliance.

The focus on planning and development activities and the improvement of the organizational and management systems made it possible for the Ministry of Works and the Department of Posts, Telecommunications and Civil Aviation to accelerate their performance to a higher standard.

The consent by the Government of Lesotho to establish a new Ministry to develop the nation's vast water resources was a harbinger of significant opportunities for enhancing the country's development. Lesotho has eventually become exemplary in making use of its water rights as one of the riparian states.

My mission to Lesotho having ended in April, 1978, I proceeded to my next assignment to Tanzania during the same month.

MINISTRY OF WORKS
KINGDOM OF LESOTHO

To all to whom these presents may come, Greetings::
We, the Minister, Permanent Secretary, Officials &
the Staff of the Ministry of Works, Kingdom of Lesotho
hereby certify that
KIDANE ALEMAYEHU, ESQ.
has performed his services as
Permanent Secretary
with diligence, distinction, competence, integrity,
compassion and forthrightness,
to the high satisfaction of all
and forever to the betterment of the Kingdom
and wish him well
in all his future undertakings.

Dated 31 March 1978   Maseru, Lesotho

_____   _____
Minister   Permanent Secretary

Certificate Awarded to me by Lesotho's Ministry of Public Works

H.E. Mr. Tim Thahane

Recollection No. 1
By The Honorable Mr. Tim Thahane, MP.

Recollections by H.E. Mr. Tim Thahane, then Director of Lesotho's Planning Department (later worked as a senior official of the World Bank followed by being Lesotho's Minister of Finance and, subsequently, Minister of Energy, Meteriology and Water Affairs and member of Lesotho's Parliament)

"My Association and Recollection of Lesotho's Developments during 1970-1982 with particular focus on the role played by the UNDP and its experts, especially Mr. Kidane Alemayehu.

Political And Economic Setting

1.1 On 4 October 1966 Lesotho which had been a British Protectorate since 1868 became independent. Completely surrounded by the Republic of South Africa whose philosophy of Apartheid it did not share, Lesotho faced a difficult political and economic environment from its large and economically and politically powerful neighbor. But, it shared common history and culture with the Black people of South Africa. As result, Lesotho faced major policy challenges and choices.

1.2 First, because of its philosophy of apartheid and denial of human rights to the black people, South Africa faced mounting pressure from independent black African States which were pressing for international sanctions and isolation of South Africa at the United Nations, and internationally. Geographic and economic realities compelled Lesotho to cooperate with South Africa as a neighbor even though politically they were worlds apart.

1.3 Second, Lesotho was dependent on South Africa for employment and income of most of its people. Over 150,000 Basotho worked in South African mines as migrant workers while another 40-50,000 worked on South African farms and industry.

1.4 Third, Lesotho received up to 30% Grant-in-Aid from the British Government annually to finance its budget and a large number of British expatriates who ran the civil service and the police.

1.5 Fourth, Lesotho had poor physical infrastructure of roads, power, water and telecommunications, schools which were owned and managed by Churches, health clinics and hospitals. Agriculture was limited to subsistence farming in the lowlands and foothills while the livestock, especially cattle, sheep and goats were reared mostly in the mountains that ranged from the low of 5,000 feet to the highest peak of about 12,000 feet.

1.6 Fifth, Lesotho had a very high literacy rate of about 60-70% but very low functional literacy. It had only one vocational school, and one artisan. This lack of technical and vocational skills was to prove a major constraint to Lesotho's economic transition and development in the early 1970s and beyond.

1.7 Sixth, Lesotho had no commercial mineral resources; no exploration had been done even though a number of Basotho were finding alluvial diamonds in the mountains and digging them using small equipment.

1.8 Seventh, unlike other African Governments, Lesotho's independence elections were won by a conservative party led by Chief Leabua Jonathan by a very narrow margin of two seats. It defeated the Popular Pan-Africanist Basutoland Congress Party led by Mr. Ntsu Mokhehle who was a contemporary of President Nelson Mandela and other freedom fighters at Fort Hare University in South Africa. This laid the foundations of political instability that characterized Lesotho's post independence history until 1993 when Lesotho's 2nd Democratic Elections took place and all seats except one were won by Basotho and Congress parties. This notwithstanding, political instability continued until 2002 when Lesotho adopted a Mixed Member Parliamentary model.

1.9 Eighth, Chief Jonathan, however, turned out to be a strong nationalist who pursued a principled based foreign policy. Though he had little education himself, he surrounded himself with educated people and proved to be a tough negotiator in later years with the South African Apartheid Regime. A key official whom Chief Jonathan appointed secretary to Cabinet or Government Secretary was, Joas Mapetla, who later became the first Mosotho Chief Justice. Mr. Mapetla held the Government together for most of Chief Jonathan's rule.

1.10 - The Economic Challenge that Lesotho faced

1.10.1   The major constraint which the independent Government of Lesotho faced was the inability to pay salaries of its civil servants from 1966 until 1971/72. Each year Lesotho Government officials had to travel to London to present its Recurrent and Capital Budgets to British Officials of the Ministry of Overseas Development who scrutinized and approved them before they could be submitted to the Parliament of Lesotho. This was most humiliating to the independent Government of Lesotho Chief Jonathan hated it.

1.10.2   Faced with this reality, Chief Jonathan assembled his small team of local economic advisers and asked them to think seriously about how to increase revenue collections so that Lesotho can get out of British Grant-in-Aid as quickly as possible. This would allow Lesotho to pursue its independent political policy unpressured by any country. It would not have to explain to anybody or state why it voted one or another at United Nations or why it established diplomatic relations with one country and not another.

1.10.3   This small team of economists turned to UNDP to assist them in two ways:
First, to finance an inventory study of the water resources of Lesotho. They had found from the review of colonial records that South African mines and industry would need water in the Johannesburg (Vaal River catchment) area in the coming years. South Africa had no readily available sources of cheap water except from The Highlands of Lesotho. The water from the Mountains of Lesotho flows in the southwest direction to the Atlantic Ocean whereas the demand for it was in the North East. However, it could be diverted to flow to the north through a series of dams and tunnels in the mountains.
Second, this team of local economists identified the lack of adminis-

trative, managerial and technical capacity in the public service as the main constraint that must be addressed as quickly as possible if Lesotho were to accelerate its economic transformation and development. They requested UNDP to provide technical experts. Sweden made available to the UNDP some fund-in-trust that could be bused to top up the local salaries of experts that were employed against established local positions in the civil service. This UNDP Operational Programme of Assistance (OPAS) was meant to finance international experts who could become operational Heads of Departments and Managers. It was under this programme that Mr. Kidane Alemayehu, an Ethiopian, came to Lesotho. Others who came under this programme included the first Commissioner of Mines and the head of Hydrological Services.

1.10.4   While this Inventory of Water Resources of Lesotho and Hydrological Data was being conducted, other transformational changes were taking place in the economic management and administration of Lesotho .These personnel appointments were to prove very determinative in subsequent economic and social advances of Lesotho.

1.11 - Establishment of Development Planning and Coordination Office and Lesotho National Development Corporation in 1969.

1.11.1   Chief Jonathan established in 1969 a Development Planning and Coordination Office to plan how Lesotho would:

- get out of British Grant-In-Aid and accelerate its social and economic development;
- coordinate all external assistance including training;
- undertake feasibility studies to export water to South Africa, even though politically the two countries were at odds politically, and to generate electricity for Lesotho;
- renegotiate the Customs Union Agreement which was originally signed in 1910 on behalf of Lesotho, Botswana, Swaziland and the then Union of South Africa.

1.11.2   Chief Jonathan appointed a young Mosotho Economist who had just completed his graduate studies at the University of Toronto in Canada, by the name of Timothy Thahane to be the Director of the Planning Office and to report to him directly. It is interesting to note that the Planning Office has remained substantially unchanged in functions until today. It is also the only office which has never been headed by an Expatriate, although it has had a number of expatriate advisers.

1.11.3   The second key institution that was established by Chief Jonathan is the Lesotho National Development Corporation (LNDC) whose mandate was:

• To promote establishment of small and large industries including mining by

(a) entering into equity with foreign investors;

(b) building industrial estates and factory shells for lease to new investors;

(c) providing loans to new companies where appropriate.

1.11.4   To find experienced chief executive for LNDC Chief Jonathan turned to a South African industrialist with whom they had been friends for years to provide him with a Chief Executive and a Chief Financial Officer. This industrialist was Dr. Anton Rupert, whose large and diversified international tobacco and luxury good's company owned investments in agriculture, mining, finance, etc. Mr. Rupert seconded as Chief Executive, Mr. Wynan Van Graan who had been in Canada in one of Dr. Rupert's companies. It was under Mr. Van Graan's leadership that LNDC took shape and Lesotho produced Wool and Mohair Carpets that won international awards in German and Italian Exhibits and, Pottery. LNDC established a Maize Milling, and negotiated exploration contracts with Rio Tinto and Anglo American, among others.

1.11.5   Chief Jonathan also appointed several other bright Basotho to key positions in the various Ministries, such as, Mothusi Mashologu and his brother Teboho Mashologu in Foreign Affairs; Moabi Mapetla in Finance; Sam Montsi in Planning and later to LNDC as Chief Executive. Sam was to succeed Thahane as Director of Planning when the latter became Ambassador and Chief Negotiator for Lesotho to EEC in Brussels for the First Lome Convention between the European Economic Commission and the African, Caribbean and Pacific States. When Van Graan left, he was succeeded by another UNDP/OPAS expert, Mr. Heinrich Bechtel from Germany who became the Managing Director and Chief Executive of the new Lesotho Bank. Other appointments included, Lengolo Monyake and his brother Moletsane Monyake in Statistics; Paanya Phoofolo and Percy Mangoaela in the

Department of Posts, Telecommunications and Civil Aviation; the small team of local economists included Tsepa Manare who obtained his Master's degree in economics from Cambridge University in the U.K; Joshua Khetla Rakhetla, who studied economics and administration at Fort Hare in South Africa and a post graduate diploma in Yugoslavia; and, Joel Moitse who did political economy at McGill University in Montreal, Canada. Others that had been sent out to Cambridge University to do a Diploma in Development Studies were Henry Ntsaba, who was appointed to the Ministry of Public Works, and David Makoae, who was appointed in the Ministry of Agriculture. Mr. Joki Kolane was appointed Speaker of the National Assembly and Mr. Tseliso Mafike Deputy Managing Director of Lesotho Bank to succeed Mr. Bechtel.

1.11.6   This early development of Lesotho illustrates the importance of:

i.   The right, focused and committed leadership;

ii.   Strong institutions; and ,

iii.   Early training and appointment of key local personnel.

1.12 - Key Aspects of The National Transitional Development Plan 1970-76 And The Identification And Feasibility Studies of The Oxbow Water Transfer Scheme To South Africa.

1.12.1   Lesotho produced its National Transitional Development Plan, 1970-76 in January 1970. This coincided with the First Post Independence Election that saw Chief Jonathan declare a State of Emergency, suspend the Constitution and rule by decree. Although the country was ushered into political instability, the key focus on development agenda remained unchanged and undisturbed.

1.12.2   The key focus of the plan was on preparing the country for sustainable development and better economic formulation and execution by:

• Creating development institutions and Ministries that can address infrastructure deficits; poor technical and vocational education and training; lack of health facilities by majority of the people; improvements needed in the Judiciary; lack of access to Telecommunications, clean Rural Water Supply, Electrification and Postal services; and, identification and preparation of water export projects that can enhance Lesotho's revenue prospects and economic and political policy options. The plan laid top priority on the implementation of the

Southern African Customs Union Agreement that had been successfully renegotiated and signed in December 1969. A major technical, economic and engineering study, which was to be undertaken was the water transfer project, known as Oxbow Project. The World Bank and UNDP were to be approached to fund and supervise the consultants.

1.12.3   The new Customs Unions Revenue sharing formula provided large amounts of revenue that enabled Lesotho to get out of British Grant-In-Aid. The revenue share for each of Botswana, Lesotho and Swaziland was calculated on the basis of this formula:

(C+E+S) all raised to the power 1.42.

Where C = Customs

E = Excise Duties

S = Sales Tax

0.42 is compensation to Botswana, Lesotho and Swaziland for the polarizing and price raising effect of being in a Customs Union with larger and highly developed economy that will always attract financial and human resources to itself due to better infrastructure institutions and services.

1.13 - Why The Plan Was Considered Preparatory

1.13.1   The 1970/71 – 75/76 plan was considered transition and preparatory because:

(a)   Many studies were to be undertaken, during the plan period such as, among others;

* The Transport Survey;

* The expansion and modernization of Telecommunication to cover the different district capitals and rural and mountain areas;

• Studies to determine the mix of air and road transport in Lesotho and how to link Lesotho by regular air service with the outside world;

• The mineral exploration;

• The country lacked technical experts in all fields and these had to be recruited to implement the plan.

1.13.2   In recruiting experts, it was decided that the expatriate staff should be diversified by nationality with preference given to United Nations Experts. Within the UNDP candidates, preference was to be given to nationalities that were not represented in the public service or were not predominant in The Expatriate Community in Lesotho. A special preference was given to selecting African experts from the Candidates presented by UNDP or The Commonwealth provided they were equally qualified. It was under this policy that;

- Dr. B.W. Taylor was selected as UNDP Representative
- Mr. Kidane Alemayehu was appointed Director of Posts and Telecommunication including Civil Aviation and later Permanent Secretary for the Ministry of Public works and Transportation.

Recollection and Perspectives of Hon. Timothy T. Thahane M.P.

2.1 After completing my Master's Degree in economics at the University of Toronto, Canada, I joined the Public Service in July 1968 as Assistant Secretary in the Ministry of Planning and Economic Development which was headed by a Dutchman from Pius XII University College, Professor Joris W. Biemans.

• Professor Biemans had been appointed at independence in 1966 with a mandate to produce a national development plan within a short-time but without professional staff and other resources to support him.

• I joined Bieman's Ministry with Tsepa Manare who had done a Masters in Economics at Cambridge University in the U.K. and Joshua Khetla Rakhetla who had studied Economics and Administration at Fort Hare University. Later we were joined by Joel Moitse who had a Master's degree in Political Economy from McGill University in Montreal, Canada.

2.2 Vigorous intellectual debates ensued as we started to discuss development and political constraints and how to approach plan formulation, priorities and strategy. The British Expatriate Civil Servants who had been left behind occupying key administrative positions at independence, were unhappy that an important office, such as, the Ministry of National.

2.3 Planning and Development did not have a British civil servant or economic adviser among its senior staff. This led to a concerted fight and representations to the Prime Minister through the British High Commissioner and the Head of the Reorganization Team, Sir Glyn Jones, former Governor of Malawi. Sir Glynn Jones advised the Prime Minister to dismiss Joris Biemans or risk a cut in British Development Aid.

2.4 Faced with these challenges, the Prime Minister decided to retire Joris Biemans, reorganize the Ministry of National Planning into a Central

Planning Office under a Director who would report directly to him. Though the youngest of the local team, I was appointed Director of Planning with an Adviser to the Prime Minister. UNDP provided support in the person of Professor Apostolos Lazaris, who later became Deputy Leader of the Greek Pan Hellenic Party or PASOIK under the late Prime Minister of Greece, Andreas Papandreos.

Why and How Kidane Alemayehu Was Recruited and Given a Key Policy Making and Decision Making Roles.

3.1 Under Prime Minister Leabua Jonathan, the Central Planning and Development Office was given broad mandate to coordinate all external assistance and applications and to assist line Ministries in the identification,, preparation, appraisal and monitoring of budget implementation. It was also given mandate to prepare, with line Ministries, project applications for external funding and then process them through the Ministry of Foreign Affairs. This mandate continues to be the same even today.

3.2 As Director of Planning, I led the team which gave me all the support in identifying a serious technical and managerial gap that existed in line Ministries which were responsible for implementing development projects and programmes, hence achieving economic growth. Lesotho received almost all its capital budget from the U.K. A large part of the capital budget (up to 30%) remained unused at the end of each year and returned to the U.K. The recurrent budget, on the other hand, was often fully utilized.

3.3 We had to submit both sets of estimates to the Ministry of Overseas Development (new DFID) for scrutiny before Government would submit them to the Parliament of Lesotho. We had to prepare our estimates and then go to the U.K t o discuss them with the officials of the Ministry of Overseas Development, now Department For International Development (DFID). These annual discussions meant that the British Government knew what the Cabinet and the Parliament of Lesotho were planning before the people of Lesotho could be informed. It also learned early about the technical assistance needed to implement the projects and programmes, and could therefore propose recruitment of such staff through Crown Agents, which recruited ex-colonial staff for placement in former overseas territories.

3.4 One of the areas identified as high priority was Postal and Telecommunication and Civil Avian Department which was headed by an Englishman by name of Mr. Heathcote. Mr. Heathcote's Deputy was a South African.

3.5 When asked to appoint or train locals to take over from the expatriates in his Department, Mr. Heathcote often claimed that there were no locals who could (a) head a technical Department such as the Telecommunications or understand the technical and legal issues involved in the International Telecommunications Union, International Postal Union or International Civil Avian Organization. He firmly believed that no local person can ever become a Pilot or Airport Controller. It was this attitude that eventually led to his dismissal by the Prime Minister when it was reported to him.

3.6 The Prime Minister directed that Mr. Heathcote should recruit young Basotho and train them as pilots and train others to replace the heads of Postal services and telecommunications as well as the lawyers in those fields. Mr. Heathcote refused and put his reasons in writing. At this point the Prime Minister asked the Cabinet Secretary, Mr. Joas Mapetla to fire him immediately and to ask me to approach UNDP to find him a replacement as quickly as possible.

3.7 Dr. Bill Taylor, the UNDP Representative and I prepared a Project Document. Bill Called the Head of ITU which was having its annual meetings and asked for a suitably qualified candidate under Swedish UN/OPAS Posts. The Head of ITU in Geneva approached the Ethiopian Minister to see if he could release one of his Senior Executives to come and head Telecommunications, Postal Services and Civil Aviation Department in Lesotho. That is how Mr. Kidane Alemayehu was nominated and accepted by the Government of Lesotho. He was the first non- Mosotho African in Public Service to be appointed a Director (equivalent to Permanent or Principal Secretary) to Head a large technical Department consisting of Postal Services, Telecommunications and Civil Aviation with strong international connections.

3.8 The appointment of Mr. Alemayehu was highly welcomed by His Majesty, the Prime Minister and the Cabinet as a whole. The appointment began a process of reducing dependence on largely a single nationality among the technical experts.

3.9 Mr. Alemayehu's first action was to introduce a clear localization policy that had two components: to recruit and train locals in relatively large numbers; and, to appoint a local to understudy each expartriate in the Department with clear time line and milestones for the local to take over. He identified two graduates for training as managers to eventually replace him as Director at the end of his contract.

What were Some of the Key Challenges/Improvements that Mr. Alemayehu Faced And Introduced?

4.1 Mr. Alemayehu's employment as Director changed the attitudes in the Department he headed. First, the locals became more assertive and self-confident. They felt that they can also head the so-called Technical Ministries just as Mr. Alemayehu had done. Second, Mr. Alemayehu also motivated locals to come forward for training as technicians, pilots, aircraft maintenance engineers, air controllers, and telecommunications engineers. He appointed Obed Nteso to head Telecommunications, Matsobane Putsoa to be head of Finance and Postal Services whose revenues were sufficient to cover their expenses and leave a surplus. He appointed Paanya Phoofolo to Head the postal services. Matsobaue was later removed by Government directive for political reasons while Nteso left for U.S.A.due to political pressures. Only Paanya and Percy remained.

4.2 The other major development was to recruit three Basotho to go for training as pilots. These were Duke Moorosi, Ntlaloe and Molapo. They were sent then to Pretoria to undergo aptitude, psychometric and other tests. They passed everything and were sent abroad for training. They were the first Basotho Pilots.

4.3 Kidane recruited a Lawyer/Scientist/Educationist Mr. Percey Mangoaela to become Head of Civil Aviation. Mr. Mangoaela decided to train as a pilot also so that he could have a better appreciation of his job. Mr. Mangoaela (now Dr. Mangoaela) later replaced Mr. Alemayehu as Director of Posts, Telecommunication and Civil Aviation when Mr. Alemayehu was appointed Permanent Secretary of the Ministry of Public Works including Water and Electricity. Dr. Mangoaela later served at the U.N. Economic Commissision for Africa as Head of Infrastructure development and at the Southern African Development Community (SADC) as Head of Infrastructure.

What was achieved under Mr. Alemayehu's Public Service?

5.1   The Second Five Year Development Plan 1975/76-1979/80 lists impressive programmes of achievements in the expansion of:
   i.   Postal Services into the rural areas;
   ii.   Expansion of telecommunications network to go along with the postal services in the rural areas and throughout the country;
   iii. Expansion of external air links including direct air links with Swaziland and Mozambique;
   iv.   Expansion of domestic airfields and purchase of aircrafts;
   v.   Introduction of regular air service between Maseru and Johannesburg, Matsapa in Swaziland and Maputo In Mozambique;
   vi.   Training of a large number of technicians at a regional training schools in Malalwi that was established with the support of U.S. Agency for International Development.

Achievements of Mr. Alemayehu as Permanent Secretary for the Ministry of Public Works and Transport.

6.1   After his excellent performance in the Divisions of Civil Aviation, Telecommunications and Postal Services, Mr. Alemayehu was transferred to the Ministry of Public Works as Permanent Secretary.

6.2   His major achievements here were:
   • Expansion and bituminization of the North-South Trunk Road from Quthing to Botha Bothe;
   • Creation of a Labor Intensive Road Construction Unit which was assisted by the World Bank in order to absorb returning miners;
   • Expansion of domestic all weather roads as well as feasibility studies for bituminizing other roads, such as Maseru- Roma; Maputsoe -Mahoteng; Maseru-Thaba Tseka;
   • Re-starting of the negotiations with South Africa on the water transfer project which was stopped for political reasons in 1971. These negotiations resulted in the joint feasibility studies for The Lesotho Highlands Water Transfer to South Africa.

6.3   I wish to say a few words about The Water Transfer Project later called Lesotho Highlands Water Project and Mr. Alemayehu's role here and his contribution.

Lesotho Highlands Water Project

6.3.1   In 1966/68 Lesotho Government applied to UNDP to conduct an Inventory of the WaterResources of Lesotho and to identify a specific scheme that would transfer water from a Dam at Oxbow in Lesotho to Eland River in South Africa. This would be a run-of-the river scheme rather than using a tunnel.

6.3.2   The World Bank was appointed an Executing Agency for this feasibility study. A U.K. firm of Consultants, Binnie and Partners was appointed to carry out the study. South Africa appointed a Consulting firm of Mr Ninham Shand who was the engineer that wrote in the 1950's about the possibility of Lesotho supplying water and electricity to South Africa. At that time South Africa needed water and not power even though technical studies showed that it will need a lot of power since it was under investing in energy and subsidizing coal production. The lead consultant that Binnie and Partners used on the Feasibility Study was Nick Payne, a British.

6.3.3   A UNDP financed French expert Dr. de Bono carried out the hydrological studies and placed rainfall measuring units throughout the mountain areas. These hydrological studies formed the basis of the design of the Lesotho Highlands Water Project Design and regime in Phase l and phase ll. It is being used to deal with the rights of the downstream users and the riparian states.

6.3.4   In 1970 Lesotho and South Africa began negotiations about the price of water from Oxbow. I was part of these negotiations which were led by our Cabinet Secretary and later Chief Justice Mr. Joas Mapetla. The team included, the Permanent Secretary Mr. Henry Ntsaba of the Ministry of Public Works and Teboho Mashologu from the Ministry of Foreign Affairs. The World Bank advisory team that had supervised the feasibility study was led by a Division Chief, Mr. Robert Dean.

6.3.5   The South African delegation was led by the Director General of Water Affairs and included Mr. Brand Fourie from the Ministry of Foreign Affairs and all senior engineers from the Department of Water Affairs.

6.3.6   Lesotho wanted a price of water that would give a Rate of Return of at least 8% while South Africa wanted to use a cost plus Royalty Method. This method when translated into Lesotho Rate of Return method gave a 5% Rate of Return. The negotiations broke down when South Africa proposed that the 3% difference be regarded as Aid from South Africa to Lesotho. Lesotho insisted that anything above 8% should be regarded as aid from South Africa to Lesotho.

6.3.7   When these negotiations broke down in 1971, South Africa proceeded with Phase II of Tugela Water Scheme which would defer Lesotho's water transfer by five years. We convened Binnie and partners, Mr. Nick Payne, who had prepared the feasibility study report and reviewed all the possible alternative schemes to Lesotho's run-of –the-river scheme. It became clear to us then that South Africa's least cost scheme was the Lesotho one. Second, it became clear that South Africa had underestimated its future demand for water and that it would eventually come back to Lesotho with a larger scheme. We therefore advised the Prime Minister to sit tight. Lesotho's water will always be there for use domestically or for export if the price is right for both parties.

Resumption of negotiations on larger Lesotho Highland Water Transfer Project

7.1   In 1974 after serving as Ambassador to the European Economic Commission for the negotiation of a Convention between ACP (African Caribbean and Pacific) States and the European Economic Commission (known as the Lome Convention), I was appointed by seventeen African countries and Trinidad and Tobago as ALTERNATE EXECUTIVE DIRECTOR to the World Bank Board. South Africa had also appointed its former Secretary for Finance, Dr. Joop De Loor, as its Principal Representative to the World Bank and IMF. Dr. De Loor and I were friends having met during the re-negotiation of the Southern African Customs Union between Botswana, Lesotho, South Africa and Swaziland and which was signed in December 1969. Common Monetary Agreement with Dr. De Loor which was later signed by Lesotho, South Africa and Swaziland in 1971.

7.2   Dr. De Loor and I often talked about the economics of the water resources of Southern Africa and the fact that South Africa will need a lot of water in the future. We saw great scope for cooperation between our two countries for the mutual benefit, peace and well-being of our peoples.

7.3   Dr. De Loor shared some of these ideas with his colleagues in South Africa. In 1976 he told me that they would like to resume the negotiations on Water Transfer Project which broke down in 1971. I contacted Prime Minister Jonathan who agreed to resume the discussion.

7.4 Dr. De Loor and I agreed to propose to our respective Governments that, the resumed discussions should be kept technical and professional and avoid introduction of political and foreign policy issues. This goal would be achieved if the negotiations are conducted under the leadership of the Ministries responsible for water affairs in each country. For Lesotho this would be the Ministry of Public Works and for South Africa the Ministry of Water Affairs. We also agreed to propose that the process should be kick-started by a high level visit of a South African Minister to his counterpart in Lesotho. The two governments agreed to these proposals.

7.5 On June 16, 1976 when the Soweto Youth Uprising took place, the South African Minister had just landed in Maseru. Lesotho Government quietly arranged for the Minister to return to South Africa and come back at a later date when the situation in South Africa was clearer. IN the meantime the officials will continue to do the preparatory work.

8. Mr. Alemayehu leads Lesotho Delegation To Cape Town To Resume Water Negotiations.

8.1 In July/August1977 the Two Governments decided to resume the discussion on Water transfer at the Officials level. Mr. Kidane Alemayehu , who was the Permanent Secretary for the Ministry of Public Works and Transport, led the Lesotho delegation to Cape Town which included among others Mr. A. M. Monyake, Permanent Secretary for Planning, Mr. J.R. L. Kotsokoane from the Ministry of Foreign Affairs. I was asked to join the delegation as Executive Director for Lesotho at the World Bank which was expected to play an important role as technical adviser to Lesotho eventually a financier. I was also expected to defend the project in the Board should there be reservations in view of the increasing political criticism and demands to isolate South Africa.

8.2 The Mandate that was given to Lesotho delegation was:

(a) to agree to sell water to South Africa provided that water was also used to generate electricity before it leaves Lesotho.

(b) South Africa should contribute financially to the costs of any feasibility studies to demonstrate its commitment to the project. South

Africa had not paid for the feasibility study of the Oxbow scheme and could, therefore, walk away from the table without losing anything..

8.3 Mr. Alemayehu, as leader of delegation did an excellent job. The project was resumed under the leadership of the technical Ministries, which is still the case today. The Rest Is History!"

H.E. Mr. Paanya Monyane Phoofolo

Recollection No. 2
By H.E. Mr. Paanya Monyane Phoofolo

Statement by H.E. Mr. Paanya Monyane Phoofolo (initially recruited to be in charge of Personnel Services, succeeded to head Lesotho's Postal Services, promoted, later, to the post of Principal Secretary for the Ministry of Transport and Communications, and, subsequently to the higher posts of Senior Principal Secretary for the Cabinet, and Lesotho's Ambassador to China and the United Nations

"It was the winter months in The Kingdom of Lesotho when I had my first encounter with Mr. Kidane Alemayehu. It was late July 1972 and he had just arrived in the country recruited through I TU (International Telecommunications Union- a U N specialized agency on telecommunications issues). I was being employed as newly recruited university graduate as Personnel Officer (Human Resources Manager) being responsible, inter alia, recruitment and all establishment matters pertaining to the divisions of the Department of Post, Telecommunications and Civil Aviation. Mr. Alemayehu was the Director of this Department which administratively was an integral part of the Ministry of Works.

As the new Director assumed his responsibilities the country was heading to its sixth year of independence from British rule and surrounded by apartheid Republic of South Africa. The country had also just gone through a turbulent election period in 1970 and was trying to go through a political healing period during 1971-1972 The Civil Service was predominantly white at most key management positions , and the Director's Department was no exception, it included expatriates from Britain and South Africa itself. Because of its untenable geographic position the services rendered by this department were dependent heavily and skewed in favour of its more economically powerful only immediate neighbour. Lesotho like all newly independent states was rightly calling for localization of all senior positions in the Civil Service and parastatal organizations. The new Director had to be seen implementing this declared government policy. Mr. Alemayehu succeeded a British called Arthur Heathcote and all key divisions in his department were occupied by expatriate personnel: R P. Jones —Postal (British); Dr. Kiderlene-telecommunications (South African); Higginson - Civil Aviation (British). There were no locals immediately under these expatriate personnel save those at the operational level. The Director wasted no time to recruit and identify suitable candidates into the department. There had been no university graduates in all these key divisions of the department save one senior assistant to the Director and he was almost due for retirement. Late 1972, I was made counterpart to Mr. Jones (Assistant Director for Postal Services) and Mr. Alemayehu arranged intensive training for me in postal matters and management in the following countries: Zambia, Japan, United Kingdom, and Switzerland . Mr. P M Mangoaela, a lawyer by training, was recruited, to understudy Mr. Higginson (Assistant Director for Civil Aviation), Ben Mokoatle to understudy the Director, Andrew Moqhali sent to Australia to pursue full-fledged engineering studies. Unfortunately Ben Mokoatle disappeared into South Africa and Mr. Mangoaela replaced him who in turn was replaced by Mr. T.J Motsohi - a graduate too. The department was taking a new phase under Mr. Alemayehu's leadership, consistent with the policies of the government of the day the postal division was the first to be localized in 1974 when I was appointed the first Mosotho to be its head. This was the time I worked very closely with the Director. The Postal division had been organized and managed (during the colonial days) as if it were an extension of the South African Post Office and the only existing main post offices were located along the border between the two countries, obviously to serve colonial interests. On the home front, under the new management, rigorous plans were, therefore, put in place to open new post offices in the ignored rural areas. Following the establishment of the planning unit and subsequent studies, funding was secured from the European Commission (EU today) to expand postal services to the people at large, particularly the rural areas. The post offices increased from 14 to 39, that is constructed and made operational during the time of our new Director (Mr. Alemayehu), ie 1972 to 1976. On the external front Lesotho reduced dependence on its neighbour; all incoming and outgoing mails, be it surface or air had to be handled and treated in accordance with international rules and regulations as stipulated in the Acts and Rules of the Universal Postal Union (also a U N specialized agency on postal matters). Lesotho for the first time participated at international fora like U.P.U Congress in Lausanne, Switzerland in 1974, Commonwealth conferences in Sri Lanka and Malaysia.

With the remarkable expansion of the postal wing under the tutelage of Mr. Alemayehu, more nationals of Lesotho were being employed to man the post offices, thus necessitating training and opening promotion prospects. A new and appropriately equipped training school built and opened. To meet the ever increasing training requirements of the division, the new Director in consultation with his counterparts in Botswana, Malawi and Swaziland, and with the concurrence of the respective governments, initiated for the establishment of a regional posts & telecom middle management school. The two specialized agencies were approached for assistance and that led to the establishment of the Multi-country Post and Telecommunication Centre in Blantyre, Malawi, the school was and continues to be managed by the four countries.

The new Director equally focused in the development of other divisions. The South African head of Lesotho's Telecoms had to go and, through I T U assistance, a new manager was sought as more Basotho were being trained at middle management and university level. Initially the successor came from the Netherlands and, through Sweden, Swedtel provided consultancy, as Mr. Alemayehu had pushed for a detailed master plan for telecommunications services in the country with emphasis in the rural areas. Rural radio communication was introduced in the country by 1974, telephone lines were increased by introducing new and modern exchanges, microwave transmission network were introduced and plans were afoot for the construction of the satellite earth station to give Lesotho total independence for its external communication and this materialized after his departure in 1976.

Telecoms was properly structured with nationals assuming higher responsibilities in planning, installation, major works and maintenance, training and finance. By 1980, the division was reasonably at a point that it was granted some autonomy becoming a parastatal organization i.e. Lesotho Telecommunication Corporation (LTC). It has since been privatized during the mid'90's.

On the Civil Aviation front, localization was speedily achieved and for the first time locals were sent for air pilot training in Nigeria and Scotland, Perth. Air traffic controllers were trained in various parts of the world with assistance of International Civil Aviation Organization (I C A O - a U N specialized agency on aviation issues). The Director pushed for the improvement of the rural airfields so as to serve people in the mountain areas where there was a dearth of roads. It was during Mr. Alemayehu's tenure of office that a new international airport was planned and indeed came to fruition in the 1980's.

An almost non-existing unit of road transport service was attached to the department to be developed and expanded. A citizen of Finland, Mr. Penti Makela was recruited to come and help with the establishment of the wing of transport & traffic. He worked on the Act and Regulations to govern the wing. Four locals with degrees in economics and transport were recruited and were posted to be the foundation of the new division of transport and traffic services."

Chapter 2

<u>UN Mission to Tanzania</u>

The UN mission to Tanzania commenced in April 1978 and its main objective was to assist the Ministry of Capital Development which was based in Dodoma but reporting directly to the country's President, Mwalimu Julius Nyerere. The Ministry's main purpose was to set the policy and strategy as well as oversee the development of a new capital city at Dodoma, located at the center of the country. The implementation of the capital city's development was the responsibility of the Capital Development Authority (CDA).[1]

The UN project was initially executed by the Department of Technical Cooperation and Development (DTCD), but in 1979 it was taken over by the United Nations Center for Human Settlements (UNCHS), otherwise known as the UN-HABITAT.

<u>Tanzania and Its Prospective New Capital City: Dodoma</u>

It was in 1973 that the people of Tanzania had decided, by referendum, "to shift the national Capital of Tanzania from Dar es Salaam to Dodoma, at the geographical center of the country, in Central Tanzania."[1] The initial objective was highly optimistic as it was intended to transfer the basic elements of the capital city from Dar es Salaam to Dodoma within ten years. However, the aim turned out to be overly optimistic. 40 years after the original referendum, the capital city continued to be in Dar es Salaam. I visited Dar es Salaam and Dodoma in December, 2011 and witnessed the fact that, by and large, the Government and all embassies were still located in Dar es Salaam. It should be noted, however, that there is a Prime Minister's office in Dodoma where occasional meetings take place but, for all intents and purposes, Government business is still operated from Dar es Salaam.

One significant institution that has been transferred to Dodoma is the country's main university which was reported to accommodate over 30,000 students and has been granted extensive land to facilitate future expansion.

The central purpose for the transfer of the capital city to Dodoma was to accelerate Tanzania's socio-economic development from the center of the country. This move was justified by various reasons including the relatively urgent need for the development of the Dodoma Region in view of its comparative poverty as well as the ease of access expected to be afforded by the central location of the new capital city to other parts of Tanzania. The issue of the need for centrality was given a high emphasis as Dar es Salaam's location at the South-eastern edge of Tanzania was obviously found to be rather remote for most of the country's populated areas especially in the context of the underdeveloped transportation network in the country. Another important factor was the relatively mild climatic condition in Dodoma compared with the highly humid and hot environment in Dar es Salaam.

1. Institutional Framework for the Development of the Capital City

The initial institutional arrangement for the development of the capital city was as follows:

    1.1 Ministry of Capital Development that operated from the President's (Mwalimu Juluis Nyrere) Office and headed by a Minister of State;

    1.2 Capital Development Authority (CDA) which operated under the overall control of the Ministry of Capital Development as a corporate body;

    1.3 Dodoma Region;

    1.4 Dodoma Municipality (capital development area).

The above institutional arrangement was changed in November, 1980 by integrating the Ministry of Capital Development into the Capital Development Authority.[2]

The main focus of the UN project and the achievements were the following:

2. Ministry's Policy and Institutional Arrangement

A careful study of the Ministry's role and responsibilities was undertaken resulting in an institutional framework whereby specific sections were established to focus on policy and planning, coordination and transfer programs, Land, and Administration and Finance Branches.

3. Planning and Urban Design Studies

With regard to planning, the Ministry conducted, with the assistance of the United Nations, detailed studies on appropriate strategies for the development of the capital city as well as the urban design of Dodoma's central district.

4. Land Use

The section was responsible for policy issues with regard to land, surveys needed for the planning and urban design needs as well as land use for various projects and settlements. This section also included valuation, land allocations, and urban issues in general.

5. Low-income Housing

As has been indicated above, Dodoma Region was among the least advantaged and needy areas in Tanzania. It was therefore recognized right at the outset that unless the development of the new capital city took into account the needs of the low-income people in the overall framework of the capital city project, Dodoma could be overwhelmed by unplanned and sub-standard settlements. A multi-disciplinary United Nations consultancy team comprising an architect/planner, a Finance specialist, and a construction/building materials engineer conducted a comprehensive study and submitted its findings and recommendations to the Government of Tanzania.

It is unfortunate to note, during my visit to Dodoma in December, 2011, that at least 70% of the Dodoma city area was occupied by unplanned/sub-standard settlements. It was obvious that the UN project's recommendations were not fully implemented.

6. Coordination and Transfer Program

The coordination and transfer program focused on the participation of other ministries and organizations and their respective roles in the transfer process. Therefore, the Ministry arranged, with the initiative and support of the UN project, joint meetings with other Ministries for briefings and discussions on the development of the capital city. It was hoped at the time that a similar coordination and information process would involve the diplomatic community as well as the private sector so that all stakeholders would be engaged in the transfer process.

7. Administration and Finance

The activities covered by this section included resource mobilization, human resources management, training, accounts, general services, etc.

Observations about Tanzania and Dodoma during 1978-'80:

In those days, Tanzania was governed by its policy of "African socialism" under the leadership of President Mwalimu Julius Nyerere and the political party he led i.e. CCM (Chama Chama Mapinduzi). Since the UN project I was leading was located in Dodoma, I had the opportunity to travel from the center of the country to other parts of Tanzania including not only Dar es Salaam but also such cities as Arusha.

I was also able to travel by car to Kenya and see that the ground realities were such that although socialism in Tanzania was more egalitarian, the overall state of the economy in Kenya was by far superior with the latter's free enterprise policy.

Because of frequent shortages of essential items including food supplies in Dodoma, one had to resort to other sources including Dar es Salaam. One particular episode I recall distinctly was the time when Dodoma ran out of essentials such as oil, sugar, salt, etc. only to discover, later, that the Dodoma Regional Manager had apparently sold off the quota for Dodoma before it left Dar es Salaam to an Indian trader. The consequence of that malfeasance for the Regional Manager was to transfer him to another Region as he was a prominent member of the CCM party.

One positive aspect that deserves mention about Tanzania in those days was President Nyerere's high integrity. I had the opportunity to meet him in Dodoma and at his special residence in Dar es Salaam. It was clear to see that, unlike most other national leaders in Africa, he actually practiced simplicity and avoided excessive waste. The difference in salary between that of the President and the lowest civil servant was relatively minor. There was no doubt that Tanzania's salary structure was such that payments to Ministers and civil servants were quite low. As an example, when the wife of my neighbor, a medical doctor and head of the local hospital, had a baby, I discovered that he could not afford to buy what was needed for the new arrival.

Another important factor that deserves mention was the fact that Tanzania made immense contributions to the liberation of African countries suffering colonialism and the South African apartheid system. Dar es Salaam was the host for an Organization of African Unity (OAU) (now African Union (AU) branch Office as well as representatives of liberation movements such as ANC

(African National Congress). Tanzania was making huge sacrifices for African liberation despite its meager resources.

The Capital City Project and Tanzania's Invasion of Uganda

It was quite obvious at the outset that the project for the transfer of the capital city to Dodoma would involve substantial amounts of expenditure in the billions of US Dollars. Tanzania's economy was, however, among the least developed in the world. As if this were not enough, international events were rendering the situation even harder. Among the serious occurrences that affected Tanzania's economy and the Dodoma project was the Tanzanian invasion of Uganda for the ousting of the former dictator, Idi Amin.

In October, 1978, exactly six months after the commencement of the UN project in Dodoma, Uganda's ex-dictator, President Idi Amin, invaded Tanzania with the intent of annexing the Tanzanian region of Kagera. Tanzania retaliated immediately with a force that was estimated to be 100,000 including members of the Ugandan opposition movements and was able to defeat Idi Amin's army despite the support it had obtained from Muamar Ghadafi, Libya's President. Tanzania's army reached Uganda's capital city, Kampala, in April 1979. Uganda was under Tanzania's virtual control until 1980 when the former President of Uganda, Milton Obote, took over for the second time.

It was clear that the combination of Tanzania's weak economy and the consequences of the war with Uganda had a devastating effect on the ambitious capital city transfer project.

New Institutional Arrangement of the Capital City Transfer Project

In view of the huge financial crises encountered, the Tanzanian Government had to take some drastic steps which included the integration of the Ministry of Capital Development and the Capital Development Authority into a single institutional entity. The project was requested for a review and recommendation on the new entity and a report dated February 22, 1981 was submitted.

As a result of the new institutional arrangement:

> "In November, 1980, the Ministry of Capital Development (MCD) was abolished and its functions were taken over by the President's Office and the CDA. Accordingly, some MCD staffs were retained in the Office of the Minister of State, and others were transferred to CDA under a new

Transfer Program Department while the rest were allocated to other Ministries."3

One of the important points of controversy referred to by both the UN project as well as an Australian renowned consultant, Sir John Overall, was the issue relating to the three key roles played, under the new institutional arrangement, by a single official i.e. as the Minister of State of Capital Development, the chairman of the Capital Development Authority (CDA), as well as the Director General of the CDA. The Tanzanian Government was alerted to the danger of a conflict of interest arising from such a situation but since I was reassigned to another project, it was not possible for me to determine the full consequences of that Government decision.

In my project (URT/77/163) report dated February 22, 1981, I submitted the detailed findings containing an assessment of the background, the prevailing situation and specific recommendations on the role of the Minister's Office. Please see Fig. 4 showing the organization chart of the Ministry of Capital Development, after its reform taking into account the project's original recommendation and Fig. 5 after the integration of the Ministry with the CDA and the project's recommendations for the achievement of accountability and transparency.

Fig. 4

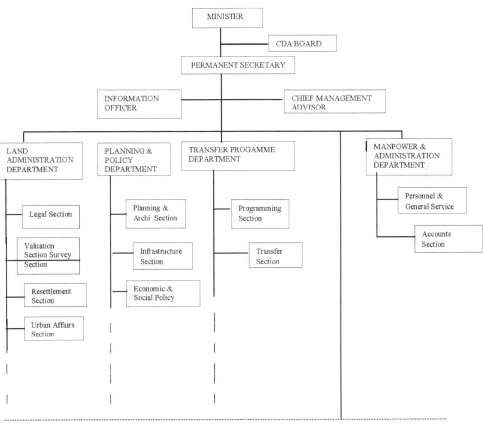

DAR-ES SALAAM OFFICE

_____Line of Hierarchy
---Co-ordination
.- Planned

Fig. 5

ORGANIZATION

OFFICE OF THE MINISTER OF STATE

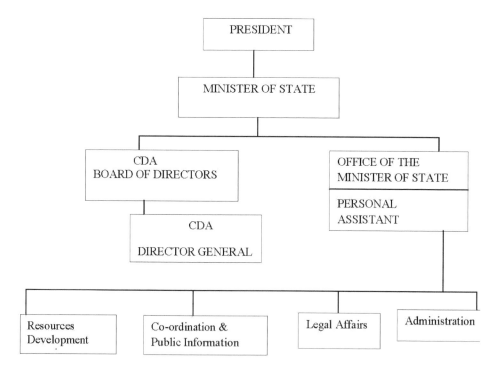

Relocation to Tanzania's Ministry of Planning

Once the process of integrating the Ministry of Capital Development with CDA was completed, I was transferred to the Ministry of Planning in Dar es Salaam to work there as a Human Resources consultant during the remaining couple of months until my contract period was concluded. During this period, it was possible to conduct a human resources survey in the Tanzanian Ministries responsible for the human settlements sector and to initiate recommendations for restructuring and development.

A Tragic Event

In March, 1981, I was asked to participate in a meeting that was arranged to take place in the Dodoma office of the Prime Minister to resolve a controversy that involved the Tanzanian Government as well as the UN Department of Technical Cooperation and Development (UNDTCD), the UN Food and Agricultural Organization (UNFAO), and the UN Development Program (UNDP). The meeting was attended by several officials of the Tanzanian Government, the Resident Representative of the UNDP, two Assistant Resident Representatives and a Tanzanian employee at the UNDP, a representative of the UNDTCD who had come from New York, a UNFAO official who had travelled from Rome, and I. Fortunately, the controversy was resolved and the meeting was concluded successfully.

During the meeting, it was decided that I remain in Dodoma for a few more days to follow-up on issues concerning my work with the Ministry of Planning. I recall that a Tanzanian employee at the UNDP came over to where I was sitting and asked whether his sister could take my airplane seat on the way back from Dodoma to Dar es Salaam. I confirmed that I had no objection as I was not flying back to Dar es Salaam that day.

I had a phone call at 7:00 am the following morning from the Deputy Permanent Secretary of the Ministry of Planning who simply enquired about my health and seemed to be relieved to know that I was alright. I learned later in the morning that the UN team that had flown from Dodoma had perished because of the plane's crash due to adverse climatic conditions. A tragic occurrence. My time was obviously not up. At the beginning of April, 1981, I was transferred to the headquarters of the United Nations Center for Human Settlements (UN-HABITAT) located in Nairobi, Kenya.

Chapter 3

Inter-Regional Consultant, UN Center for Human Settlements (UN-HABITAT) (April 1981-July 1982)

At the conclusion of my mission to Tanzania, first in Dodoma under the Ministry of Capital Development, followed by a few months assignment with the Ministry of Planning in Dar es Salaam, I was transferred to the headquarters of UN-HABITAT in Nairobi and commenced work there at the beginning of April, 1981.

The task assigned was to work as an Inter-Regional Consultant to provide institutional development services in the human settlements sector as needed by various countries. This assignment lasted one year comprising missions to Malawi, Botswana, Swaziland, Nigeria, The Gambia, and Uganda.

With the exception of Nigeria, the consultancy missions typically covered the concerned Ministries including those dealing with local government, public works, urban planning and development, housing, building materials and construction, land surveys and management, transport and communications, relevant education and training, related administration and finance, etc. In the case of Nigeria, the focus was on its new capital city, Abuja.

Each consultancy mission lasted a period of 1-2 months and the strategy followed was:

1. The identification of the current organizational arrangement, staffing, plans and work programs of the institutions in the human settlements sector;

2. The assessment in depth of the organizational adequacy to meet the

policy, planning, development, operation, and other technical, administrative, and financial needs of the institution;

3. The assessment of the human resources capability on the professional, sub-professional, and artisan levels in order to meet current and foreseeable development needs;

4. Recommendations for a systematic and sustainable resources development, especially the organizational and human resources requirements.

Being an African Consultant: An Advantage!

Since my consultancy missions in the various countries occurred only a few years after their respective political independence, the level of welcome and sense of cooperation was highly gratifying. Examples of these occurred in Malawi and Nigeria.

When I reported for work at the UNDP a day after my arrival in Lilongwe, Malawi's capital city, I was stunned by the Resident Representative's statement informing me that my mission was unfortunately not going to proceed because it required an advance notice of three months for a program that my work required, namely, meetings with some eight Ministries and organizations. The UNDP Resident Representative simply continued with his other work after dropping his bombshell remark. According to him, I should pack up and fly back to Nairobi empty handed.

What I had to do was to use the Malawi Government telephone directory and call the office of the Senior Permanent Secretary (head of the civil service) who fortunately received my call and listened to the purpose of my mission and the work program I needed to be arranged. A period of silence followed my explanation which appeared to me at the time as if it were an eternity and was about to repeat myself when I heard the official's voice in my own language, Amharic, welcoming me to Malawi! He had apparently studied at and graduated from the Haile Selassie I University in Addis Ababa. He graciously arranged the full program and called me back within one hour and enabled me to proceed with my mission.

The event that took place in Nigeria concerned the Minister of Planning. Following the UN consultancy mission to Abuja, the new capital city, along with an associate from Canada, it became essential to brief the honorable Minister. Again, the UNDP Representative informed us that, without an advance arrangement requiring months, it would be impossible to arrange a meeting with the Minister. What I had to do was visit the Minister's secretary and explain our purpose to him. He told us to wait a bit and went to the Minister's office and returned a short while later to inform us that he was ready to see us right away!

A similar positive attitude was displayed in the other countries where I undertook my missions.

The Case of Uganda [1]

Since the basic objectives, methodologies, and expected outcomes of the various missions were similar, despite the differing local circumstances, the report on the mission to Uganda is presented hereunder in summary, for the purposes of this book.

The one-month mission to Uganda commenced on October 11, 1981, only ten months after the return of President Milton Obote's Government to power following a period of turmoil under the Idi Amin regime which grabbed power, through a military coup d'état, on January 25, 1971 until it was, in turn, overthrown on April 11, 1979 with Tanzania's military support. It took nineteen months, up to December 10, 1980, to achieve a degree of stabilization including the holding of a democratic election which resulted in bringing President Milton Obote back to power.

In view of the huge crises that prevailed due to the military clashes between the Tanzanian and Ugandan armies, the lack of security and stability, the extensive looting, destruction of properties, etc. that took place especially in the main city, Kampala, my UN mission was, in fact, part of the stabilization process. Among the symptoms of the situation confronted during my mission to Uganda were the daily occurrences of gun shots heard in the area and, therefore, the special concern for personal security that had to be observed, the difficulty of finding minimally acceptable restaurants and hotel accommodation. A particular challenge that required physical fitness was the need to walk up eleven floors to the Ministry of Planning offices as the lift was not working and electricity supply was in any case unreliable. The mission was, therefore, undertaken in an environment not dissimilar with a military field operation.

In this regard, I fondly remember the great hospitality extended to me by the local manager of the Ethiopian Airlines, Mr. Besrat and his wife, Alemnesh, without whose wonderful hospitality life in Kampala would have been rather unbearable.

Uganda's Context in 1981

In addition to the then somewhat unstable situation, Uganda's economy was in dire straits mainly due to the mismanagement by the overthrown Idi Amin regime. Institutions in the private and public sectors were in a state of turmoil. Therefore, the new Milton Obote regime was engaged in the process of achieving stability while establishing the basic institutional framework that would enable the provision of basic services and the execution of a strategy that would enhance the country's development performance.

The overall strategy was to bring about a speedy recovery of the shattered economy in Uganda with the following objectives:[2]

1. To achieve national unity, political stability and security;
2. To improve agricultural productivity;
3. To adjust the structure of the economy by raising the level of industrial and mineral production and by broadening the export earning sector to reduce dependence on coffee as well as the contribution to GDP by the agricultural sector to 45% by 1990;
4. To pursue a more equitable incomes policy;
5. To embark on an extensive policy of integrated rural development;
6. To be self-sufficient in trained middle level manpower and achieve over 75% of high level manpower needs by 1990;
7. To reduce the population growth to 2.5% per annum and the subsistence sector from 40% to less than 20% by 1990;
8. To embark on the development of "cheap energy with particular emphasis on hydro-electricity and renewable sources of energy";
9. To rehabilitate and expand infrastructural facilities such as housing, transport and communication.

The Human Settlements Sector in General

The following are usually considered to be the key areas of human settlements activities:

1. Physical and land use planning for an integrated rural and urban development including the formulation of detailed strategies for the most optimum use of land and other resources for agriculture, mining forestry, industries, transport and communications, urbanization etc. in a manner that reflects social equity;
2. Housing with particular reference to the needs of the majority i.e. low-income people;
3. Infrastructure and services such as water, sewerage, energy including

renewable sources of energy for rural development, health, education, transport and communications, commerce, etc;

4. The construction industry;
5. Housing and building finance with particular emphasis on the needs of low-income people;
6. Science and technology including research and dissemination of information with particular reference to upgrading of low-income dwellings and infrastructure;
7. Institutional development including administrative structures, human resources planning and development.

Status of The Human Settlements Sector in Uganda in 1981

Uganda's population, in 1981, was 12.6 million of which only 7% lived in the urban areas. The population in the urban areas was increasing at 8.7% per annum.

Uganda's public services comprised 28 ministries and 126 parastatal (semi-government) organizations. The main ministries dealing with the human settlements sector were the Ministry of Planning and Economic Development, the Ministry of Housing and Urban Development, the Ministry of Lands, Minerals and Water Resources, Ministry of Health, Ministry of Education, Ministry of Rehabilitation, Ministry of Works, Ministry of Transport, and the Ministry of Local Government.

The private sector in the human settlements sector included 17 architectural, and 10 quantity surveying firms as well as numerous construction companies.

Due to the mismanagement encountered during the Idi Amin regime, the human settlements sector including the concerned institutions had suffered serious development reverses. Therefore, it was obvious that there was an urgent need for the formulation of appropriate policy, strategy, and an action plan in order to stimulate the development of the human settlement sector and, for that purpose, enhance the country's human resources capacity.

Uganda's human settlements sector was marked by diverse circumstances. On the positive side, Uganda was endowed with huge natural assets, including its mostly pristine environment, its rich agricultural, water, energy, and human resources potential. Uganda's significant potential stems from the fact that as a country that is the source of the White Nile, it could play a pivotal role in the development of the region as a whole in the context of the Nile Basin.

The human settlements arrangement comprised, in general, three major regions:

1. The relatively more developed and urbanized areas around Lake Victoria covering central, southern and south-eastern districts which have rich agricultural lands as well as heavy and evenly distributed rainfall. Most of the major towns, industries, commerce, and services were concentrated in that area. The country's major agricultural products: coffee, tea, sugar, livestock products, fish, crops, etc. were obtained substantially from this region.

2. The Western and south-Western High Lands although relatively less developed than the Lake Victoria Crescent, were also endowed with rich agricultural land and heavy and evenly distributed rain during most of the year making them suitable for the production of tea, coffee, cotton, banana, food crops, etc. Minerals such as copper, cobalt, salt, cement, tin, barley, wolfram, iron and gold were located in that zone.

3. The North, North-West and North-East Zone were the least urbanized and had less economic infrastructure than the above two. The rainfall was less reliable making them vulnerable to drought conditions. Nevertheless, most parts of the area were suitable for cotton, tobacco, food crops and livestock.

On the other hand, the constraints facing Uganda in the human settlements sector were also immense.

The main challenges were the following:

1. There was a huge disparity between the urban and rural areas in terms of income, provision of infrastructure and services as well as investment and employment. All these favored the urban areas which, therefore, attracted high rates of migration from the rural areas.

2. In accordance with Uganda's Land Decree No. 3 of 1975, land was state owned. The Uganda Land Commission held the land on behalf of the state. The decree required a customary landowner to apply for a lease over his holding.

3. In addition to the destruction caused by the devastating war, neglect, and the heavy looting that prevailed in several urban centers during the final Idi Amin days, the haphazard system of urban development had resulted in increased unplanned or slum settlements.

4. The extensive damages to housing that occurred in certain urban areas such as Masaka, Mbarara, etc, the mismanagement and deteri-

oration of the building materials industry, lack of adequate housing finance, especially for low-income people, prohibitive construction costs, etc. the housing backlog in Uganda was extensive. It must be stated, however, that although Uganda did not have a comprehensive national housing policy it, nevertheless, had conducted studies, with the assistance of a Commonwealth Team of Experts, on its 10-year (up to 1990) housing need which was estimated to be 330,000 of which 80,000 was expected to be within the urban sector. In Uganda's 1980 context, that need was quite extensive.

5. Despite Uganda's abundant natural water and energy resources, their availability including sewerage services was grossly inadequate. This was reflected in the fact that people in rural areas had to travel great distances to fetch water and the few water boreholes and pumping stations had fallen into disrepair during the previous decade due to lack of maintenance and spare parts. Water supply in urban areas had also deteriorated sharply. The report by the Commonwealth Team of experts mentioned in item 4 above, revealed that whereas Kampala had an estimated demand for water of 41.4 cu.m/annum, its designed intake capacity was 43.8 m.cu.m./annum while the actual intake and output was, sadly, only 26.3 m.cu.m./annum. The UNCHS/HABI-TAT 1981 report had stated:[3]

"The Government strategy includes the rehabilitation of existing water supply schemes which is in progress, and the improvement of water quality and supplies in urban and rural areas. It is also Government objective to supply potable water to all within a radius of a maximum of 1.6 miles by 1990. With regard to sewerage, only 12 towns in Uganda have such a system covering a maximum of 40% connection. Poor maintenance and lack of spare parts have rendered the system ineffective. Steps are underway to rehabilitate the system. At the same time, it is planned to engage in low-income sanitation using more technology in urban and rural areas. The 10-year plan indicates that a total of 380 professional sub-professional staff will be required by 1990 for water development."

6. With regard to energy, Uganda's main sources were hydropower, wood, and imported oil. Of these, the most significant was hydropower supplied from the Owen Falls station with a capacity of 150 MW of which 31 MW was exported to Kenya. A previous study had indicated that Uganda could generate 2,500 MW hydropower, from

the White Nile River which could transform its rural economy as well as contribute to the development of neighboring countries. It had also been indicated that Uganda could exploit its alternative sources of energy including biogas, sun, wind, geo-thermal, etc. Its abundant forest reserve was also considered a reliable source of charcoal for use in rural areas.

7. The transport and communications facilities were also depleted due to the breakup of the East African Community as well as the neglect by the overthrown Ugandan Military regime. All the services were in a serious state of disrepair and highly inadequate. Roads were in poor condition. Inland waterways were damaged due to unattended heavy flooding. Insufficient equipment, facility, and resources rendered the railways, telecommunications, postal and civil aviation services inadequate. Therefore, there was a desperate need for urgent improvement of the transport and communications infrastructural services.

8. Uganda's institutional capacity for the human settlements sector comprised government ministries, parastatal (semi-governmental) organizations, and the private sector. The ministries operating in the human settlements sector were the Ministry of Housing and Urban Development, the Ministry of Local Government including urban authorities, and the Ministry of Lands, Minerals and Water Resources. The Ministries catering for infrastructural services included the Ministry of Transport, Ministry of Power, Posts and Telecommunications, Ministry of Industry, Ministry of Health, Ministry of Education, Ministry of Commerce, Ministry of culture and Community Development, Ministry of Information and Broadcasting, Ministry of Marketing and Cooperatives, and the Ministry of Supplies. Parastatal (semi-governmental) organizations included the National Housing and Construction Corporation, the Housing Finance Company of Uganda, the National Water and Sewerage Corporation (actually for Kampala, Jinja, and Entebbe), The Uganda Cooperative Savings and Credits Union (with 400 participating unions and 200,000 members as well as 40 Marketing and Cooperative Unions for about 1 million farmers), and the Reconstruction and Development Corporation.

9. Although the private sector[4] suffered major reverses during the Idi Amin regime, it nevertheless continued to play a significant role in the development of the human settlements sector. Among the reasons

for the setback in the private sector was the forced exodus of the Asian community due to the military government's policy. In 1981, the main elements of the private sector within the human settlements sector comprised:

Consultants	No. of Firms
Quantity Surveying	10
Architectural	12
Valuation and estate management agents	6
Structural engineering	6
Electrical	4
Land surveying	4
Contractors*	4
Civil engineering	5
Structural and Building	45

*The above were the ones which were registered with the Ministry of Housing and Urban Development. It was reported that there were numerous others which were registered under the Companies Act.

As stated then by the Minister of Housing and Urban Development, the Hon. Eng. A.P.N. Waligo, the private sector contributed 80% of all housing developments. The Ugandan government embarked on the policy of strengthening the private sector so that it could play a major role in the progress required for the human settlements development in general. The issuance of legal instruments was designed to facilitate private investments including the attraction of funding from foreign sources.

10. The human resources development institutions[5] catering for the human settlements sector comprised several educational and training entities including the renowned Makerere University with its various faculties such as electrical, mechanical, and civil engineering. In 1981, the enrollments were 41, 56, and 68 respectively. The other institutions included the Uganda Technical College, the Directorate of Industrial Training, the Survey Training School, the 5 Technical Institutes run by the Ministry of Education, certain secondary schools with courses in technical subjects, Technical schools, Community Development Carpentry and Bricklaying Training Centre, the Management Training and Advisory Centre, the Institute of Public Administration, the Uganda College of Commerce, the National

Teachers' College, the 30 Teacher Training Colleges, and the National Research Council. In general, the outputs in terms of human resources were inadequate compared with Uganda's development needs. Details are provided hereunder.

HUMAN RESOURCES NEEDS FOR THE HUMAN SETTLEMENTS SECTOR IN UGANDA

In order to undertake the human resources survey in a comprehensive manner, careful studies were made of the current staffing and vacancy levels, previous surveys [6], [7] and recommendations as well as international standards for determining the requirements. In general, what came out clearly was the conclusion that Uganda was in desperate need of professionals, sub-professionals and artisans in order to fully meet its development needs. Another clear constraint in human resources capability was the low ratio between the professional, sub-professional and artisan/clerical level categories.

In the report by the Commonwealth Team of Experts (1979) [8], it was indicated that in 1977 the Ugandan Government public service comprised 40,839 (70.7%) Ugandans, 225 (0.4%) non-Ugandans, and 16,678 (28.9%) vacancies. The report further indicated that there was a shortage of professional and technical capability, an excessive number of vacancies, and a need for an effective policy and development strategy for the human resources sector. The Team also recommended the establishment of a National Manpower and Training Council to advise the Ugandan Government on human resources, education, training employment and incomes policies and strategy.

Methodologies for Forecasting Human Resources Needs;

Among the methodologies considered for determining the human resources needed for the human settlements sector in Uganda was the recommendation by the UNCHS consultant, Sir John R. James [9], who had concluded that at least one planner would be required for every 100,000 population. He had also indicated that there was a need for a minimum of 300 junior professional level staff.

Another study that was considered was the one conducted in 1973 by the ECA (Economic Commission for Africa) consultant, Prof. R. Vagale who had determined that there were an average of five physical planners per million population in the British Commonwealth countries. Taking into account the fact that the United Kingdom had 57 physical planners per million population while Sri Lanka had a mere 0.6 per million, Prof. Vagale had recommended between 8 to 10 physical planners per million population for developing countries. He had also recommended that, based on the technology at that time, there would be a need for maintaining a ratio of 1:3 between professional physical planners and sub-professional level staff.

In 1981, Uganda had a population of 12.6 million and the number of planners was 22 i.e. 1.7 planners per million population. Therefore, based on the above recommendations, Uganda required 109 additional planners in 1981. The projection, taking into account the population forecast by the Ugandan Ministry of Planning, was a requirement of 169 physical planners in 1990 needing an additional 147 planners for the anticipated population of 16.9 million. With regard to the requirement of sub-professional level staff, since the surveys conducted were not comprehensive, it could only be indicated that a total of at least 441 such human resources would be required by 1990.

Ratio of Human Resources Requirements Among Professionals and Sub-professionals

One of the most important factors taken into account was the determination of the ratio among professional and sub-professional human resources in a manner that would be relevant to Uganda's realistic conditions. In order to achieve this objective in a well considered and in-depth manner, I undertook consultations with the following pertinent institutions in government, semi-government, and private sectors:

1. Ministry of Planning and Economic Development;
2. Ministry of Housing and Urban Development;
3. Ministry of Industries;
4. Ministry of Rehabilitation;
5. Ministry of Education;
6. Ministry of Public Service and Cabinet Affairs;
7. Ministry of Health;
8. Ministry of Works;
9. Ministry of Labour;
10. Ministry of Culture and Community Development;
11. Ministry of Cooperatives and Marketing;
12. Ministry of Lands and Surveys;
13. Ministry of Cooperatives Development;
14. National Water and Sewerage Corporation;
15. Water Development Department;

16. National Housing and Construction Corporation;
17. Housing Finance Company;
18. Association of Uganda Professionals;
19. Faculty of Technology (Makerere University);
20. Association of building and Civil Engineering Contractors;
21. Management Training and Advisory Centre;
22. Uganda Technical College;
23. Statistics Department;
24. Survery Training School;
25. Directorate of Industrial Training;
26. Building Materials Research (Ministry of Housing and Urban Development);
27. Census Bureau;
28. National Research Council;
29. Kitara Enterprises Limited;
30. Kampala City Council.

Ratio of Human Resources on the Professional, Sub-professional and Artisan Levels

With regard to the determination of the appropriate human resources ratio, I stated in my project report [10]:

> "The ratio among related technical and administrative professions may vary from country to country depending, among other things, on the level of economic development and activity, and the extent of manpower development. In the case of Tanzania, for example, the ratio of 1 Planner: 1 Valuer or Land Economist: 2 Surveyors: 2 Architects: 1 Building Economist: 1 Sanitary Engineer was adopted. In order to arrive at an appropriate ratio in the context of Uganda, several approaches were considered. Previous studies were not helpful. Relations among existing establishments or filled posts were not meaningful either. Therefore, the accumulated experience of Senior officials in the Ministry of Housing and Urban Development, namely, the Permanent Secretary (also an Architect), the Chief Quantity Surveyor, and the Chief Planner, officials of the Ministry of Lands and Surveys as well as the chairman of the Association of Uganda Technical Profession-

als was considered to be the best to formulate the ratio which was agreed to be as follows:

(i) Ratio among professionals:
1 Planner: 2 Architects: 1 Quantity Surveyor: 2 Water and Sanitary Engineers: 1 Land Economist/Valuer: 2 Land Surveyors: 3 Building Engineers: 1 Housing Finance Specialist/Economist: 3 Housing administrators/Cooperative Specialists: 1 Foreman: 5 Masons: 2 Carpenters: 3 Plumbers: 2 Electricians: and 3 Painters totaling 16 Craftsmen.

(ii) Ratio on the professional, sub-professional and craftsman levels:

Category	Professional :	Sub-Prof. :	Artisan
Physical Planner	1	2	4
Land Economist/Planner	1	2	4
Quantity Surveyor	1	2	-
Building Eng. (site)*	1	4	64

*Each Building Engineer is considered, on the average, capable to handle 4 projects which require 4 sub-professional personnel who in turn require, for each project:

Water and Public Health Eng.	1	2	5
Land Surveyor	1	3	6
Architect	1	2	4
Accountant/Economist	1	3	6
Housing Administrators	1	4	8

Application of First Principles

In addition to the use of the above methodology, other means of estimating the human resources requirements for Uganda's human settlements sector were utilized. These comprised the use of first principles on the basis of general estimates to meet population based needs for urban and rural requirements.

It was noted that in 1981, there were 32 urban settlements with populations varying from 2,000 to over 300,000. The need for 39 Physical Planners was determined on the basis of a formula of one Physical Planner for a population of 25,000 in the urban areas. For the rural areas, the estimate was one planner per 100,000 populations. On this basis, the number of available and expected supply, as well as the anticipated requirements were determined for the professional, sub-professional, and artisan levels in the fields of physical planning, architecture, water/public health engineering, quantity surveying, land economics/valuation, building engineering, housing finance/ economics/ accounting, and housing administration and cooperatives. It was estimated that a total of 3,700 professionals, 7,050 sub-professionals and 39,000 artisans would be needed by 1985. However, according to the project's study the human resources expected to be supplied with the existing capacity in Uganda was a mere 274 on the professional level, 444 on the sub-professional level, and 10,080 on the artisan level by 1985. The expected supply of human resources was to come from Uganda's educational and training institutions as well as those returning from abroad. The local institutions that were considered were Makerere University, Institutions abroad where Ugandan students were studying, Uganda Technical College, Ministry of Education's Technical Institute, Technical Schools, and Vocational Training Schools.

Survey of Human Resources Capacity and Needs in the Human Settlements Sector

Another approach that was also used was a field survey of human resource requirements by obtaining responses, utilizing a format with specific guidelines, from 30 organizations in the Government, Semi-government, and private sectors.

Human Resources Requirements

After a careful consideration of all the above methodologies including the actual human resources capacity available during 1978, 1979, and 1980, and the forecasted supply by 1985, the additional requirements for the human settlements sector, for the years 1981-85, 1986-90, and 1981-90, were determined and submitted by the UNCHS project for 71 relevant posts on the management/supervisory, professional, sub-professional, and technical/artisan levels.[11] Examples of estimates of human resources requirements by 1990 included 329 Physical Planners, 142 Architects, 193 Building Surveyors/Engineers, 152 Land surveyors, 102 Quantity Surveyors, 140 Water and Sanitary Engineers, 152 Land Surveyors, 341 Engineers, 220 Valuation and Estate Managers, 54 Administrators, 254 Economists/Accountants, etc. as well as a total of 11,624 sub-professionals and artisans required to assist the various professionals.

Factors Taken Into Account

At the same time as the above survey was being conducted, other relevant factors were taken into account. These included the overall status of the human settlements sector, Uganda's urbanization process which was increasing at 8.7% per annum, the strategy for economic development, the status and capacity of the education and training institutions, the status of the concerned Government, semi-government, and the private sectors, and the improvements of policy and systems needed to advance the progress of the human settlements sector.

Collaborative Review and Conclusion

The main organizations that were closely involved in the human resources review process were the Ministry of Planning and Economic Development, the Ministry of Housing and Urban Development and the Ministry of Local Government. The Ugandan officials who participated closely in the whole process were Dr. Lubega, the Permanent Secretary from Ministry of Housing and Urban Development, Dr. Y. Okulo-Epak, Chief Planner, from the Department of Regional and Town Planning, Miss. S. Keera, Housing Officer, Mr. Wairama-Dembe, Housing Economist, and Miss. A. Kalibbala, an Urban Sociologist.

Taking into account the various estimates, the survey results as well as the various relevant factors, the following human resources requirements were recommended

	Available	Needed
Physical Planners	22	150
Physical Planning Assistants	6	300
Architects	55	300
Architectural Assistants	15	600
Water & Public Health Engineers	29	300
Engineering Assistants	59	600
Quantity Surveyors	24	150
Quantity Surveying Assistants	2	300
Land Economists/Valuers	8	150
" " " Assistants	36	300
Land Surveyors	40	300
" " Assistants	197	900
Building Engineers	7	450
" " Assistants	257	1800

Need for a Human Settlements Policy and Strategy

In order to ensure that the human resources needs were formulated in an appropriate context, it was recommended that a comprehensive policy, development strategy and action plan should be formulated for the medium- and long-terms needs for the human settlements sector within the framework of Uganda's national plans.

The needs for the implementation of the development strategy would also incorporate the financial, human and other resources needed during the medium- and long-terms. However, for the short term, it was recommended that existing institutions be strengthened while placements should be found in African and other education and training centers in fields of study which are of critical importance for the development of the human settlements sector. Examples of such education and training institutions in Africa, Asia, etc. were provided. It was further recommended that for this purpose, the Ugandan Government seek assistance from the UNDP and other multi-lateral and bilateral sources to meet its needs for the formulation of appropriate policy, strategy, and action plans for the human settlements sector and the required capacity.

Among the recommendations submitted for the longer-term was the establishment of additional vocational training institutions in order to produce the increased number of sub-professionals and artisans needed for the human settlements sector. Another recommendation was for the Ugandan Government to explore the possibility of establishing a regional human settlements education and training institution in collaboration with other African countries in compliance with an OAU (Organization of African Unity) (currently AU: African Unity) resolution adopted at the Heads of State conference in Nairobi in June 1981 (No. CM/Res. 893)

UNDP's Assessment of My Report

At the conclusion of my one-month consultancy mission in Uganda, a 67-page report was submitted with six annexes. The UNDP Resident Representation, Mr. Ferhand Scheller, stated in the letter to the then Executive Director of UNCHS: [12]

> "I would like to give you a brief statement on the one month mission of Mr. Alemayehu to Uganda.
> From the time he arrived here Mr. Alemayehu was determined to produce a report which would not just sit on the

shelf. Rather he said he wished to produce some practical recommendations which could be implemented within the context of UNDP's resource picture and the Government of Uganda's development priorities.

This I believe he has done. Evidence of the enthusiastic and constructive approach he took to his mission can be seen in the large number of organizations he contacted in the field and in the size and quality of the report he finished and presented to a final debriefing meeting before he left Kampala. The Permanent Secretary of the Ministry of Planning in a letter written to us stated his Government "particularly endorse(s) his practical approach" and that his report had "generated keen interest". He goes on to express his appreciation to UNCHS/HABITAT for "this extremely useful consultancy service."

Mr. Alemayehu drafted a variety of well thought out recommendations for improving the quality of manpower in the human settlement sector. There is no need to detail them as I am sure Mr. Alemayehu is himself available for debriefing. The type of technical assistance and training mentioned in the report tallies well with the Government's planning perspective and are basically modest in their cost."

Chapter 4: United Nations Assignment

ASSISTANCE TO THE MINISTRY OF PUBLIC WORKS AND HOUSING IN THE UNITED ARAB EMIRATES (UAE)

At the conclusion of my contract as an Inter-Regional Consultant with UNCHS (HABITAT) in July 1982, I migrated to USA and commenced living in Los Angeles along with my family. My intention was to take a much needed rest to be followed by a consultancy service. I had hardly settled down when I received a call early one morning from UNCHS (HABITAT) in Nairobi asking me to undertake a one-month consultancy service at the UAE (United Arab Emirates) Ministry of Public Works and Housing. This was a complete surprise as I had no such plans myself. Later, I discovered that I was in fact nominated for the consultancy by the Ministry's Director of Planning, Mr. Faisal Al-Gurg, with whom I had a brief meeting in Nairobi when he was there to attend a UNCHS conference and had a discussion about my experience in various countries especially Lesotho, Tanzania, and some other countries.

I accepted the UNCHS offer and proceeded to Dubai, UAE, the city where the Ministry was located and commenced my consultancy in October, 1982. The consultancy was focused on the Ministry's institutional development needs including its organization and human resources capacity. To my further surprise, two weeks after the commencement of my consultancy service, I was informed by the Ministry that I was in fact needed for a two-year contract. It was obvious that the consultancy service was a sort of trial or introductory period for the Ministry. By then, I had a pretty good idea about the Ministry's institutional challenges and the leadership and felt comfortable enough to accept the invitation to serve as a UN expert for an extended period. Therefore,

On my right: H.E. Mr. Ahmed Jasim Al Abduli, Deputy Minister of the UAE Ministry of Public Works and Housing. On my left: H.E. Mr. Qassim Sultan, then Director General of Dubai Municipality; and other officials.

what was originally intended to be a one-month (October/November, 1982) consultancy ended in being followed by an over two-year contract service during January, 1983 to March 1985.

During the one-month consultancy, the Ministry's overall policy, plan, operation, organizational arrangement, human resources, administrative system, coordination with other Ministries, and Municipalities as well as its performance were reviewed. It was discovered that the Ministry was facing serious challenges in virtually all aspects. Therefore, the main recommendations that were presented to the Ministry included the following:

1. The need to strengthen the Planning and Monitoring Office reporting to the Deputy Minister, as a staff function, in order to:
    a. Initiate an appropriate policy, strategy, plans (short-, medium-, and long-term) and work programs;
    b. Apply a systematic performance monitoring system;
    c. Establish and apply an effective system for coordination with other federal ministries and institutions as well as the seven Emirates operating within the national federation;
    d. Arrange a system for the compilation, analysis, and reports of statistical data;
    e. Submit monthly, quarterly, and annual progressive reports in a manner that constructive corrective measures would be generated in a timely manner;
    f. Strengthen and undertake the Ministry's public relations activities;
    g. Enhance the Ministry's information systems and the application of an advanced computer technology;
    h. Establish an effective organization and methods unit in order to assist departments in the restructuring and streamlining of their activities for the achievement of an increased effectiveness and efficiency;
    i. Provide an effective institutional support to the Deputy Minister in issues involving inter-departmental considerations and ad hoc studies;
2. The need for the establishment of an effective training unit for enhancing the Ministry's human resources capacity;
3. The improvement of the Ministry's other organizational arrangement (detailed charts were provided) with regard to its various responsibilities including the development and maintenance of federal roads,

buildings, design, tendering and contracting activities, administrative and financial services;

4. The need to improve the Ministry's human resources capacity on the professional, sub-professional and artisan/clerical levels;
5. The assignment of local counterparts to the experts serving within the Ministry;
6. The need for a delegation of authority; and
7. The need for the application of an efficient classification system, with appropriate criteria and standards, with regard to consultants and contractors in the private sector.

Prior to the submission of the above recommendations, an in depth review was conducted concerning the UAE's federal and local government arrangements and the role of the Ministry. The consultancy process facilitated the participation of 20 Ministry officials including the Deputy Minister, Assistant Deputy Ministers, Directors, Managers, some professionals, three UN experts, a consultant, and a contractor from the private sector as well as three officials of the United Nations Development Program.

As stated above, I was requested to continue with my service, as a UN Expert and Team Leader, which I commenced at the beginning of January, 1983.

Organization and Management of the UAE Ministry of Public Works and Housing:

History in Brief

The UAE comprises a federation of seven Emirates, namely, Abu Dhabi, Dubai, Sharjah, Ajman, Umm Al Qwain, Fujairah, and Ras Al Kahimah and was established in 1971 after it obtained its independence from British colonialism during which it was referred to as the "Trucial States". Under the UAE's federal system, the Ruler of Abu Dhabi is ex-officio President of the country whereas the Ruler of Dubai is the Vice-President and Prime Minister.

In accordance with the UAE constitution, the main federal institutions included the Supreme Council of the Union comprising the Rulers of the various Emirates; the President, Vice-President and Prime Minister; a Council of Ministers with a Prime Minister, a Deputy Prime Minister and Ministers appointed by the Supreme Council; and a Federal National Council with 40 members assigned by the various Emirates i.e. 8 from Abu Dhabi, 8 from Dubai, 6 from Sharjah, 6 from Ras Al Kahimah, 4 from Ajman, 4 from Umm Al Qwain, and 4 from Fujairah.

The scope of federal activities included the country's defense; interior; foreign affairs; public works; Finance; foreign trade; education; higher education and research; culture, youth and development; health; justice; energy; economy; labour; social affairs; Presidential affairs; and environment and water. However, the level of autonomy at the Emirates level was extensive as it included a full mandate over their respective natural resources such as oil, gas, water, land, etc. as well as the local trade, industry, public works, housing, education, health, and other infrastructure. The federal budget was provided for, in the most, by the more endowed Emirates, namely, Abu Dhabi and Dubai.

In 1985, UAE's total population was 2.2 million of which 80% was from foreign countries. In 2010, the population increased to 8.26 million and the local (citizen) population decreased to 11%. This is an amazing feature in the international context as some countries e.g. Switzerland get so concerned that they conduct referendums as, in their view, they considered it a national issue when the expatriate population reached 10%!

In the early 1980's, UAE was dependent on oil as it contributed nearly 60% of its GDP.

According to a 1981 UN project report on housing, it was noted that 50% of the UAE's population was living in sub-standard housing characterized by overcrowding, lack of utilities, poor design, building materials and sanitation facilities.

The main functions of the Ministry of Public Works and Housing were the design, construction and maintenance of federal roads, federal office buildings, national housing, and the required coordination with and assistance to local authorities in the human settlements activities.

During the early '80's, the Ministry was facing several serious constraints which made it difficult to perform its tasks effectively. These included the lack of a clear policy, strategy, plan, and program, a weak organizational set-up, inadequate human resources development and dependence on expatriate staff (45% on the professional level), over-centralization, lack of clear functions and job descriptions, lack of adequate coordination with local authorities and other Ministries, lack of adequate administrative, financial, operational, and information systems, etc.

UN-HABITAT's PROJECT ASSISTANCE

At the request of the Ministry and funding by the UNDP, a UN-HABITAT project was, therefore, initiated comprising a Senior Management Expert/Chief Technical Advisor (CTA), a Housing Expert, a Road Expert, a

Building Expert, and a Contracts Analyst. Consultancy services in finance, and environmental development were provided as assistances by UN-HABITAT and UNEP (UN Environmental Program).

On the Ministry's side, the UN project's plans, programs, and activities were coordinated by Mr. Faisal al-Gurg, then Director of Studies and Planning. His recollections of events in those days are presented hereunder as "Recollection No 3".

As Senior Management Expert/CTA, my role was to supervise the project activities and ensure the delivery of the outputs required from the other experts as well as perform the institutional development items which were my area of responsibility. For the purpose of this book, I will dwell extensively on my assignments.

Ministry of Public Works & Housing Organization

The Ministry's actual organization can be seen in Fig. 6. It can be observed clearly that the organization reflected a highly haphazard and uncoordinated situation. For example, there was a manager for housing reporting to the Minister as well as the Deputy Minister while there was another Department of Housing and Construction reporting to the Deputy Minister. Another example of such an organizational weakness was the Studies and Planning office which was again reporting to the Deputy Minister as well as to the Assistant Deputy Minister for Technical Affairs. A third example was the Town Planning Unit which was reporting to the Studies and Planning office while a Physical Planning Agency was supposed to be present reporting to the Minister.

Following an in depth study of the Ministry's overall responsibilities as well as the review of each sector, department, and section, the organization chart shown as Fig. 7 hereunder was recommended and accepted by the Ministry and the concerned federal organization i.e. the Ministry for Cabinet Affairs which had a mandate on civil service institutional arrangements.

Among the many institutional reforms reflected in the Ministry's new organization were:

- The establishment of a separate sector, under the leadership of an Assistant Deputy Minister, for one of the Ministry's most important responsibilities, namely, public housing;
- The clear delineation of the responsibility for the studies, planning, training, international relations, and information systems to be managed under a directorate operating as a staff function under the Deputy Minister;
- The establishment of a separate testing and research section to oper-

ate as a staff function under the Assistant Deputy Minister for Technical Affairs;

- The placement of the Physical Planning Section to operate under the Assistant Deputy Minister for Housing instead of the previous confused situation whereby it had been subjected to a dual supervision i.e. under the Director of Studies and Planning as well as the Assistant Deputy Minister for Technical Affairs;
- The streamlining of the administrative and financial services.
- The restructuring of the Ministry's building directorate into its distinct components, namely, design, and construction services;
- The elevation of the important services related to roads to a department level; and the streamlining of the administrative and financial services.

Administrative Improvements

The following administrative improvements were also undertaken:

1. Descriptions of functions were prepared for each Department and Section;
2. Job descriptions were prepared for each job in the Ministry;
3. Identification of human resources and development needs;
4. Arrangement of the following training programs:

   a. Assignment of UAE national counterparts to UN experts and facilitating training for them including the following:

       i. For Mr. Shawki Mukhthar in contracts management training in Malta, U.K. and Kuwait;

       ii. For Mr. S. Al Amoodi in building materials testing and research training in India and Australia;

       iii. For Mr. Anwar Badri in road maintenance in USA; and

       iv. For Mr. Ali Sultan in housing in Singapore.

   b. Arrangement of the first training seminar at the Ministry on the subject of "Project Execution" for 14 trainee engineers from the Ministry and presentations by UN project staff, the Ministry's professionals, and the private sector;

   c. A seminar on legal aspects of project management conducted by a UN expert for 34 participants from the Ministry, 12 from other ministries, and 8 from the private sector;

   d. The project also initiated symposia on other important subjects: "The nature and Characteristics of Soils in the UAE and Foundation

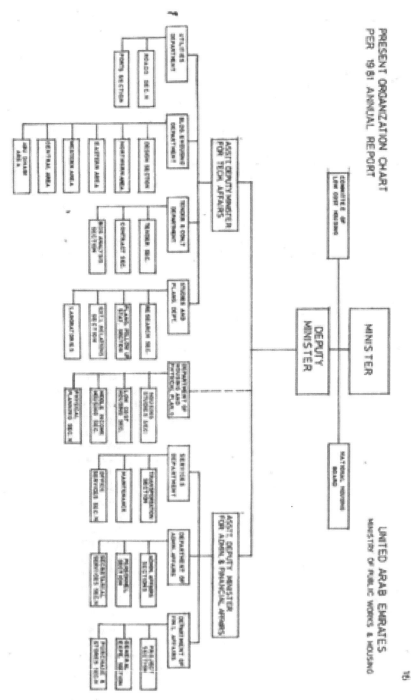

Fig. 6

Actual Organization of the UAE Ministry of Public Works and Housing - 1981

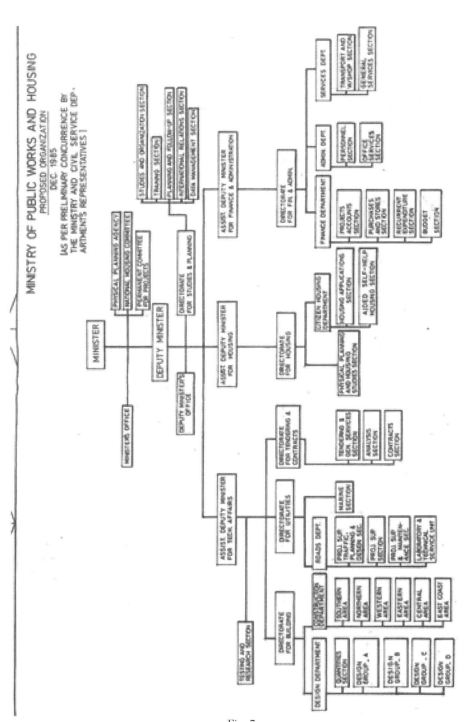

Fig. 7
Proposed Organization for the UAE Ministry of Public Works and Housing

Engineering", and "Road Maintenance".

5. The review and improvement of the Ministry's programming and monitoring system in order to facilitate the reporting, analysis, and timely corrective measures including the use of computerized systems;

6. An improved performance appraisal system with clear criteria aimed at enhancing efficiency and effectiveness;

7. Facilitating, with the project's initiative, the following consultancy services:

(a) A UN-HABITAT Housing Finance consultant (Mr. G. Tessema) who recommended the establishment of a Housing Finance institution;

(b) UNEP (UN Environmental Program) consultants (Mr. Saleh M. Osman and, later, Mr. N. Gabremedhin) who proposed an assistance program for the Ministry;

(c) A UNDP consultant (Dr. M.S. Matta) who recommended the establishment of an improved information system and training.

Other Project Support Services during 1983-85

On top of my responsibilities as Senior Management Expert/CTA, I was assigned the following additional tasks, with the mutual agreement of the Ministry of Public Works and Housing and the UNDP:

1. At the request of the Government of Qatar and the UNDP in Qatar, a 2-month mission was conducted for a study of Doha Municipality's institutional development needs;

2. I undertook a one-month UNDP consultancy service at the UAE University at Al Ain in response to its request for assistance concerning its institutional development needs;

3. I acted as Officer-in-charge of the UNDP in the absence of the Resident Representative;

4. I also reviewed a consultancy report on the organization and management of Abu Dhabi Municipality and made various recommendations for improvements.

Further Assistance to the Ministry of Public Works and Housing

The first phase of my service with UN-HABITAT's project assistance to the Ministry of Public Works and Housing (UAE) ended on December 31, 1985. The second phase of my service, through the UNDP and UN-HABITAT, occurred during February, 1992, at the request of the Ministry of Public Works

On my left: H.E. Mr. Qassem Sultan, Then Director General of Dubai Municipality and on my right: H.E. Mr. Faisal Al-Gurg, then Director General of the Sheikh Zaid Housing Program.

and Housing, and the concurrence of Dubai Municipality. I was then working as UN Senior Management Expert/CTA at Dubai Municipality in a project executed by UN-HABITAT.

The Minister of Public Works and Housing, His Highness Sheikh Rakadh Bin Salem Bin Rakadh, issued an Administrative Order No.Q/W/91 dated 21st October 1991 according to which a committee was established comprising:
Kidane Alemayehu, UN Senior Management Expert/CTA, Advisor;
Engineer Ali Hamed Al Shamsi, Director of the Housing Department;
Mr. Ibrahim Abd Almalek, Director of Financial Affairs Department;
Engineer Faisal Abdalla Al Gurg, Director of Studies and Planning Department;
Engineer Zahra Salman AlAboudi.

The study committee undertook its task during February-March, 1992 and submitted its 128-page report under a covering letter dated March 24, 1992. The comprehensive study covered not only the Ministry's internal situation at that time but also the needs of all other concerned Ministries as well as the various municipalities (20 organizations). Aside from various consultative meetings, formal surveys were undertaken involving those organizations as well as the Ministry's staff.

After assessing the challenges, constraints, and opportunities, identified from the various findings and responses, the committee submitted various recommendations in detail including the following:

a. The need for the establishment of a national housing policy, strategy and action plan; a National Housing Board; a housing fund to be converted eventually into a Housing Bank;

b. The need to make the National Physical Planning Agency operational;

c. The need for the formulation of a national policy and action plan for the development and maintenance of a federal infrastructure system including roads, utilities and harbors;

d. The need to allocate adequate resources for the repair and maintenance of federal buildings;

e. The need to strengthen the Ministry's research and quality control capabilities through allocation of adequate financial and human resources;

f. The need to enhance the Ministry's human resources development and training as well as the establishment of a Technical Training Centre within the Ministry for its benefit and the needs of Municipalities, consultants and contractors;

g. The need to privatize the Ministry's design, construction, and maintenance services, wherever possible, by making use of capable consultants and contractors;

h. The need to define the respective roles of the Ministry and Municipalities so that they would operate in mutual support and harmony;

i. The need to empower the Ministry with a higher authority so that the excessive bureaucracy arising from the involvement of the Ministries of Finance, State Audit, and the Minister of Planning even for minor purchases would be minimized;

j. The need to apply an internal delegation of authority within the Ministry with adequate or effective controls;

k. The need to provide adequate office facilities including the required information and documentation system, space, etc;

l. The need for improving the Ministry's performance appraisal systems;

m. The need for streamlining the Ministry's organization in two phases with a special focus on strengthening public housing, tendering and contracting, building design and development, and the offices of the Minister and Deputy Minister.

My UN service with the UAE Ministry of Public Works and Housing was concluded after the above consultancy input was delivered. For more details regarding my role at the Ministry, please have a look at the following statement of recollections by the then Director of Studies and Planning of the Ministry, Mr. Faisal Al-Gurg.

H.E. Mr. Faisal Al-Gurg

H.E. Mr. Faisal Abdulla Al Gurg worked at the U.A.E. Ministry of Public Works and Housing (MOPWH) from 1976 till 2008 at various management levels including his role as the Ministry's Director of Planning. He was subsequently promoted to the post of Director General of the Sheikh Zaid Housing Program until his retirement.

Recollections of Mr. Faisal Abdulla Al Gurg:

"I met Kidane Alemayehu in Nairobi, Kenya in 1982 for the first time during a UNDP Habitat meeting.

During the meeting I was impressed by Mr. Kidane Alemayehu. United Nations proposed him to support us in the United Arab Emirates. Accordingly, we as MOPWH, offered him a role with the Ministry as a Consultant for one month which was accepted by him. When we returned back to UAE, we asked the UN to second him for one month. Accordingly, Kidane joined the Ministry of Public Works and Housing during October – November 1982.

After the one month, the Ministry of Public Works asked the UN to extend Mr. Kidane's work for three years contract as a United Nations Senior Management Expert and Chief Technical Advisor (CTA) starting from January 4, 1983.

During his time at the UAE MOPWH, a delegation from the Ministry of Public Works from the State of Qatar attended one of the meetings held in United Arab Emirates. The State of Qatar Ministry's delegation were impressed with Mr. Kidane's proposals, orientations and ideas and as a result offered him a position with them in Qatar. The U.A.E. MOPWH agreed to second him for one month to work in Qatar. Also, Dubai Municipality requested us to second him for one month where we did.

Also, Mr. Kidane worked for UAE University at Al Ain for one month where he developed the organizational structure and internal regulations.

At the end of his 3 years sojourn with MOPWH, and after long negotiations between UNDP and Dubai Municipality and Qatar, we recommended him to join Dubai Municipality. UNDP asked Mr. Kidane to speak to Mr. Qassem Sultan,

Director General of Dubai Municipality for 15 minutes. Accordingly, and after this call, Mr. Kidane joined Dubai Municipality for a period of 15 (Fifteen) year service.

Mr. Kidane developed the MOPWH in terms of productivity and efficiency. It is worth to say that the important contributions of the project was the introduction of staff training on important public works and housing issues; and collaboration between the MOPWH, other concerned Ministries, and various Emirates.

In addition he supported us in the selection of experts and he developed our organizational structure and internal regulations. He also assisted in establishing the Institute of Administrative Development in the UAE by implementing his studies, reports and experiences.

It was a great asset to the U. A. E. government having Mr. Kidane Alemayehu, and his contributions had a great effect to all other departments by taking advantage of his experiences."

CHAPTER 5

DUBAI'S AMAZING TRANSFORMATION

The transformation of Dubai from a small fishing village as late as the 1950's to its present status of an internationally recognized cosmopolitan, "best practice city" is a phenomenal achievement. I will attempt to present Dubai's actual situation not so long ago as well as the process that was followed by Dubai Municipality in the city's amazing progress.

The question many visitors to Dubai raise is how such an extremely fast development was achieved. The most frequent presumption is that Dubai's phenomenal growth was due to its oil resources. However, this assumption could not be farther from the truth. Although Dubai has some oil resources, it is quite limited making it less than 10% of the Emirate's GDP. If there is one factor that could be singled out to explain Dubai's tremendous achievement in such a short time, it is leadership. The Emirate has been blessed with excellent leaders, especially the late Sheikh Rashid Bin Saeed Al-Maktoum, the former ruler of Dubai Emirate, as well as his sons Sheikh Maktoum Bin Rashid Al-Maktoum (late) and the current leader of Dubai Emirate, Sheikh Mohammed Bin Rashid Al-Maktoum. Their vision and strategy coupled with their ability to deploy competent executives such as H.E. Mr. Qassim Sultan as Director General of Dubai Municipality and other local staff enabled the formulation and application of appropriate policies, strategies, plans, programs and management systems that finally facilitated the achievement of the Emirate's development.

On my right: H.E. Mr. Qassim Sultan, then Director-General of Dubai Municipality, and other officials at my farewell party in Dubai.

Dubai in the 1950's[1]

A 15-Minute Interview Results in a 15-Year Cooperation between the UN and Dubai Municipality

As stated above, towards the end of 1985, I was busy preparing my final report on the UN project assisting the Ministry of Public Works and Housing when I received a telephone call from the UNDP Resident Representative, Mr. Akram Qursha, based in Abu Dhabi, asking me to meet with the then Director General of Dubai Municipality, Mr. Qassim Sultan, to brief him about my mission to Doha Municipality in Qatar. Since I was under pressure to conclude my final report and preparations for my transfer to Doha as agreed among the Government of Qatar, the UNDP, and UN-Habitat, I was, frankly, reluctant to spend time on other issues such as the requested briefing. However, Mr. Qursha, was rather insistent and assured me that it should not take more than 15 minutes.

When I reached the office of Mr. Qassim Sultan at Dubai Municipality, he was already waiting for me and I took exactly 15 minutes to brief him about the study at Doha Municipality including the background information, methodology, action plan, findings, and recommendations. When I returned to my office a short while later, the phone was ringing and it was, again, from Mr. Akram Qursha who informed me that Mr. Qassim Sultan had called him and strongly requested that I continue my UN service within the United Arab Emirates as advisor to Dubai Municipality. Thus, the fifteen-minute interview ended up in becoming a 15-year (1986-2000) United Nations service to Dubai Municipality.

The UN project was entitled "Institutional Support to Dubai Municipality" and comprised, eventually, numerous experts and consultants supervised by me as a team leader with a title Senior Management Expert/Chief Technical Advisor (CTA), covering virtually all sectors of the Municipality. The project's achievements were largely due to the tremendous effort exerted by the experts, consultants and specialists as well as the local counterparts and the decisiveness of the Municipality's officials.

An introductory statement by the then director of the Technical Cooperation Department of UN-Habitat, otherwise known as the United Nations Center for Human Settlements (UNCHS), Mr. Daniel Biau, is provided in the following pages as Recollection No. 4.

Who is Daniel Biau?

Born in France, Daniel Biau graduated in 1974 from the prestigious Ecole Nationale des Ponts et haussées in Paris as a Civil Engineer specialized in urban

Dr. Daniel Biau

planning. He also holds a PhD in African Sociology from Sorbonne University. He has worked for the United Nations from 1988-2011 as a senior expert in housing and urban development policy. In this capacity, he has provided advice to more than 60 countries in all regions of the world and published many articles on urban issues. Daniel Biau has been Deputy Executive Director and Director of the Regional and Technical Cooperation Division of UN-Habitat, the City Agency of the United Nations (www.unhabitat.org) headquartered in Nairobi, Kenya. He is now an independent consultant (danielbiau.webnode .com) and has recently published a book based on his UN experience: "Le Pont et la Ville" (the Bridge and the City).

Recollections No. 4 by Mr. Daniel Biau:

"Urban Policy-making, a key role of the United Nations"
I have worked for more than thirty years in international cooperation on housing and urban development. I have managed the technical cooperation Division of UN-Habitat from 1994-2011, established the network of UN-Habitat Offices around the world, initiated the World Urban Forum in 2002, the State of the World's Cities Reports, directed a number of global programmes, guided the drafting of international guidelines and dozens of technical reports, visited and advised more than 60 countries. I joined the UN by political ideal, impressed by its mandate and the respect it deserves, committed to bring my contribution to the cause of the World Peace and Development.

At UN-Habitat I realized that the urban agenda was too broad to be an international priority. This explains why during the last decades, the United Nations system has tried to give it some focus and to link it to clearer or simpler priorities such as sustainable development, democratic governance or poverty eradication. This has not worked very well in terms of resource mobilization and overall visibility. But it has allowed better understanding of the on-going urban transition, to identify and highlight local policy options and to advise a number of governments on the best ways and means to develop and implement housing and urban strategies.

In fact the urbanization process of the developing world has been less chaotic than forecasted by the media. Many countries are managing their urban development relatively well, particularly in Asia, the Arab States and Latin America. Ideas and good practices have been shared, adapted and successfully applied in a number of emerging economies. Of course many other countries, particularly the Least Developed Countries (LDCs), are lagging behind and are unable to address the slum crisis. But the urbanization of our planet should not be seen as an outright disaster. It has both positive and negative features.

The Urban Agenda covers by essence a cross-sectoral and multi-disciplinary field, and has to be related to many aspects of the economic, social, environmental, cultural and political life. It has to provide the territorial dimensions of a number of societal challenges that the UN system tries to bring together at the global level, in an often scattered but consensual manner. This might be the weakness of the urban agenda: because it is too wide it cannot stand on its own and needs to be subsumed under - or associated with - more popular and fashionable topics (such as climate change). But then it may lose its explanatory power, comprehensiveness, and political value. Therefore urban specialists have no choice but to frequently restructure this agenda in various ways to reach the world leaders.

I have followed these periodical changes in the urban discourse with some cynicism; I have also contributed to formulate that discourse. I have seen physical projects replacing master-planning in the 70s, then urban management replacing projects in the 80s, then the birth of the governance paradigm, the increasing emphasis on local authorities, the abandon of "shelter for all" and its resurrection in the anti-slum Millennium Development Goal, the death of traditional urban planning and the appearance of strategic planning at the turn of the century, the continuous divorce between experts advocating participatory and incremental upgrading and politicians adept of slum eradication, the recent revival of climate change and green energy concerns, the permanent and rather fruitless search for simple monitoring indicators, the gender equality credo and its subsidiary debate on mainstreaming vs. direct women empowerment, the youth bulge vs. ageing societies, and last but not least the unbelievably persistent and absurd question on how to stop (for good!) rural-to-urban migrations.

At the City Summit (Istanbul, June 1996) governments argued about urban governance concepts and later refused that UN-Habitat be called "the City Agency". They did not understand what was underway. Now they have moved forward. They have agreed that they must decentralize powers and resources to local authorities. Many cities have adopted a City Development Strategy approach, by implementing participation and partnership principles as key ingredients of renewed urban planning. Only a few have upgraded the urban slums but many, particularly in Asia, have improved the material lives of slum-dwellers by relocating them in the suburbs. Slums remain a major problem in only two sub-regions, South Asia and Sub-Saharan Africa. The rest of the developing world has progressed slowly but steadily and cities are better in spite of their tremendous growth. The urban population of the developing world increased from 1.35 Billion in 1988 to 2 Billion in 2000 and 2.8 Billion in 2013. However cities have been able to cope and to become effective engines of development in most regions of the planet.

Dubai constitutes a good example of this evolution. When I joined UN-Habitat in 1988, I was surprised to discover a project entitled "Institutional Support to Dubai Municipality". In my mind the Emirate did not need any UN assistance. This was true in financial terms but untrue in technical terms. At that time Dubai was already well-known for its wealth, but the city, with its 400 000 inhabitants, had only limited managerial abilities. Its leaders were fully aware of the need to strengthen, modernize and "nationalize" the municipal administration. This is why they had requested UN inputs, a technical assistance seen as objective, neutral, highly qualified and cost-effective. Under the visionary leadership of Qassim Sultan and the perseverant and efficient direction of Kidane Alemayehu, the support project was implemented over ten years. It involved many experts and was very successful. Dubai's urban management capacities have become first-class, at par with other national companies such as Emirates Airlines. In 1996 Dubai was recognized as one of the best managed cities in the Middle-East and created, in partnership with UN-Habitat, an international Best Practice Award on urban management. Today the agglomeration counts 2.4 Million people, a six-fold increase in 25 years. In spite of some hiccups and controversial investments in recent years it has become one of the leading cities of the world.

What role did we (and other international agencies active within UN-Habitat field of expertise) play in the positive evolution of towns and cities around the planet? How did we help or influence the urban transition? We implemented many projects but they were only drops in the enormous bucket of urban initiatives. They were useful but with limited quantitative impact, they did not address the magnitude of the needs.

I believe that our influence has been essentially political and ideological. Ministers and Mayors came to Nairobi and to other meeting places and heard experts repeating the same messages over and over again. In their countries our experts adapted the same messages to city-specific situations. Reports, guidelines, films, websites, pamphlets, articles, informal discussions, site visits, and training sessions resulted in an overall change of mindset towards housing and urban issues. Country projects were seen as demonstrations of new approaches, not as ends in themselves. They gave us the required credibility and allowed our recommendations to be taken seriously, not always followed but always kept in mind as references. We have effectively built national and local capacities that were essential to translate our advices into concrete improvements, as evidenced in Dubai. We have been an implicit think tank rooted in country realities, not a research network but a "policy-making organ" as so nicely characterized by the UN jargon. I am convinced that we have played a progressive role by spreading and testing valuable ideas and concepts which were just a step ahead of standard policies and helped in due course politicians to respond better to the needs and expectations of their peoples. We have probably contributed to realize the ambitions of the UN Charter by linking and bridging "We, the peoples" and "We, the governments" in our area of work.

There is room for optimism but certainly not for complacency. Still millions of people live in abject poverty, corruption is widespread, wars, violence and disasters destroy human lives and settlements, the urban environment is badly polluted, social inequalities divide our agglomerations in ghettos, international cooperation is under-funded, and African cities are lagging behind. The combat for better cities and better life must therefore go on. And the UN should continue to play a strategic role in this endeavour."[2]

Dubai Emirate and Dubai Municipality (1950-1979) [3]

Dubai Municipality is one of the major government organizations within Dubai which is one of the seven Emirates in the federation of the United Arab Emirates, frequently referred to in its acronym UAE.

According to the still applicable UAE federal law, the President of the country is, ex-officio, the Ruler of Abu Dhabi while the Vice-President and Prime Minister is the Ruler of Dubai. The major governmental structures in the UAE comprise: (i) a Rulers' Council which includes the leaders of the seven Emirates; (ii) parliament of assigned members; (iii) a federal cabinet with Ministries focusing on various government services such as foreign affairs, defense, justice, health, trade, public works and housing, transport and communications, etc; and (iv) the local authorities of the various Emirates each of which is headed by the respective Ruler.

Dubai Municipality is a government unit within Dubai Emirate similar to other such organizations including the Department of the Dubai Police, Emirates Airlines, Dubai Courts, Dubai Customs, Dubai Health Department, etc.

According to Mr. Qassim Sultan, the former Director General of the Municipality, Dubai Municipality was established as an institution in "the early 1950's" and its major purpose was to keep the city clean. By 1962, the Municipality's capacity and services expanded covering health, engineering, administrative and financial activities. Among the services provided by the Municipality during the early 1960's, the following were reported to be "the most important":

"1. Organizing and cleaning public areas and inspecting hotels;
2. Taking care of public health and inspecting outlets selling food and beverages;
3. Planning the city and monitoring the implementation of the general planning;
4. Licensing buildings and supervising craftsmen;
5. Establishing and inspecting slaughterhouses and shops;
6. Paving public roads and maintaining them as well as building public squares and bridges;
7. Establishing and supervising public bus services;
8. Planting trees along roads and in public parks and sports grounds;
9. Fire-fighting and operating fire stations; (and)
10. Establishing and supervising graveyards."

Among the other important developments in the 1960's, mention should be made of the Municipal Council in 1961 and, later in 1965, the appointment of

A major part of Dubai in 1980 and 2012

Sheikh Hamdan bin Rashid Al-Maktoum, son of the then Ruler of Dubai Emirate, Sheikh Rashid bin Saeed Al-Maktoum, as the head of the Municipal Council.

The change in leadership coupled with the discovery of Dubai's off-shore oil resources as well as the UAE's independence set in motion an accelerated development process which resulted in the implementation of several projects that facilitated the basic infrastructure network to transform the city into an urban center. Some of the important projects that were reported to have been completed during the 1970's include the following:

> "1971 Dubai International Airport;
> 1972 Port Rashid;
> 1973 Rashid Hospital;
> 1975 The Deira Corniche and sea front;
> 1975 The Shindaga Tunnel;
> 1979 Deepening the Creek (between Deira and BurDubai);
> 1979 Jubel Ali Port;
> 1979 Dubai Dry Dock;"

In 1974, the organizational arrangement of Dubai Municipality comprised three sectors, namely, Engineering, Health, and Financial & Administrative Departments.

In 1979, the still in use Dubai Municipality headquarter building was in-augurated by Britain's Queen Elizabeth II.

Dubai Emirate's population was a mere 38,000 in 1959, and 70,000 in 1968. As its development increased, its population mushroomed to 276,000 in 1980; 498,000 in 1990; 862,000 in 2000; 1.9 million in 2010; and 2.1 million: (2013 estimate). It should be noted also that according to the Dubai Government Statistics Center's population report for 2010, there were over a million[4] additional people working in Dubai but living elsewhere. Thus the total population in Dubai during the day time is over 3 million, a huge increase from only 20 years ago.

Project's Initial Focus

The initial focus of the UN project was on the review of the Municipality's overall organization as well as each section's set-up, functions and systems and initiate an appropriate reform including the identification of the required capacity. The Municipality's 1986 organization chart [6] can be seen in Figure 8.

It can be observed from the chart that the Municipality was over centralized. For example, 20 sections and various offices were reporting directly to the Director General. With such an excessive span of control, and, at the same

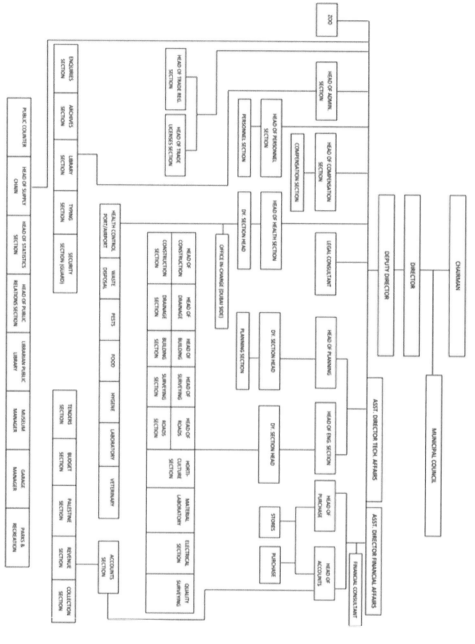

Fig. 8: Organization Chart of Dubai Municipality

time, with virtually no delegation of authority, it was impossible to provide the required level of service efficiency as well as project planning, implementation and control. For instance, it was noted that the Director General had to approve personally the issue of each trade license three times: (a) to decide on whether an application should be considered, in principle; (b) to review and decide on whether the required information about an applicant was adequate; and (c) finally to decide on the actual approval of the trade license. It was, therefore, essential to streamline the Municipality's organization, define the functions of each Department and Section as well as identify the required jobs with descriptions of the respective duties and responsibilities, required qualification and experience as well as authority, where appropriate.

Dubai Municipality and Its Collaboration with the United Nations

In 1986, at the commencement of the project, Dubai Municipality had both positive as well as highly challenging circumstances. The main positive aspect was the fact that there was a leadership in place in the person of Mr. Qassim Sultan as Director General of the Municipality, and few support staff, who were capable and highly motivated to bring about the required institutional development in the Municipality under the overall directive of the chairman, HH Sheikh Hamdan Bin Saeed Al Rashid Al Maktoum. On the other hand, it was recognized that the Municipality was operating under severe institutional constraints.

The Municipality lacked a comprehensive policy with clear directives and regulations, strategy, an action plan, program, definition of systems, functions, performance standards and assessment methods, accountability and transparency. In essence, it lacked the systematic and sustainable institutional instruments needed for the ambitious vision that the leadership aspired for and the high level of efficiency required by a competitive city.

Among the most serious challenges faced by the Municipality was the extremely weak human resources situation. There was no training capacity. Only 30% of the staff on the management and supervisory levels comprised local citizens. Most of the expatriates on these levels were also not fully competent for their duties and responsibilities. It was evident that the Municipality required a comprehensive and an in depth review and a fundamental transformation. In addition, it was noted that, especially among the local staff, there was a huge gender gap; women were very under-represented.

The Municipality lacked numerous essential management tools that would enable it to compete globally. These included lack of appropriate policies, plans, programs, clear performance measures, a customer oriented municipal service, the application of preventive maintenance systems, use of modern information systems, effective internal controls that would ensure transparency and accountability, systematic use of efficiency methods to enhance revenue and decrease/avoid waste, effective public relations measures, regulations and procedures that would facilitate efficient processes, systematic delegation of authority with an effective control, sustainability with the utilization of the Emirate's own human resources, etc. Therefore, as a result of several management weaknesses that were prevalent in the Municipality, its overall performance was considered inadequate. Consequently, the Municipality needed expert assistance from the United Nations.

At the request of Dubai Municipality, a UNDP project was submitted by me for execution by UN-Habitat. The first phase of the project was entitled, as stated above, "Institutional Development of Dubai Municipality" (ref. No. UAE/85/012). This was followed-up later by the Project UAE/92/002, as a second phase and, finally, Project UAE/98/005 as the third phase. The UN project staff comprised 4 experts, 16 consultants, and 7 specialists with varying contract periods as needed. The list of the UN staff who served under the project can be seen hereunder:

Kidane Alemayehu, Senior Management Expert/Chief Technical Advisor (CTA)

Experts:
1. Dr. Maher Stino, Planning Expert;
2. Mr. John Ward, Environment Expert;
3. Dr. Waheed Uddin, Roads Pavement Expert;

Consultants:
1. Mr. Samir Selloum, Legal Consultant;
2. Mr. M Halwani, Finance Consultant;
3. Mr. S. Nimry, Stores Consultant;
4. Mr. A. Akrouk, Library Consultant;
5. Mr. M. Haider, Statistics Consultant;
6. Mr. D. Armstrong, Transportation Consultant;
7. Mr. N. J. Nuttal, Waste Management Consultant;
8. Mr. M. Qrunfleh, Horticulture Consultant;
9. Dr. Tahani el-Erian, Archives Consultant,
10. Mr. A. F. Galamallah, Archives Consultant;

11. Mr. M. Itayem, archives Consultant;
12. Mr. Jon Ward, Environment Protection Consultant;
13. Dr. Ahmed Ragheb, Public Relations Consultant;
14. Mr. B. Parnell, Advertisement Control Consultant;
15. Mr. Mokhtar Abdul-Kader Saleh, Building Regulations Consultant
16. Mr. G. Konecny, Survey Consultant

Specialists:
1. Mr. S. Al Monthiri, Organization and Methods (O&M) Specialist;
2. Mr. M. Duheidal, Job Analyst;
3. Dr. B. Sandouka, O&M Specialst (Admin. & Fin);
4. Dr. Ali al Asam, O&M Specialist (Tech);
5. Dr. Qrunfleh, Horticulture Specialist;
6. Mr. Ahmed Nuseirat, Human Resources Specialist;
7. Mr. Iyad Usta, Job Analyst.

Support Staff
1. Mrs. Wafaa (Secretary – Arabic);
2. Mrs. Sabina Fernandes (Secretary – English);
3. Mr. Raid Khleif (Translator: Arabic/English)

Main Counterparts (UAE Nationals)
One of the important methods applied by the project in the development of the local capacity was by ensuring that every expert and consultant had at least one local counterpart to closely follow and learn from the various activities and outputs for the purpose of gaining additional knowledge and experience as well as sustainability in dealing with the work after the departure of the UN staff.

Some counterparts were also provided with additional formal training (more on this item under the subject of human resources).

My main counterpart staffs were the following:

Mr. Mohammed Julfar, Head of the Administrative Development Office, after Mr. Talal Khoori left the municipality (now Assistant Director-General for Financial Affairs); and

Mr. Talal Khoori, first Head of Administrative Development Office (now running his own private business).

The project objectives, activities, inputs in terms of experts, consultants and specialists, the required outputs and the achievement of the required tangible impact, evolved in accordance with the Municipality's actual needs. The basic objectives of the project were to enhance Dubai Municipality's self-reliance, efficiency, and effectiveness through appropriate policies, development goals and plans as well as the application of innovative and pragmatic institutional mechanisms including systems, regulations, comprehensive and integrated plans, programs, and monitoring tools in all its undertakings.

Some of the specific objectives incorporated in the UN project documents (UAE/85/012; UAE/92/002; UAE/98/005) included the following:

- To strengthen the Municipality's capacity and self-reliance in various human settlements areas, particularly town planning, development and provision of urban services;
- The continued development of Dubai Emirate in an accelerated and integrated manner including the provision of efficient services while maintaining effective control on urban improvements, building construction, commercial and industrial activities, public health , infrastructural, and environmental services;
- To enhance the Municipality's self-reliance and sustainability with efficient administrative and financial systems with appropriate institutional development mechanisms including adequate internal controls that assure transparency and full accountability;
- To streamline the Municipality's organization and simplify its procedures with clear regulations and manuals of operation with suitable training programs locally and abroad.

The main outcomes of the UN project activities with the close participation of the local counterparts and the decision making officials of the Municipality are presented hereunder.

Institutional Development Impact on Dubai Municipality

Dubai Municipality has achieved a significant, positive impact as a result of its sustained and substantial institutional development effort in collaboration with the United Nations. The United Nations project reviewed in depth all the Departments, Sections, Offices, and Units comprehensively in terms of their policy, organization, systems, operational methods, resources including financial, human and other assets. The credit for the achievement of the organization's huge institutional development goes to the officials and staff of the Municipality for their hard work, decisiveness, and perseverance.

H.E. Mr. Qassim Sultan

On my right: Mr. Mohammed Julfar and on my left Mr. Talal Khoory

Sustainability and Self-Reliance

The views of the then Director General of Dubai Municipality, Mr. Qassim Sultan, are presented hereunder as Recollection No. 5.

Recollection No. 5
by H.E. Mr. Qassim Sultan, then Director General of Dubai Municipality

"It is a pleasure to write these few lines as an expression of my deepest gratitude to the UN–Habitat agency and to Mr. Kidane Alemayehu.

The UN-Habitat agency team together with Mr. Alemayehu at the realm (partnered with Dubai Municipality) worked tirelessly from 1985 to 2000 to guide and assist the Dubai Municipality in order to improve its practices on both the administrative and technical levels. They provided expertise and diligently managed technical support which contributed in achieving tremendous success and improvement at Dubai Municipality.

Additionally, Mr. Alemayehu's immeasurable personal guidance in helping me improve Dubai Municipality's performance was crucial to the great successes achieved in our practices, which mainly focused on self-reliance, increased efficiency, the cost cutting practices, and an increase of revenue resource

In the mid-Eighties, and after I took over the reign of Dubai Municipality in 1985 as Director; we conducted a number of studies and surveys to determine areas that needed improvement in our rapidly growing city.

In order to complement and continue Dubai's growth momentum, we sought the expertise of the United Nations Development Program (UNDP) to partner with and aid us in providing efficient services and putting into place an organization with an effective workforce and working methodology. With the assistance of United Nations Development Program experts in the fields of environment, public health, urban planning, laboratories, agriculture, and management development, we formed joint committees made up of those experts working alongside Emirati municipality employees to plan and execute the tasks at hand.

Attaining the set objectives involved several key tasks:

- Starting by putting in place organization structure in order to set up preliminary requirements of work ahead.
- Reviewed and developed manuals, job descriptions and descriptions of functions of municipality personnel.
- Improved, streamlined and developed effective standard procedures as well organized the legislation pertaining to commercial registration and licensing.
- Improved, streamlined and developed effective standard procedures as well as organized the legislation and licensing procedures pertaining to the management of building and housing.
- Improved, streamlined and developed effective standard procedures as well as organized the legislation and licensing procedures pertaining to town planning and land surveying.
- Improved, streamlined and developed effective standard procedures as well as organized the legislation pertaining to public health services including nutrition and environment.

Starting from right: H.E. Mr. Qassim Sultan, Director General of Dubai Municipality, H.E. Mr. Waly Endow UNCHS Executive Director, Mr. Daniel Biau, head of UNCHS Department of Technical Cooperation and Development, Mr. Akram Qursha, UNDP Resident Representative, and myself.

- Conducted studies designed to improve employee efficiency across all departments, especially those departments with a large workforce such as agriculture, environment and public health.
- Developed an information technology system to be applied to all departments and which is designed to facilitate and improve customer service.

I look back on these achievements with the greatest pride and deepest appreciation for Mr. Alemayehu and people from UNDP.

My best wishes to Mr. Alemayehu for continued successes in all his current and future endeavors."

Project Outputs

It would take several books to relate the detailed studies and recommendations by the UN project staff as well as the actions taken by the Municipality during the 15-year period of collaboration between the Municipality and the United Nations. For the purpose of this book, the following main areas of focus are presented to provide a glimpse of the process which facilitated Dubai's transformation into a major, global and cosmopolitan city.

1, Organizational Reform

The project's initial focus was on the Municipality's organization, policy, plans, systems, functions, and capacity. This was undertaken in a comprehensive and systematic study of each section based on which, a more streamlined organization chart as well as the required functions were proposed and implemented. As a result of the organizational review, there were several improvements achieved including the following:

- The span of control under the Director General was reduced substantially thereby enabling more focus on vital policy issues and decision making;
- The establishment of an administrative and quality systems development office in order to ensure a continued effectiveness and efficiency

in the Municipality on all levels;

- The establishment of an effective internal control system and capability thereby avoiding corruption and waste;
- The integration of related services e.g. the planning, building control, and housing activities; environmental activities such as public health (preventive), drainage and irrigation, public parks and horticulture, and environment protection services; public transportation and other infrastructure services, etc. in order to achieve the required full coordination and effectiveness;
- The establishment of an effective external affairs office to deal with international issues involving the Municipality;
- The establishment of Municipal centers in various key locations throughout the Emirate of Dubai in order to provide its services in close proximity to the public;
- The establishment of a modern and effective information technology including GIS (Geographic Information System) that greatly facilitated the provision of efficient municipal services;
- The establishment of a customer service center where, for instance, an applicant for a building permit, would find all the offices concerned with its processing at one location;
- The establishment of a municipal training center;
- The establishment of other important offices for public relations, and legal services.

It should be noted that the initial revised organization continued to be reviewed and adjusted to meet Dubai's evolving needs. Three of the organization charts [7] can be seen in Figs. 9, 10 and 11 for the years 1994, 2002 and 2011:

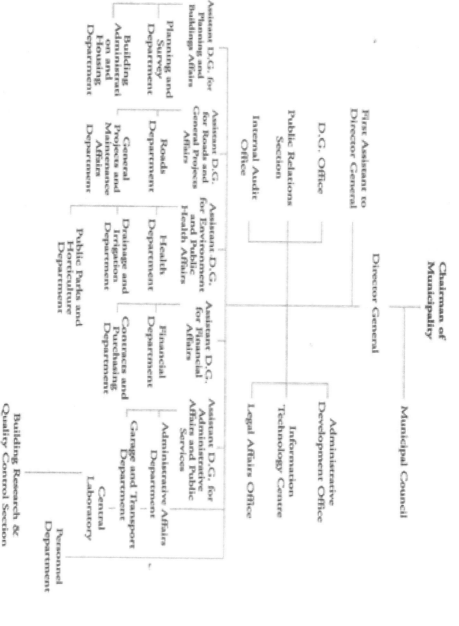

Fig 9 : Dubai Municipality's Organization Chart in 1994:

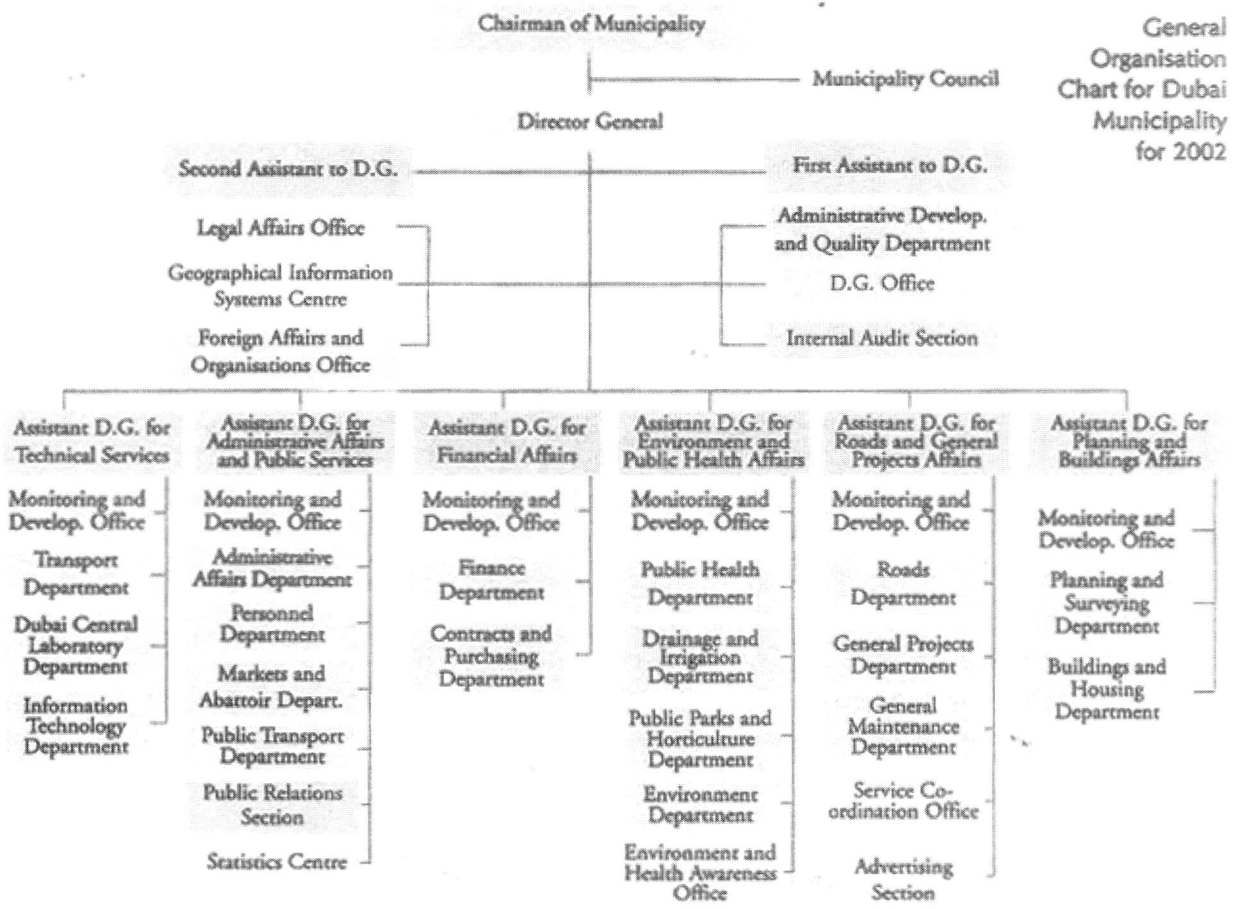

General Organisation Chart for Dubai Municipality for 2002

Chairman of Municipality

Municipality Council

Director General

First Assistant to D.G.

- Administrative Develop. and Quality Department
- D.G. Office
- Internal Audit Section

Second Assistant to D.G.

- Legal Affairs Office
- Geographical Information Systems Centre
- Foreign Affairs and Organisations Office

Assistant D.G. for Technical Services
- Monitoring and Develop. Office
- Transport Department
- Dubai Central Laboratory Department
- Information Technology Department

Assistant D.G. for Administrative Affairs and Public Services
- Monitoring and Develop. Office
- Administrative Affairs Department
- Personnel Department
- Markets and Abattoir Depart.
- Public Transport Department
- Public Relations Section
- Statistics Centre

Assistant D.G. for Financial Affairs
- Monitoring and Develop. Office
- Finance Department
- Contracts and Purchasing Department

Assistant D.G. for Environment and Public Health Affairs
- Monitoring and Develop. Office
- Public Health Department
- Drainage and Irrigation Department
- Public Parks and Horticulture Department
- Environment Department
- Environment and Health Awareness Office

Assistant D.G. for Roads and General Projects Affairs
- Monitoring and Develop. Office
- Roads Department
- General Projects Department
- General Maintenance Department
- Service Co-ordination Office
- Advertising Section

Assistant D.G. for Planning and Buildings Affairs
- Monitoring and Develop. Office
- Planning and Surveying Department
- Buildings and Housing Department

Fig 10

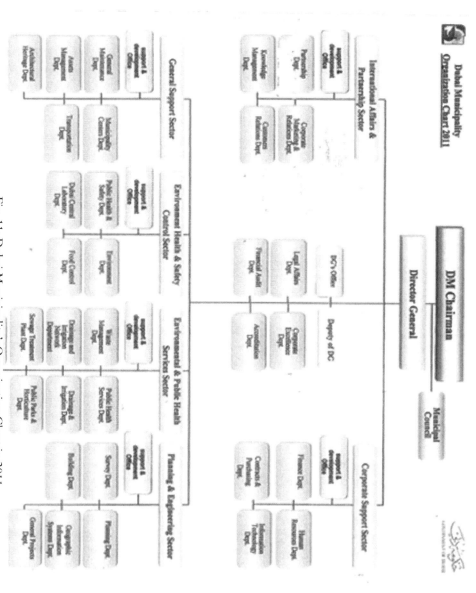

Fig. 11: Dubai Municipality's Organization Chart in 2011

Certain important reforms included the following:

1.1 **Administrative Development Office**

One of the important policy decisions made by the Municipality was to establish a framework for its systematic and sustained evolution through the Administrative Development Office reporting to the Director General. In addition, Follow-up and Development Offices were established in each sector in the Municipality which made it possible to undertake a systematic monitoring of each Department's working methods and performance. Such systematic and continued monitoring made it possible to identify any constraints in a timely manner thereby making it possible to initiate preventive and corrective measures as appropriate.

The project assisted in the training of qualified UAE nationals to be assigned to the various development offices. For some of them, training was arranged in other countries including, USA, Europe, Australia, etc. where they could gain an advanced knowledge and skills in their respective fields of municipal service.

As a result of applying such an institutional capacity, it was possible to initiate pragmatic methods for improving service efficiency and customer/public satisfaction, timely implementation of plans/projects, enhancing revenue, reducing expenditures through cost-effective methods, and the strengthening of the Municipality's human resources capacity.

This institutional capacity also reviewed the Municipality's policy, systems, regulations, procedures, and resources systematically in order to achieve its continued evolution and development.

The Administrative Development Office functioned as a complement to the internal audit capacity which focused on the control of financial and material resources whereas the former was concerned with institutional issues.

Dubai Municipality's experience was that this service was cost-effective as the benefits gained from improved service efficiency, control of expenditure, and revenue enhancement as a result of the institutional reforms were much higher than the expenditure incurred for the Administrative Development, and Follow-up and Development Offices. The Municipality's financial performance details are provided under the subject of financial management on page 115.

1.2 <u>Planning and Building Affairs</u>
This sector was responsible for planning, control of plan execution, land surveying, building control, advertisement control, and public housing. The sector resulted from the reorganization process and was led by Mr. Abdella Al-Ghaith as Assistant Director General. The UN expert who supported this sector was Dr. Maher Stino for the planning functions, while Dr. Gottfried Konecny served as a consultant for the land surveying activities.

Planning
The formulation of a comprehensive strategic plan was one of the most important systems that enabled the Municipality to achieve an accelerated development of Dubai Emirate and the city. Moving away from a static approach of urban development in terms of a classic master plan to a dynamic and strategic concept facilitated an evolving human settlements progress. This was one of the fundamental reasons for Dubai's phenomenal growth in such a short time. To this must, of course, be added Dubai's leadership capacity that was blessed with the highest integrity, bold vision and commitment to an internationally competitive standard of urban facilities and service efficiency.

With the support of the UN expert, Dr. Maher Stino, the Planning Department was initially reorganized into an Urban Planning Section comprising two units, namely, comprehensive planning and execution and monitoring ; a Projects Section with two units: project planning and monitoring; construction monitoring; a Surveying Section with three units: property surveying monitoring and geographic information systems. In addition to guiding the formulation of a comprehensive strategic plan for Dubai Emirate, the project

Dubai Municipality Expenses and Revenues 1990-2010
(In UAE Dirhams)[1]

Fiscal Year	Salaries	Current Expenses	Capital Expenses	Projects	Total Expenses	Revenues
2010	998,236,670	462,192,917	54,917,598	2,106,460,415	3,621,807,600	4,756,828,194
2009	1,032,915,976	534,279,230	115,273,192	2,652,110,538	4,334,578,937	4,569,295,691
2008	1,029,202,331	568,338,652	222,805,041	1,734,211,957	3,554,557,981	4,966,776,049
2007	812,807,475	468,198,740	198,465,977	923,619,325	2,403,091,517	3,946,566,580
2006	674,861,995	496,602,949	115,876,658	1,408,261,497	2,695,603,098	3,311,294,559
2005	749,325,790	533,503,232	109,776,109	1,171,944,919	2,564,550,049	3,351,867,422
2004	620,206,290	402,927,749	102,684,295	1,026,048,776	2,151,867,110	2,326,919,681
2003	540,008,430	374,561,563	210,490,038	1,235,014,211	2,366,074,242	1,758,811,877
2002	477,063,349	405,085,886	126,017,640	962,695,429	1,970,862,304	1,472,008,283
2001	441,064,676	447,549,205	70,568,387	1,058,426,629	2,017,608,897	1,288,375,368
2000	399,001,852	367,289,919	74,549,296	1,475,787,401	2,316,628,468	1,152,413,947
1999	353,875,089	234,898,517	63,283,134	1,307,114,815	1,959,171,555	1,216,996,410
1998	329,782,011	473,031,540	86,709,922	1,187,829,946	2,077,353,418	982,599,687
1997	305,875,576	191,923,429	80,426,071	1,099,299,713	1,677,524,789	676,850,267
1996	293,116,388	178,140,228	92,683,958	1,044,384,895	1,608,325,469	587,947,807
1995	271,939,539	227,924,456	32,419,607	679,346,861	1,211,630,463	436,286,604
1994	255,999,328	207,463,431	20,399,474	787,578,177	1,271,440,410	361,001,097
1993	249,659,255	260,596,534	43,202,716	948,366,277	1,501,824,782	310,826,430
1992	229,941,692	169,500,445	19,959,426	849,597,002	1,268,998,565	304,380,191
1991	214,362,024	203,555,969	42,588,346	535,185,262	995,691,601	280,482,018
1990	179,309,047	81,452,292	39,879,770	459,079,849	759,720,958	201,651,524
1985	122,977,242	252,253,640	11,557,932	399,900,725	786,689,539	119,606,635

facilitated various essential instruments including a zoning ordinance, a detailed manual of operation and provided direct training to local counterparts in planning and monitoring systems and methodologies.

Eventually, the Advertisement Control Section was transferred to the Planning Department with two units, namely, Advertisements Permits and Monitoring and Advertisement Workshop. This Section's phenomenal performance in terms of adopting appropriate regulations and procedures, the introduction of new technology utilized in Dubai resulting in the transformation of the city's visual image, the tremendous increase in the financial revenues from advertisement control, etc. reflected positively the real benefits achieved from the application of modern systems gained from a UN consultant as well as a local counterpart, Mr. Mohammed Nuri, who was trained in the field in other countries.

Among the numerous instruments initiated for the improvement of the urban planning system, mention can be made of the following:

a. The first 5-year plan in the Municipality's history;
b. A manual of operation for the Planning Department;
c. A zoning ordinance adopted and widely disseminated;
d. Urban designs of numerous localities in Dubai Emirate;
e. An improved Execution Planning Section for a more efficient handling of public transactions; and
f. Regular training of the planning staff.

Planning Execution

Eventually, the unit under the Planning Section responsible for execution functions was elevated to a section level for monitoring the execution of the approved plan in close collaboration with other concerned Sections including Building Control.

Building Control

Another area of service that registered a significant improvement was building control. The building regulations, operational systems, and resources were reviewed comprehensively and made consistent with the structural planning policy, the provision of efficient and effective services resulting in the achievement of high standards of safety as well as architectural and environmental excellence.

Dubai's Urban Design (presented by the GIS Center)

Whereas it had taken weeks to process applications for building permits, Dubai Municipality was able to reduce the time to an average of a few days by adopting efficient management systems including the dissemination of the requirements for the different types of applications as well as the use of appropriate information technologies.

Typical to other sections, here also, the use of qualified nationals and their continued training had a huge, positive impact.

Land Surveying
One of the most important contributions to the improvement of the Municipality's services was in the land survey sector, with the assistance of a consultant, Prof. Gotfried Konecny. With his assistance and counterpart staff including Mr. Mohammed Zeffin, the following main outputs were achieved:

a. The establishment of a GIS Center;
b. Transformation of survey data to DLTM projection;
c. Control densification;
d. New line mapping;
e. Ortho-photo applications and updates;
f. Cadastral fitting;
g. Modern GPS developments;
h. Geoid determination;
i. Formulation of a survey law and code of practice; etc.

The survey code of practice was prepared by the UN Survey Consultant, Prof. G. Konecny in a detailed and comprehensive manner including:

- the survey law and regulations;
- organization of the survey tasks;
- horizontal control surveys comprising horizontal reference datum, projection coordinates, global positions system, angular measurements and electronic distance measurements, reductions of distances and directions to coordinate grid, traverse closures and network adjustments, astronomic measurements, and monumentation of horizontal control points;
- Vertical control surveys comprising vertical reference datum, leveling, monumentation of benchmarks, trigonometric heightening, barometry, and global positioning system heights;

- Property survey tasks comprising types of land, designation of land, site plans, affection plans, demarcation, expropriation, and disputes;
- Property survey methodology comprising global positioning, angular and electronic distance measurements, and tape measurements;
- Mapping methods comprising analog photogrammetry, digital photogrammetry, ground surveys by angular and electronic distance measurements, and ground surveys by tape;
- Map records comprising basic topographic maps, cadastral maps, planning maps, derived maps, utility maps, and digital map records;
- Property records including ownership documents, ownership registers, and maintenance of cadastral records;
- Underground and overhead utility records comprising utility records, and maintenance of utility records;
- Engineering surveys comprising earth works, utility corridors, coastal protection, and microwave corridors;
- Gravity and Geophysical surveys comprising gravity, and geophysical exploration;
- Environmental surveys and remote sensing comprising mineral exploitation, hydrology, and waste;
- Navigation systems comprising hydrography, and air traffic;
- Military mapping comprising military restrictions

Among the most important aspects of the institutional development with regard to land surveying was the use of improved technology including the computerization of the Section's activities as well as the introduction of the Geographic Information System (GIS) and the advent of the Global Positioning System (GPS). These facilitated the accurate and efficient registration, processing and servicing of land related services thereby accelerating Dubai's development.

Advertisement Control

The Advertisement Control Section was initially operating under the Trade Licensing Department. In 1993, it was transferred to operate within the Planning Department. It coordinated effectively with the planning, and for the licensing and control of advertisements in Dubai. The services including the processing activities of applications for various types of permits for advertisements including those in public places, roof-top signs, pathways, roads, building fronts, etc. The introduction of new techniques such as mupies, unipoles, electronic advertisements, vehicle advertisements, double sided sign boards, etc. greatly expanded the Section's services.

The Section was assisted by the UN project consultant, Mr. B. Parnell, with Mr. Mohammed Al-Nuri as the local counterpart. The consultant drafted the appropriate regulations, and detailed procedures as a manual of operation which were reviewed by the Municipality and fully implemented. A comprehensive training was arranged for the counterpart, Mr. Al-Nuri, in various countries including Spain and Turkey as well as USA (an advanced management course at the University of Pittsburgh). He eventually took over as Section Head and brought about very impressive changes resulting in the use of modern advertisement systems and technologies in Dubai.

The Section ensured that advertisements in Dubai complied with established standards including the required cultural, aesthetic, linguistic, and geometric stipulations.

The Section's services included the processing of permits for advertisements as well as service providers licenses and their renewal as well as monitoring through systematic inspections and control, and the provision of workshop services to meet the public's need for advertisement facilities.

One of the success indicators of the Advertisement Section was its significant achievement in its financial performance. Whereas the Municipality's annual revenue from Advertisement control services was a mere $150,000.00 in 1986, it shot to over $2 million by 2000 and $6 million by 2010. This performance is one of the indicators of Dubai's success story. It has demonstrated that a city has the capacity to make use of its advertisement space in an aesthetic and streamlined manner, in the context of a dynamic economic development framework, while profiting significantly from the provision of efficient services. Dubai's advertisement service environment has become known as a best practice and attracted trainees from other countries and cities.

Housing

One of the important areas of service that the Municipality focused on was public housing. In addition to the formulation of a comprehensive housing policy, the Municipality was engaged in providing direct assistance to needy citizens in terms of the required land, and financial grants for housing construction and related infrastructural services.

The Municipality ensured that the public housing it provided met the people's social, cultural and economic needs and standards. In addition, assistance was provided by the Municipality for additions as well as maintenance needs. Advice was also provided for housing design, construction and maintenance.

1.3 Roads and General Projects Affairs

This sector was responsible for Dubai Emirate's roads, general projects, and maintenance activities. It was led by an Assistant Director General, Mr. Matar Al Tayer with the support of two UN experts, Mr. Farook Khalifa (Highways Engineer) and Dr. Waheed Uddin who was a Pavement Management Expert.

Roads Department

The Roads Department comprised the study, design, construction, and operation of roads in accordance with the Municipality's plans and standards. The sections operating within the Department were the following:

Roads Planning Section

This Section undertook detailed studies and formulated plans and designs for all types of roads including highways, bridges, tunnels, flyovers, road exits, public car parks, pedestrian crossings, etc. It also collected statistical traffic data for the determination of street lighting and related road safety services.

Roads Construction Section

This Section dealt with the implementation of the approved road projects as well as the operation and maintenance of Dubai Emirate's roads network and related facilities.

Traffic Technology Section

This Section was responsible for the operation and management of the Emirate's central traffic control system including the traffic signals for the purpose of ensuring an efficient traffic flow as well as the overall road safety.

Lighting Section

This Section took care of the roads lighting as well as the maintenance of the traffic lighting facilities. It ensured their efficient operation through effective preventive and corrective maintenance operations.

Car Parks Section

This Section dealt with the control of public park areas including metered parking facilities as well as their efficient maintenance.

General Projects Department

This Department was responsible for the study, design, construction, and monitoring of the Municipality's general projects including buildings, parks, public facilities such as libraries, landscaping, marine protection, coastguard, markets, and numerous other urban structures.

General Maintenance Department

This Department was responsible for the planning of maintenance activities including buildings, utilities, roads, and related facilities.

Buildings and Utilities Maintenance Section

This Section was responsible for the maintenance of buildings, road lighting facilities, and all structures requiring electro-mechanical, and civil engineering services.

Roads Maintenance Section

This Section dealt with maintenance activities requiring asphalting and soil works, paving and repairs of roads and traffic signals.

1.4 Environment and Health Affairs

This sector was one of the major activities in the Municipality. It was led by Mr. Hussain Lootah as Assistant Director General. Mr. Lootah is the current Director General of the Municipality. Later, the post of Assistant Director General for the Sector was taken over by Mr. Mohammed Salem Mohammed Bin Mesmar. The sector was responsible for preventive public health services, drainage, irrigation, public parks, horticulture, and environmental protection.

Public Health Department

This Department was responsible for preventive health services including food control, monitoring of hotels and restaurants, markets, abattoirs, and monitoring employees deployed in providing such services.

Dubai Municipality Clinic

This Section was responsible for monitoring staff providing health related services to the public. Such employees were required to be health clearance at the clinic on a regular basis.

Food Control Section

This Section was responsible for the control of hotels, restaurants, and all other food outlets.

Markets Section

This Section was in charge of monitoring all food related markets to ensure public health and safety.

Food Laboratory Section

This Section was responsible for the testing of food samples and providing the findings for the purpose of facilitating the required control.

Veterinary Services Section

This Section was in charge of controlling all veterinary related activities in Dubai.

Environment Department

This Department was provided with significant support by the United Nations through Mr. Jon Ward. The main counterpart was Eng. Salem Mohammed Bin Mesmar.

Waste Management Section

Collection, delivery, and treatment of waste was the responsibility of this Section

Pest Control Section

This Section was responsible for the control of all types of pests as well as stray animals including dogs and cats.

Environment Section

This Section was responsible for ensuring the formulation of appropriate policy and regulations as well as control concerning the environment in Dubai. The UN expert was instrumental in the drafting of the regulations as well as the manuals of operation and the training of the required staff.

Drainage and Irrigation Department

Drainage and Irrigation Network
This Section was responsible for pumping stations, irrigation operations, electrical and mechanical maintenance and related workshops and general services.

Sewage Treatment Plant Section
This Section's activities included the operation of the treatment and maintenance of the treatment plant as well as related laboratory and general services.

Development and Monitoring Section
This Section's responsibility was covering the continued monitoring and development of the drainage and irrigation services.

Public Parks and Horticulture Department
This Department was assisted greatly by a UN specialist, Dr. Qrunfleh.

Horticulture Section
This Section's responsibility included the implementation of horticultural projects as well as cultivation and maintenance of horticulture on Dubai's roads and public areas.

Horticulture Services Section
The services of the section comprised the operation of nurseries as well as the provision of advisory and general services including maintenance activities.

Parks and Gardens Section
The operation and maintenance of the various parks in Dubai as well as the Ladies' Club were the responsibility of this section.

Zoo Section
This section catered for the care of animals at the Dubai zoo and related administrative and general services.

1.5 Financial Affairs
This sector was responsible for financial, contracts and purchasing affairs.

Finance Department
The UN consultants that assisted this Department were Mr. M. Halwani (Finance), and Mr. S. Nimry (Stores).

The Sections under this Department were:

- Accounting Section
- Treasury Section
- Compensation Section
- Fees & Revenues Section
- Budget Section

Contracts and Purchasing Department
The Sections under this Department were:

- Purchasing Section
- Stores Section
- Tenders, Contracts and Cost Control Section

1.6 Administrative and General Services Affairs
This Sector was responsible for human resources, general services, markets and abattoirs, public relations, and transportation services. It is currently led by Mr. Obaid Salem Al Shamsi.

Administrative Affairs Department
This Department was initially managed by Mr. Mohammed Obaid Al-Mulla who was my first local counterpart. He was instrumental in several important issues including his collaboration in the review of the Department's organization, functions, and staffing as well as attracting suitable nationals to be recruited by the Municipality.

The organizational review with the assistance of the UN project resulted in the establishment of an Administrative Affairs Department with four sections personnel, garage, museum, documentation and four zonal centers reporting to a Director.

The Department was assisted by various UN personnel: Mr. A. Akrouk (Library), Mr. D. Armstrong (Transportation), Mr. M. Haider (Statistics), Dr. Ahmed Ragheb (Public Relations), Dr. Tahani el-Erian (Archives), Mr. A.F. Galamallah (Archives), and Mr. M. Itayem (Documentation).

With Dubai Municipality's continued restructuring of the sections under this Department were increased and eventually comprised the following:

- Administrative Services which was responsible for security and monitoring, building cleaning, general services, and communications;
- Libraries;
- Statistics;
- Zonal Municipal Centers (at Al-Karama, Umm Suqeim, Al-Rashidiya, and Hatta);
- Customer Service Center;
- Public Relations;
- Transportation.

Personnel Department

This Department was assisted by UN personnel i.e. Mr. Ahmed Nuseirat, Mr. M. Duheidal, and Mr. Iyad Usta. The main local counterpart was Mr. Ahmed AbdelKerim.

The Sections were the following:

- Policies and studies;
- Human Resources and planning and deployment;
- Human Resources Development;
- Compensation and Services;
- Salaries, benefits, services, housing, employee transportation, time-keeping, etc.

Markets and Abattoirs Department

The Sections were the following:

- Markets
- Al Hamriya Vegetable and Fruit Market
- Al Rashidiya Central Market
- Al Hamriya Central Market
- Nayif Market
- Fish Market – Deira
- Fish Market – Bur dubai
- Livestock Market
- Abattoir which was responsible for public services and maintenance.

1.7 **General Technical Services Affairs**

This sector was responsible for information technology (computer systems), laboratory, and road transport services.

Information Technology Department

- E-Government Services Section which was responsible for the planning, design, development and support of e-Government services;
- System Development Section which was responsible for systems planning, design, development and support of systems;
- Office Automation Section which catered for office automation programmes, support and training services.

Dubai Central Laboratory Department

- Engineering Materials Laboratory Section which was responsible for construction, building materials, and chemistry services;
- Food and Environment Laboratory Section which was responsible for the environmental, microbiological, and chemistry services;
- Consumable Laboratory Section which was responsible for precious metals and jewelry, electrical equipment, and chemistry and physics services;
- Standardization Section which was undertaking measurements, standardization, and maintenance as well as support services;
- Inspection and Certification Unit which was responsible for granting permits.

Transportation Department

- Transport Services Section which was responsible for road transport planning, marketing, operations, public services, and accounting as well as the control boat transport (Abra) services;
- Workshop Section which provided maintenance (preventive and corrective) as well as manufacture of certain vehicle parts;
- Administrative Services Section which provided purchasing, stores, and fuels supply services as well as the required labourers.

1.8 **Dubai Municipality's Organizational Evolution**

During the period following the conclusion of the United Nations project support, the organization of Dubai Municipality continued to evolve based on its strategic requirements and development needs. The Municipality's latest (2011) organization chart (including the senior staffing) can be seen in Fig. 11.

Compared with the 1994 organization chart, the main changes reflected in the 2011 version are:

- The special focus and strengthening of international relations and partnership including customer relations, corporate marketing, partnerships, and the so-called "knowledge management" functions;
- The integration of the support services as a staff function including the human resources management, financial affairs, information technology, as well as contracts and purchasing activities;
- A special focus on quality management including corporate excellence, and accreditation; and
- Legal services.

It should be noted here that the audit services were kept to operate under the Director General's office.

2.Human Resources Development: The Essence of Sustainability and Self-Reliance

One of the most important contributions of the United Nations project assistance to Dubai Municipality was in the area of strengthening the latter's sustainability and self-reliance.

In 1986, Dubai Municipality was facing severe human resources constraints including the following:

- Only 30% of the management and supervisory staff were local citizens;
- There was no capacity or system for training purposes;
- The regulations were weak and inadequate;
- There was a huge gender imbalance: the municipality had only 16 local female staff being only 4% of the total local staff;
- There were no job descriptions as well as descriptions of functions for the various departments, sections, and units;
- There was no performance appraisal system including a mechanism for motivating staff for a higher performance;
- There was no position classification system;

- There was no appropriate salary scale in addition to the fact that payments were low compared with the UAE Federal salary system;
- There was no system for arranging local counterparts, wherever needed and possible, to be assigned to expatriate staff;
- There was no policy for attracting UAE citizens for employment by Dubai Municipality.

In view of the above significant constraints, the project expert i.e. myself assisted by a few specialists including Job Analysts i.e. Mr. Ahmed Nuseirat (later a senior advisor in the office of the Ruler of Dubai), Mr. Iyad Usta, Dr. Ali Al Asam, Dr. Bahjat Sendouka, and Mr. M. Duheidal as well as local counterparts such as Mr. Mohammed Obaid Al-Mulla, Mr. Ahmed Abdelkerim, etc. exerted a great deal of effort for the production of the following:

1. The organization of the Personnel Department with descriptions of functions for the department, each section, and unit;
2. 17 regulations were formulated and applied on various human resources subjects including recruitment, transfer, promotion, discipline, acting, training, allowances, duty travel, etc;
3. Job descriptions were prepared for each post in the Municipality in consultation with the respective managers, supervisors, and incumbents;
4. A new position classification was introduced based on the approved job descriptions and qualification requirements;
5. A competitive salary scale was introduced after a comprehensive field survey including payments to employees in the federal ministries of the United Arab Emirates;
6. Various allowances to compensate staff for various services;
7. A performance appraisal system was introduced in order to motivate staff for higher excellence;
8. A committee was established in which I participated as a member to recruit local (UAE) citizens with the necessary education to be assigned to various posts including being counterparts to expatriate staff with a view to the achievement of a systematic localization. It is interesting to note that some of the young graduates who were recruited in those days have progressed to high prominence including one (H.E. Mr. Mohammed Al Gargawi) who eventually became a federal Minister of Civil Service Affairs. Others such as Mr. Mohammed Julfar, Mr. Salem Mismar, Mr. Saleh Amiri, Mr. Ahmed Abdelkerim, etc.

became Assistant Director Generals within Dubai Municipality. Still others reached various levels of prominence holding administrative, financial, and technical posts and many of them replacing expatriates.

9. Localization of key posts held by expatriates was one of the important objectives pursued by the Municipality. Accordingly, whereas only 30% of the management and supervisory staff were locals in 1986, by the time the project completed its task in 2000, over 90% of such posts were held by local staff.

10. One other major human resource constraint was the very low number of local female staff within the Municipality. In 1986, there were only 8 female staff (3%) compared with 237 male nationals. As a result of the project's encouragement and the Municipality's positive action, the number of local staff increased substantially. In 1993 the number of female staff shot to 156 (16.5%) while the number of male local staff had increased also to 785. By 1998, the number of local female employees (266) became 25% of all local employees in Dubai Municipality. In 2008, the number of female employees soared to 931 being 44% of the Municipality's local staff. For more details, please see Fig. 12. It is important to note also that female employees achieved promotions to senior posts including Ms. Hawa Bastaki, Director of the Dubai Central Laboratory, Ms. Zohoor Al –Sabbagh, Director of

Fig: 12 Dubai Municipality's Local (Citizens) Staff

Year	Male	Female %	Total
1985	237 97%	8 3%	245 (100%)
1993	785 87%	156 17%	941 (100%)
1998	798 75%	266 25%	1064 (100%)
2004	1725 71%	702 29%	2427 (100%)
2008	1185 56%	931 44%	2116 (100%)
2010	1153 55%	928 45%	2081 (100%)
2011	1173 54%	986 46%	2159 (100%)

Public Health Services Department, etc. Although the Municipality would need to exert more effort in providing increased opportunities to its competent female staff's promotion to leadership posts, its achievement over the last thirty years can be considered exemplary especially in the context of Middle Eastern overall conditions with regard to gender equality.

11. Another major contribution by the project assistance that was of fundamental importance to the Municipality was the special focus on human resources development. Initially, the focus was on the assignment to and training of local counterparts by each UN expert and specialist. The training comprised: (a) the daily exposure of the counterparts to the activities and outputs of the respective experts, consultants and specialists; and (b) the arrangement, for most of the counterparts, of a properly structured training (usually 1-2 months) in other countries including Australia, USA, UK, The Netherlands, Canada, etc. in their respective fields of activity. The other major development was the establishment of the Municipality's training center which provided the much needed skills in administrative, financial and technical fields.

3.Performance Indicators

One of the fundamental and strategic institutional development measures taken by Dubai Municipality was the establishment of performance indicators for each Department, Section and Unit, after a comprehensive study and detailed consultation with all the concerned staff and based on the Municipality's objectives, strategies and plans. Typically, the presentation included the objectives, the respective indicators, reporting period, target actual performance and, where possible, benchmarks from other appropriate sources (countries/organizations).

As a sample some performance indicators formulated with the project's support for the Horticulture and Parks Department is provided in Annex (1).

The application of the performance indicators along with a systematic monitoring greatly enhanced the Municipality's efficiency, accountability and transparency thereby also achieving the satisfaction of customers i.e. the public with the organization's services.

4. Delegation of Authority

A major constraint faced by the Municipality was the fact decisions on virtually every aspect of its operations, especially the services needed by the public were highly centralized. This highly bureaucratic centralization had negative effect on the Municipality's service efficiency resulting in the limited development impact.

The following examples can be cited to illustrate the above point:

- The Municipality's Director General was required to personally sign applications for trade licenses three times:

    ◦ To decide whether the application should be accepted and considered or not;

    ◦ To decide, in principle, whether the application should be approved or not after all required procedures have been completed; and

    ◦ To sign the trade license issued in the applicant's name.

- As a result of the improved institutional development including the restructuring of the Trade Licensing Section, the establishment of the required standards and procedures as well as the use of competent staff, it was possible for the Director General to delegate his authority, with the exception of few sensitive items, to the officials in the Section. This enabled a fast processing of the applications thereby greatly enhancing Dubai's development into a global, cosmopolitan city.

- The other major area that was highly centralized within the Municipality was related to decisions related to financial issues. The maximum amount that the Director General was permitted to approve was merely Dh. 50,000.00 (US$14,000.00). Decisions on higher amounts had to be submitted to the Chairman of the Municipality. This had, obviously, a very negative effect.

- One of the tangible examples which illustrate the farsightedness and wisdom of Sheikh Maktoum Al-Maktoum, the chairman of Dubai Municipality was that he delegated his authority, for budgeted matters, to the Director General who, on his part, further delegated financial authority to the lower echelons of Municipal officials up to even Unit Head levels as appropriate, depending on complexity, capacity, accountability, and transparency.

- Other requirements for delegation of authority were studied in every department, section, and unit and detailed submissions were made by the UN project in collaboration with counterpart staff. Once decisions were made by the Director General, the delegation of authority was declared through formal administrative orders or, in certain cases, regulations.

A sample of the project proposals of delegations of authority for tendering and contracting activities can be seen in Annex 2.

5. Decentralization of Services

One of the most important achievements of the Municipality was the decentralization of its services to the various areas of the Emirate with the objective of providing its services in close proximity to the public, the customers for whom it is established to serve.

The following Zonal Centers were established with all the key Municipal services needed by the public along with the required human resources and facilities:

*Karama Center;
*Rashidiya Center;
*Um-Suqaim Center;
*Hatta Center;

6. Accountability and Transparency

One of the serious constraints facing the Municipality in 1985 was the lack of an effective internal control system. As a result, corruption was rampant especially among some of the expatriate staff who were apparently supplementing their low salary with ill-gotten gains. The local officials were aware of the situation and were using police/security systems to track and catch the culprits. However, since there was no institutional system in place, it was difficult to prevent the occurrence of corrupt practices. Therefore, the following corrective institutional measures were taken to effectively deal with the issue:

6.1 The establishment of the Administrative Development Office (later part of the Administrative Development and Quality Department) which among other things, monitored systematically the efficient execution of the approved organization, systems (including committees), authority, resource utilization, etc.

6.2 The Internal Control Office which performed regular financial audit of all Departments and Sections. In addition, the Municipality was audited by HH The Ruler's Office.

6.3 A Quality Management Section was established to conduct public opinion surveys and to Enhance customer satisfaction by mainstreaming quality management systems throughout the Municipality.

6.4 Follow-up and Development Offices were established in each Sector of the Municipality, led by an Assistant Director General, to closely follow-up the timely implementation of various directives, to facilitate effective internal and external coordination as well as to initiate continued improvements.

6.5 Suggestion schemes including a 24-hour telephone service were established with the aim of obtaining opinions, queries, and any ideas from the public as to the Municipality's service quality and customer satisfaction.

6.6 The establishment of clear regulations, procedures and performance standards together with the application of modern technology enabled the Municipality to make the public aware of its systems thereby facilitating compliance and service efficiency.

7. Service Efficiency and Cost-effectiveness

The Municipality accorded a high priority to the achievement of increased service efficiency in virtually all its fields of activity coupled with pragmatic applications of cost-effective measures including improved working methods, appropriate resource utilization, etc. with the support of the UN project. Some examples of this achievement are the following:

7.1 The reduction of the time taken to process applications for trade licenses from an average three weeks to 1-2 days;

7.2 The reversal of the crisis in terms of an unacceptable down time of the Municipality's vehicles by introducing systematic preventive servicing and maintenance as well as efficient applications of corrective repairs methods. It is interesting to note here that when the work on the project's study commenced at the Municipality's Garage, the Section did not even have a record of the number and type of vehicles parked in the compound awaiting repairs.

7.3 The formulation and application of a clear policy, regulations and procedures related to human resources facilitated fair standards resulting in a better management and enhancedemployee morale.

7.4 Efficiency measures applied by the Municipality in various departments resulted in some significant financial and resources savings including over 400 excess personnel from the Horticulture and Parks, and 80 from the Garage and Transport Departments as well as 150 support staff such as Driver, Clerks, Assistants, Helpers and Labourers in various Departments. A sample of performance measures formulated for the Horticulture and Parks Department is provided as Annex 1.

7.5 The application of double shifts in the use of the same buses resulted in significant financialsavings by avoiding the purchase of additional vehicles.

7.6 Other significant cost reductions were achieved including, for instance, payments for overtime was cut down from 8 to 1 million Dirhams per annum.

7.7 The Municipality established a Costing Unit within its Budgets Section in order to apply an effective cost control system.

7.8 One of the most important factors in the achievement of the Municipality's accelerated service efficiency was the application of modern technology systems which facilitated an easy access to the information on policy, strategy, systems, regulations, and procedures by both the Municipal staff, and the public as appropriate.

8. Sustainability and Self-Reliance

Dubai Municipality was able to achieve a high degree of sustainability and self-reliance through the application of diverse institutional development measures and a strong campaign in attracting, training and utilizing local human resources. The following can be mentioned as examples:

8.1 Financial Performance

During the period of the UN project's assistance, the Municipality's financial performance improved significantly. In 1985, the Municipality's revenue (US$ 33 million) was only 20% of its recurrent expenditure (US$ 160 million). 80% of the Municipality's recurrent expenditure as well as the full amount of its capital and project expenditures (US$96 million) were funded from the central budget under the Dubai Emirate's Ruler's Office. By 1990, the revenue ($55 million) rose to being 77% of the recurrent expenditure ($71 million). The Municipality's capital and project expenditure for 1990 was $137 million. The Municipality's 2000 revenue reached $316 million covering its recurrent expenditure ($ 210million) and its capital expenditure ($21 million) as well as part of its project costs (total: $404 million). By the year 2004, the Municipality's revenue had reached $638 million exceeding its recurrent expenditure of

$280 million plus the capital expenditure of $28 million as well as its project costs of $281 million i.e. total expenditure of $589 million. In 2010, the comparative figures were: Revenue: US$ 1.3 billion; total expenditure: US$ 992 million including recurrent: $400 million; capital: $15 million; and projects: $ 577 million. (Source: Finance Department, Dubai Municipality).

8.2 Formulation of Policy and Regulations

With the assistance of the UN project, Dubai Municipality formulated policies, strategies and action plans for its various operations as well as regulations and working procedures. Examples are as follows:

*Planning and execution policy, strategy, regulations and procedures
*Survey law and code of practice;
*Zoning ordinance;
*Advertisement control and procedures;
*Building regulations and procedures;
*Projects Execution procedures;
*Minor works procedures;
*Environmental protection regulations and procedures;
*Hotel classification regulations and procedures;
*Food control systems and procedures;
*Horticultural activities regulations and procedures;
*Tendering and contracting regulations and procedures;
*Budgeting regulations and procedures;
*Purchasing regulations and procedures;
*Stores regulations and procedures;
*Garage administration procedures;
*17 Personnel regulations, and procedures;
*Documentation systems and procedures;
*Stores regulations and procedures;

8.3 Manuals of Operation

Manuals of operation were prepared for the various major operations of the Municipality containing the above regulations, systems, and directives including the performance indicators and delegation of authority aimed at providing efficient service and accelerated development.

8.4 Evolving Development

The Municipality's paradigm shift towards being a customer-service oriented institution, its systems of quality control, administrative development and continuous monitoring, its policy of accountability and transparency, its application of efficient and modern information technology systems enabled it to evolve its policy, strategy, systems and operations with the changing circumstances and needs based on its vision of making the Emirate a global center of commerce, industry, tourism and urban services.

Support to other organizations

In addition to Dubai Municipality and with the approval as well as UNCHS/HABITAT, the UN project provided assistance to other organizations as follows:

a. The United Arab Emirates (UAE) University: project formulation for UN assistance in institutional development (by K. Alemayehu);

b. The Development Board (UAE) review and recommendations regarding the entity's organization and systems development (by K. Alemayehu);

c. The Central Government Garage (Dubai Emirate): organization and systems development (by K. Alemayehu);

d. The Dubai Emirate Transport Corporation: organization and systems development (by K. Alemayehu);

e. The Ministry of Public Works and Housing: organization and systems development (by K. Alemayehu);

f. The UAE Federal Environment Agency: support in environmental legislation and strategy) (by Jon Ward).

9. Dubai Municipality: A Best Practice

As a result of the Municipality's tremendous strides in urban development, it was accorded recognitions by various international and local institutions including the following:

9.1 The UNCHS Scroll of Honour;

9.2 The Arab Towns Organization awards for environment protection, safety and conservation;

9.3 The ICCC (International Council for Caring Communities), an affiliate of the United Nations Development Program, an Award for Pioneering Leadership;

9.4 The Dubai Award for Government Excellence (operated by the Government of Dubai Emirate);

9.5 Cannes International Water Award;

9.6 Arab Housing and Urban Ministries Council Award for Best Housing Project;

9.7 Arab Towns Organization: Architectural Heritage Award;

9.8 United Nations: Membership of the UN Advisory Committee of Local Authorities;

9.9 United Nations appointment of Dubai Municipality's Director General, H.E. Mr. Qassim Sultan as Goodwill Ambassador for the UN Center for Human Settlements (UNCHS/HABITAT).

10. International Award For Best Practices

10.1 International Conference on Best Practices

In view of Dubai Municipality's exemplary performance, with the Director General's concurrence, and the approval of UNCHS/HABITAT, the UN project initiated an international conference on best practices which was held in Dubai in 1995. It was attended by 914 delegates from 95 countries. The conference was highly successful on sharing expertise in best practices related to the urban environment. It adopted a "Dubai Declaration" (Annex 3) which endorsed the

With H.E. Mr. Hussain Lootah, current Director General of Dubai Municipality.

establishment of the Dubai International Award for Best Practices to Improve the Living Environment. (www.dubaiaward.ae) (www.bestpractices.org).

10.2 Dubai International Award for Best Practices to Improve the Living Environment

As the name indicates, this international award was established jointly by Dubai Municipality and UNCHS/HABITAT with the objective of improving the living environment. The UN project played a key role not only in initiating the award but also in developing its policy, objectives, systems, regulations, and procedures in close collaboration with Dubai Municipality and UNCHS/HABITAT. Some of the main elements of the international award are as follows:

Purpose
The purpose of the award is to recognize and enhance awareness of outstanding and sustainable achievements in improving the living environment as per the basic criteria established by the Second United Nations Conference on Human Settlements (Habitat II) and the Dubai Declaration.

Award Cycle
The Award is presented every two years during the World Habitat Day.

The Award
The Award comprises a total amount of $360,000.00 provided by Dubai Municipality and distributed among 12 winners comprising 10 Best Practices, one for a successful transfer of best practices, and one for an individual who has been selected for contribution to best practices.

Criteria
The criteria for being considered for the award are:

i. Positive and tangible impact in improving the living environment;
ii. Partnership between at least two actors;
iii. Sustainability and continuity in effecting changes in relevant policy, legislation, strategies, systems, etc;
iv. Leadership and community empowerment;
v. Gender equality and social inclusion;
vi. Innovation within the local context and transferability;
vii. Actual transfer.

<u>Eligibility</u>
The award is open for competition by the following:

i.   Government organization or agencies such as SIDA, USAID, etc;
ii.   National Habitat committee or Focal Points;
iii. Multilateral agencies (United Nations Agencies, the World Bank, etc.)
iv. Cities, local authorities or their associations;
v.   Non-governmental organizations (NGO's);
vi. Community-based organizations (CBO's);
vii. Private sector;
viii. Research and academic institutions;
ix. Media;
x.   Public or private foundations;
xi. Individuals submitting specific initiatives or projects meeting the Best Practice criteria.

<u>How to Apply</u>
Information on how to apply can be obtained at: http://www.dubaiaward .ae (Dubai Municipality) or http://www.bestpractices.org (UNCHS/HABITAT).

<u>Award's Institutional Arrangement</u>
The award is managed under the following institutional arrangement:

i.   Best Practices Partners carefully selected (see list in Annex 4) institutions which receive submissions and determine their suitability for consideration based on their preliminary assessments as per the approved criteria;
ii.   A Technical Committee comprising international professionals in the field of human settlements to assess each best practice submitted by the partners as per item e.i. above and select up to 100 Best Practices to be included in the database and up to 40 best practices for consideration by an international jury of experts;
iii. An International Jury of five highly reputed experts selected jointly by Dubai Municipality and UNCHS/HABITAT to select the award winners.

H.H. Sheikh Hamdan granting me an award certificate in recognition of my service concerning the Dubai International Award. On his left is H.E. Mr. Qassim Sultan, then Director-General of Dubai Municipality and on his right is Mr. Danel Biau, Director of UNCHS' Technical Co-operation Department.

Photo of Certificate Awarded to me for my contribution to the Dubai International Award

<u>Award Winners</u>

The first award was granted in 1996 and since then similar awards took place every two years. A total of 92 awards were granted up to 2012. The database for the Best Practices has reached over 4,000 and the number of countries that participated in the submission of best practices has exceeded 150. Some regions such as Latin America have established their respective regional best practices centers.

11. CONCLUSION

Dubai Municipality is a success story by international standards. More than anything else, what Dubai Municipality has clearly demonstrated is the fact that a leadership with the courage and unbounded vision, firm principles of accountability and transparency and the wisdom to apply modern systems of management, technology and methodologies would achieve positive results. The Municipality's ability to formulate sound policies, strategies, systems and action plans have enabled it to transform Dubai from being a mere fishing village less than half a century ago to its present international cosmopolitan center of commerce, tourism and industry competing with urban centers such as Hong Kong, Singapore and other such renowned cities.

Although Dubai's phenomenal urban development can be seen from the physical structures including its extensive network, extra-ordinary buildings, and its bustling economy, there are other elements that make the city unique. Examples of these include the following:

1. After establishing sound policies and standards, the Municipality applies its operations in a highly customer-oriented service efficiency. This is undertaken through the use of modern technologies, customer service centers, responsiveness to customer complaints and opinions, etc.

2. The Municipality monitored and applied competitive international standards of planning systems as well as efficiency such as the time taken to process trade licenses, and applications for building permits.

3. What is particularly interesting about Dubai is the fact that the number of local citizens i.e. "Emiratis" comprises less than 10% of Dubai's total population. When countries such as Switzerland engage in anxious cycles of national referenda whenever the number of foreigners exceeds 10% of its total population, Dubai is exemplary in welcoming an expatriate population from over 100 countries reaching over nine times the number of its own citizens. The experience of Dubai cer-

tainly deserves a special attention by the international community including the United Nations.

4. The evolution of a small town in a desert environment to a global city, meeting all the required criteria including the social, economic, financial, and security standards as well as the transformation of the area into an environmentally free, and historically relevant architecture, renders Dubai Municipality a best practice worthy of emulation.

5. Among the clear lessons learned from the Dubai Municipality experience is the fact that an international outlook for institutional development including the use of United Nations services as well as exposure to experiences of other cities/countries would greatly facilitate an accelerated development.

12. Future Challenges

Despite its significant, fast progress, Dubai Municipality still faces various challenges including the following which could be of interest to other similar cities:

1. In this age of globalization and in the context that Dubai's declared mission is to be a world class commercial and financial center, it is essential that the Emirate keeps constantly engaged with its commitment and action to maintain and improve its competitive edge.

2. It is essential for Dubai Municipality to enhance its utilization of international standards and criteria including the ones enunciated in Istanbul+5, the UN Human Development reports, Local Agenda 21, and other standards established by UNCHS/HABITAT to improve and monitor the Municipality's performance in a reliable and systematic manner.

3. It is vital that Dubai Municipality applies the highest levels of accountability and transparency. This includes the release of information on performance results to the public irrespective of levels of achievement. This author noted with concern a recent (October 2013) response by one of the Municipality's senior officials that information on performance results was confidential. An efficient Municipality would have the data and be proud to show it off.

4. The process of quality management, performance measures and benchmarking needs to be intensified requiring an enhanced level of exchange of information globally and continued service improve-

ments. An institutional capacity to help in formulating such performance standards, monitoring systems, and systems for preventive/corrective systems would be of great importance to Dubai Emirate.

5. The continued empowerment of line staff through regular training, decentralization, delegation of authority, and improvement of the technology, regulations and procedures is an essential element for the achievement of a sustainable and accelerated development.

6. Enhancing the Municipality's outsourcing through rigorous tendering and contracting as well as cost control systems could result in the achievement of increased efficiency.

7. The challenge from Dubai Emirate's continued population growth will demand the development of more effective environmental protection systems, additional infrastructural services, etc. which all need the enhanced use of strategic structural development plans and implementation processes.

8. The Emirate's use of large numbers of expatriate laborers needs a continuous improvement in the formulation and application of basic human rights including a housing policy meeting basic standards.

9. The Emirate has so far applied traditional systems of governance. In view of the increasing number of educated local nationals, it would be appropriate to consider the possibility of introducing democratic systems facilitating more participation in governance.

10. Although the Dubai International Award for Best Practices to Improve the Living Environment has achieved great strides in accumulating thousands of best practices in its database, its original intent of transferring the best practices for the achievement of practical improvements in living conditions will need to be applied systematically. For this purpose, it would be essential to review the Award's objectives, mission, strategy, criteria, etc. so that its future focus would be on achieving a tangible impact through a systematic transfer of best practices for improving living conditions in various countries.

Annex 1

Performance Measures For Parks & Horticulture Department
2333 Parks Section

No	Objective	Performance Measursure - Indicator	Performance Measure - Target	Actual Post Performance - 1996	Actual Post Performace - 1997	Actual Post Performance - 1998	Bench Mark - Source	Bench Mark - Perf	Comments
1	Provide and develop effective services at public parks	Population of Dubai city. Total park area (hectares). Park area per 000' population. Number of opinion surveys conducted.	833,682 500 0.60 1	701,065 457 0.65 1	786,493 474 0.60 1	805,468 475.9 0.59 2	Statistics Centre Phoenix	0.72 (1997)	Awaiting results from Public Relations Section (PRS).
		Assessment by Park visitors of the services, facilities; Very good. Good/Fair. c. Unsatisfactory	60% 30% 10%	- - -	33% 40% 27%	Awaiting tabulation of results by PRS			Data are being tabulated by PRS.
		1.6 Number of drowning cases	Reduce by 30%	480	229	91			Improve education, awareness methods and safety standards.
		1.7% of rescue cases to cases of drowning.	100%	99.6%	98.6%	99%			Improve safety standards and increase monitoring
		Number of accidents (annual) Deaths Injury Other	Reduce by 30%	2 -	3 13	2 55			Due to non-observances of swimming instructions.

No	Objective	Performance Measursure - Indicator	Performance Measure - Target	Actual Post Performance - 1996	Actual Post Performace - 1997	Actual Post Performance - 1998	Bench Mark - Source	Bench Mark - Perf	Comments
		Number of complaints and suggestions received (annually).	Increase by 50%	42	45	62			Increase number of suggestion boxes in parks.
		0% of complaints looked into on the same day.	80%	70%	75%	80%			
1		Number of inspections for public hygiene.	2	2	3	3			Increase field and control inspections.
2		Litter control and % daily performance.							
3		Number of recreational programmes conducted.	14	6	8	9			Connected to Recreational Programmes Office.
4		Number of beautification projets completed.	6	-	3	4			
5		Number of recreational campaigns and programmes: Number of publications and leaflets issued; Number of TV recreational campaigns and programmes; Number of newspaper recreational campaigns and programmes; Number of radio recreational campaigns and programmes.	2 4 4 4						In co-operation and co-ordianation with PRS and the Recreation and Recreation Progammes Office.

No	Objective	Performance Measursure - Indicator	Performance Measure - Target	Actual Post Performance - 1996	Actual Post Performace - 1997	Actual Post Performance - 1998	Bench Mark - Source	Bench Mark - Perf	Comments
6		Total visitors to major parks (ticket sales).	2,200,000	2,136,064	1,805,650	1,170,479	Portland	2,005,623 (1997)	Expected increase in park visitors due to in-clusion of open beaches and neigh-borhood parks.
		Average daily number of visitors;	5,000	1,380	4,000	4,910			
		Average daily visitors on Fridays;	25,000	18,000	23,000	19,980			January-July 1997
		Average daily visitors on public holidays;	80,000	60,000	76,249	49,986			
		Number of visitors to Mamzar Park.	560,000	549,833	515,654	320,835	548,378		
		Number of visitors to Creek Park	250,000	231,999	241,578	304,192	250,487		Increase due to DSF.
		Number of visitors to Mushrif Park;	300,000	281,206	280,926	141,304	267,187		
		Number of visitors to Safa Park;	550,000	514,486	422,000	186,382	344,339		January-July 1998
		Number of visitors to Jumeirah Beach Park.	470,000	462,873	434,570	209,109	345,259		
		Number of visitors to Neighour-hood Park; (approx.)	280,000	-	100,000	220,465	279,600		Approxi-mate fig-ures due to no ticketing.
		Number of visitors to Open Beach	300,000	-	125,272	200,301	386,400		
		Number of visiting school to students.	100,00	95,967	80,000	40,315	98,974		
		Total number of park visitors	2,800,000							Increase due to new proj.

No	Objective	Performance Measursure - Indicator	Perform-ance Measure - Target	Actual Post Per-formance - 1996	Actual Post Per-formace - 1997	Actual Post Per-formance - 1998	Bench Mark - Source	Bench Mark - Perf	Com-ments
2	Human Re-sources De-velopment	Total man-power % Number of training courses In-house Local External Total number of sick leaves; Total days of sick leave to total number of employees	513 45% 5 10 2 290 0.57	480 - 257 0.54	496 30% 340 1-1.5	497 33% 213 0.43			Give no-tice and warnings to employ-ees with many sick leaves. Exert more ef-fort to re-duce rate.
3	Ensure the provision of efficient cost effective services	Total parks revenues	13,600,000	12,192,420	11,508,677	6,938,156			
		Entrance charges rev-enues; Rev-enues from games; Other revenues; Revenues of Mushrif Park; Revenues of Mamzar Park; Rev-enues of Creek Park; Revenues of Safa Park; Revenues of Jumeirah Park Total general expenses (salaries, al-lowances and recurrent ex-penses)	9,200,000 2,400,000 2,000,000 1,750,000 3,400,000 1,300,000 2,400,000 800,000 16,000,00 0	10,821,280 - 1,371,140 1,021,876 3,807,384 1,351,209 2,072,395 - 16,071,54 2	7,558,151 2,533,156 1,404,570 1,040,707 3,828,058 1,471,165 1,869,019 1,882,295 14,541,57 7	5,055,365 1,386,794 52,290 551,270 2,557,311 1,733,215 1,045,015 7,125,084		',	Rent of fa-cilities, ad-vertiseme nts and subscrip-tions. Expected cost in-crease re-sults from opening of Ladies Club + some neigh-bourhood parks.

No	Objective	Performance Measursure - Indicator	Performance Measure - Target	Actual Post Performance - 1996	Actual Post Performace - 1997	Actual Post Performance - 1998	Bench Mark - Source	Bench Mark - Perf	Comments
		Capital expenditure; % cost recovery (of overheads) from total revenues; % of administrative cost to operating cost;Overhead cost; Average visitor per capita annual cost (Dhs); Average annual capital cost (Dhs); Number of vandalism cases against property.	1,200,000 85% Not available do – 5.7 19 Reduce cases by improving control.	1,453,872 76% 7.1 23	1,350,698 76% 6.6 20	596,910 97% 6.6 21	US Cities	$53	Data will be provided from January 1998.
4	Ensure the provision of efficient maintenance to park utilities and facilities.	Total area (hectares) planned to be maintained; Averages are maintained per labourer park facilities.	500 0.98 9,500,00019 000 121	457 0.95 - -	474 0.95 9,203,356 9,146 113	496 0,96 9,630,516 19,416	Phoenix Philadelphia	22,080	Awaiting the handover of new projects.
		% of mowing completed to planned time; 0% of pruning completed to planned time; 1% of gardening completed to planned time; 1% of gardening completed to planned time; (hectares); Total maintenance cost; Average maintenance cost per hectare; Total green cover area planned for maintenance; %of preventive maintenance of utilities and facilities completed to planned; Average utilization (hours) of park facilities; Actual time spent in maintaining.	100% 100% 100 135 - 48,600	- - - - - -	75% 75% 75% 135 - 48,600	98% 90% 98% 135 0.79 Annually 48,600			Develop and provide modern mowing equipment and increase productivity. Data will be provided from January 1999. Depending of Replacement parts must be made continuously available in order to achieve objective.

Annex 2

The Proposed Authority Tendering & Contracting

No 1	Subject Supply Contracts	Current Authority	NoAuthority Under the Law No 6/97	Proposed Authority
1.1	Authority to initiate a tender for supplies of budgeted items	Concerned Dept. Director Adm. Order 103/80	Concerned Department Director Art. 15	Concerned Section Head within the requirements of Art. 15
1.2	Authority to nominate from the register of importers and suppliers	Concerned Dept. Director Adm. Order 103/80	Concerned Department nominates the companies from the register and Director of CPD approves. Arts. 9,10 & 11 of the Law	Concerned Department nominates the companies from the register and Director of CPD approves.
1.3	Authority to decide on the method of selecting contractor for supply contracts: (a) Public Tender	The Director of CPD Adm. Order 103/80	(a) The DG up to Dhs 5,000,000/-	(a1) The ADG(FA) up to Dhs. 2,000,000/- (a2) Director of CPD up to Dhs. 1,000,000/-
	(b) Limited Tender		(b) The DG up to Dhs. 2,500,000/-	(b1) The ADG(FA) up to Dhs. 1,000,000/- (b2) Director of CPD up to Dhs.500,000/-
	(c) Negotiation		(c1) The DG up to Dhs.1,000,000/- (c2) Director of CPD up to Dhs. 250,000/-	(c1) The ADG(FA) up to Dhs. 500,000/- (c2) Director of CPD up to Dhs. 250,000/-
	(d) Director Agreement		(d1) The DG up to Dhs. 250,000/- (d2) Director of CPD up to Dhs. 50,000/- Article 6 of the law.	d1) The ADG(FA) up to Dhs. 100,000/- (d2) Director of CPD up to Dhs. 50,000/-
1.4	Aughority to approve invitation to tender for budgeted items: (a) to advertise in the press of supply of items (b to approve the short listed companies to be contacted	(a) Director of CPD proposes & Director-General approves. (b) Director of CPD. Admin Order 103/80.	Director of CPD, according to Arts. 9, 18 & 19 of the law.	Director of CPD.
1.5	Authority to approve the period of submission of tenders	No current authority C.P Director of CPD proposes and DG approves.	Director of CPD, according to Arts. 9 & 19(3) of the law.	Director of CPD.
1.6	Authority to approve extension of time to submit the tender	No current authority C.P Director of CPD proposes and DG approves	Director CPD, according to Art. 9 of the law	Director of CPD.

No 1	Subject Supply Contracts	Current Authority	NoAuthority Under the Law No 6/97	Proposed Authority
1.13	Authority to exempt from the performance bond.	No current authority C.P (DG)	(A) Director of CPD if delivery period under the contract does not exceed (15) days and for companies in which the government has a share of not less that 50%. Arts. 9 & 32 of the law. (B) DG upon a proposal from Director of CPD for exemption of foreign contracts. Art. 32 of the law.	(A) Director of CPD if delivery period under the contract does not exceed (15) days and for companies in which the government has a share of not less than 50%. (B) DG upon a proposal from Director of CPD for exemption of foreign contracts.
1.14	Authority to sign contracts. (a) Public Tender (b) Limited Tender (c) Negotiation (d) Direct Agreement	No current authority C.P 1. DG (above Dhs. 2 million 2. ADG(FA) up to Dhs. 2 million 3. Director of CPD up to Dhs. 400,000/-	(a) The DG up to Dhs. 5,000,000/- (b) The DG up to Dhs. 2,500,000/- c-1 The DG up to Dhs. 1,000,000/- c-2 Director of CPD up to Dhs. 250,000/- d-1 The DG up to Dhs 250,000/- d-2 Director of CPD up to Dhs. 50,000/- Art. 6 of the law	For all contracts: The ADG(FA) up to Dhs 5,000,000/- Director of CPD up to Dhs. 1,000,000/-
1.15	Authority to renew contracts	C.P Director General	The concerned authority under Art. (6) of the law	The concerned authority as on item 1.3 above
1.16	Authority to increase or decrease quantity of goods in a contract.	C.P Director General upon recommendation of Director of CPD. Adm. Order 103/80.	TNC propose and the concerned authority under schedule of Art. (6) approves Arts. 6 & 48 of the law	TNC propose and the concerned authority approves under item 1.3 above.
1.17	Authority to authorize payment to suppliers of goods	No current authority C.P Director of CPD on production of required documents.	The concerned authority under schedule of art.(6) Arts. 6 & 35 of the law	The concerned authority as on item 1.3 above, subject to the recommendation of the take-over Committee.
1.18	Authority to grant additional grace period to suppliers	No current authority C.P DG	Director of CPD propose DG approves Art. 55 of the law	Director of CPD propose DG approves
1.19	Authority to exempt from penalties	No current authority C.P (Director-General)	TNC Propose and Director General approves Art. 49 of the law	TNC Propose and Director General approves
1.20	Authority to issue penalties	No current authority with respect to supplies Fines are levied automatically as per conditions of fines provided for in the contract or as recommended by the Director of concerned Department and approved by the Director of CPD	Automatically without identifying the authority as per Art. 55 of the law	DG approves as proposed by the concerned authority under 1.3 above
1.21	Authority to approve release of bonds of deposit for suppliers	No current C.P Director of CPD	The concerned Dep. Propose and Director of CPD approves Art. 34 of the law	The Head of TC&CC Section in accordance with standard procedures

No 1	Subject Supply Contracts	Current Authority	NoAuthority Under the Law No 6/97	Proposed Authority
1.22	Authority to terminate the contract	No current authority C.P (Director-General)	Director of CPD propose and the concerned authority under Art. (6) approves Arts. 6, 52 of the law	Director of CPD proposes and the concerned authority under 1.3 above approves
2.1	Minor Projects			
2.1.1	Authority to initiate and execute minor projects including invitation to contractors, opening tender envelopes, decision and issue of awards (subject to minimum 3 proposals from the approved list of contractors registered at the CPD and budgeted funds).	Concerned Department Director for amounts up to Dhs. 50,000 Over Dhs. 50,000 standard procedures are applied Adm. Order 218/96	The DG and the Director of CPD in accordance with the authorities under Art. (6)	The Diretor of Concerned Dep. For contracts up to Dhs. 250,000/-
2.1.2	Authority to award contracts for Minor Projects	ADG concerned with respect to contracts not exceeding Dhs. 2,000,000/- under the same conditions as above, while contractors are invited by CPD.	DG and Director of CPD as per authority under article (6).	Concerned ADG for contracts up to Dhs. 2,000,000/- under the same conditions as above while CPD invites contractors provided that: 1. At least3 tenders 2. Budgeted project 3. Only approved contractors registered at the CPD are invited.
2.1.3	Authority to sign contracts for minor projects.	1. Director of CPD for contracts up to Dhs. 400,000 2. ADG(FA)for contracts up to Dhs. 2,000,000. Adm. Order 218/96	The DG and th Director of CPD in accordance with the authorities under Art. (6)	1. Director of CPD for contracts up to Dhs. 1,000,000/- 2. ADG(FA) contracts up to Dhs. 2,000,000/-
2.2	Major Projects			
2.2.1	Authority to initiate a tender of a budgeted project	Concerned ADG for projects up to Dhs. 4,000,000 (Subject to prior approval of Technical Committee)	Not specified (Article 15)	1. Director of Concerned Dep. For contracts up to Dhs. 3,000,000/- 2. Concerned ADG for contracts up to Dhs. 5,000,000/- NB: subject to the approval of the Technical Committee
2.2.2	Authority to approve the method of tender for a budgeted project	No current authority C.P DG	The concerned authority under Art. 6 of the law	1. Director of concerned Dep. For contracts up to Dhs.3,000,000/- 2. Concerned ADG for contracts up to Dhs. 5,000,000/-
2.2.3	Authority to approve invitation letters for tender for budgeted projects: (a) To advertise in the press for prequalification and provision of consultancy service competition and execution of works. (b) To invite from among short listed contractors or consultants to be contacted.	C.P (a) DG (b1) Director of CPD for in-house projects + minor projects +Dubai School projects + Demolition projects. (b2) Director-General for other projects (subject to list approved by Director General)	Director of CPD, according to Arts. 9, 18 & 19 of the law	Director of CPD

No 1	Subject Supply Contracts	Current Authority	NoAuthority Under the Law No 6/97	Proposed Authority
2.2.4	Authority to approve the period of submission of a tender	Concerned Dept. Director in agreement with the Director of CPD. Adm. Order 103/80	Concerned Department propose and the Director of CPD approves to the maximum of (6)) days. Arts. 9 & 19(3) of the law	Concerned Department propose and the Director of CPD approves to the maximum of (60) days.
2.2.5	Authority to approve extension of time for submission of a tender	No current authority C.P 1. As requested by 30% of companies who purchased tender documents. 2. Concerned Dept. Director + Director of CPD.	Director of CPD approves the extension on a request from the concerned Department. Art. 9 of the law	Director of CPD approves the extension on: (1) A request of 30% of companies who purchased tender documents. (2) A request from the concerned Department.
2.2.6	Authority to approve extension of tender validity.	No current authority C.P Concerned Department Director in agreement with the Director of CPD	Director of concerned Department propose and the Director of CPD approves. Arts. 9 & 23 of the law	Director of concerned Department propose and the Director of CPD approves.
2.2.7	Authority to open tender envelopes for projects.	1. Finance & Tender committee (DM Council). 2. CPD jointly with the concerned Dept. Admin. Order 103/80 Admin. Order 336/90	The Tendering & Negotiation Committee according to Arts. 25, 39 & 42 of the law	The Tendering & Negotiation Committee
2.2.8	Authority to approve project tender analysis result for contractors.	For project up to Dhs. 2,000,000/- by the Concerned ADG when views of the projet consultant, concerned Dept. and CPD agree. Adm. Orders 33, 34 & 35/95	The Tendering & Negotiation Committee recommends and the concerned authority approves as per article (6) of the law. Art. 31 of the law	Director of Concerned Dept. for contracts up to Dhs. 2,500,000/- the Concerned ADG for contracts up to Dhs. 5,000,000/- in the event that the views of the project consultant, concerned Dept. and CPD agree.
2.2.9	Authority to approve Letter of Award or Acceptance	C.P D.G	The Concerned Authority under schedule of Art.(6) Art. 31 of the law	The concerned ADG (letter to be forwarded through CPD).
2.2.10	Authority to sign contracts for projects.	Director-General	The Concerned Authority under Arts.6 & 35 of the law	1. ADG (Finance) for contracts up to Dhs. 5,000,000/- 2. Director of CPD for contracts up to Dhs. 2,000,000/-
2.2.11	Authority to approve and sign payment certificates.	Current practice a. Interim payment certificate are signed byconcerned Dept. Director, Head of TC & CC &Finance Dept. b. Penultimate & Finalpayment certificate asper bove (Auditor tomake a thorough checking prior to payment). Admin Order 118/89	Payment certificate to be checked finically and technically, approved by the Consultant and the Technical Department. Art. 64 of the law	Interim payment certificate a. Consultant prepares b. TC&CC check and sign c. Finance Dept. for payment (copy to concerned Dep.) ADO Proposal As above but the concerned Head of section sign after Consultant Penultimate & Payment Certificate: a. prepared by Consultant b. signed by Concerned Dept. Director. c. Checked by TC&CC d. Final check by Finance Dept.

No 1	Subject Supply Contracts	Current Authority	NoAuthority Under the Law No 6/97	Proposed Authority
2.2.12	Authority to utilize funds from the provisional sum.	a. Up to Dhs. 150,000/- by the concerned Dept. Director b. Unlimited amount to be approved by the Concerned ADG (With prior approval of the Consultant and CPD subject to available funds within the approved Provisional Sum). Adm. Orders 118/89 & 172/91	No provision in the law concerning this authority.	a. Up to Dhs.50,000/ - by the concerned Section Head. b. Unlimited amount by the Concerned Dept. Director.(With prior approval of the Consultant and CPD subject to available funds within the approved Provisional Sum). Arts. 35 & 64 of the law
2.2.13	Authority to approve Variation Orders within approved budget.	. U to Dhs. 50,000/- by the concerned Dept. Director jointly with the Director of the CPD. b. Unlimited amount by the Concerned ADG (with prior approval of the Consultant & CPD) Adm. Orders 118/89 & 33, 34, 35/95	Variations should be proposed by the TNC and approved by the Concerned Authority under schedule of article (6 of the law based on the recommendations according to Art. 48(8).	a. Up to 50,000/- by the concerned Section Head jointly with Head of TC& CC Section. b. Up to Dhs. 50,000/- by the concerned Dept. Director jointly with the Director of the CPD. c. Unlimited amount by the Concerned ADG. (With prior approval of the Consultant & CPD).
2.2.14	Authority to approve claims: Extension of time	ADG subject to: 1. Extension not to exceed two additional months. 2. Within 10% of contract amounts, up to Dhs. 500,000/- for contractor and Dhs. 200,000/- for consultant.(Subject to prior approval of CPD), A/O. 33, 34, 35/95.	TNC propose and DG approves. Art. 66 of the law	Concerned ADG For claims not exceeding two months and to the maximum of 10% of the contract sum and a limit of Dhs. 500,000/- for contractor and Dhs. 200,000/- for consultant. Concerned Dept. Director For claims not exceeding two months and to the maximum of 10% of the contract sum and a limit of Dhs. 250,000/- for contractor and Dhs. 100,000/- for consultant. (all above subject to recommendations of the consultant and with prior approval of the CPD)
2.2.15	Authority to approve fixing or release of deposits. A. Bid Bond B. Performance Security Bond	A1 Bid bond will be fixe by Director of CPD and automatically released by TC&CC once performance guarantee is submitted A2 Released by the Director of CPD ifrender of contractor is ranked 4th or her in price among tenders. B1 Fixed by Director of CPD B2. Released automatically upon presentation by contractors of the final completion certificate.	A. Bid Bond will be fixed or released by the Director of CPD in Accordance with Art. 24 of the law. B1. Performance Security Bond will be fixed by the Director of CPD in accordance with Art. 32 of the law. B2. Performance SecurityBond may be released upon proposal by the Handing Over Committee and the approval of the DG. Art. 70 of the law	A1. Bid Bond will be ixed or released by TC&CC once performance guarantee is submitted A2. Bid bond will be reeased by the Director of CPD for tenderer whose price is higher than 3rd rank. B1. Performance Security Bond will be fixed by the Director of CPD. B2. Performance Security Bond may be the Handing Over Committee and the Approval of the DG.
2.2.16	Authority to issue penalties to consultants and Contractor.	By the concerned Department Director.	The Director of CPD on a proposal by the Director of the Concerned Dept. Art. 65 of the law	The Director of CPD on a proposal by the Director of the concerned Department.
2.2.17	Authority to cancel penalties.	Director General upon recommendation of Director of CPD. Adm. Orders 103/80	The DG upon recommendation from TNC. Arts. 49 & 65 of the law	The DG upon recommendation from TNC.
2.2.18	Authority to approve completion certificates for DM projects.	By the concerned Department Director.	The DG as recommended by the Handing Over Committee. Arts. 67 & 70 of the law	The DG as recommended by the Handing Over Committee.
2.2.19	Authority to reject unacceptable consultancy output/contract work.	By the concerned Department Director.	The Handing Over Committee and the approval of the DG. Art. 67 & 70 of the law	The Handing Over Committee and the approval of the DG.

Annex 3

Dubai Declaration

Forward

The Dubai Declaration was originally formulated at the Dubai International Conference on Best Practices to Improve the Living Environment organized by the Dubai Municipality in association with the United Nations (UNCHS/HABITAT) in Dubai, U.A.E. during 19-22 November, 1995. 95 countries and 914 participants from all over the world attended the Conference. 28 best practices were presented at the conference by industrialized as well ad developing countries and thus gave the first flavor of the vast international potential for practical mutual assistance through the sharing of transferable and replicable expertise and achievements of excellence.

The Dubai Declaration was later formally adopted by the UNCHS/HABITAT conference in New York during February 1996. The Dubai Declaration has been adopted by the United Nations as well as by the World Association of Cities and Local Authorities (WACLA) at the HABITAT II Conference held in Istanbul, Turkey during 3-14 June, 1996. The Declaration is referred to in both the HABITAT Agenda (Istanbul Declaration) and the WACLA (Istanbul Declaration). It can be truly said that the Dubai Declaration gave birth to the international concept of sharing Best Practices for the accelerated development of the human settlements section. The Declaration represents a clear expression of the aspirations, hopes and strategies by Governments, Local Authorities, NGOs and CBOs for the improvement of the living environment for the benefit of humanity well into the 21st century through the application of an international system of recognizing and disseminating best practices.

The Dubai Declaration is noteworthy for another extremely important outcome, namely, the establishment of the Dubai Award for Excellence in

Improving the Living Environment. This Award is referred to in item 7 of the Dubai Declaration and was established under the directive of H.H. Sheikh Maktoum Bin Rashid Al Maktoum, Vice-President and Prime Minister of the United Arab Emirates and Ruler of Dubai. The Award comprises of a total of U.A. $400,000 to finance the biennial event honoring the Best Practices to be chosen by a UNCHS Technical Advisory Committee as well as an international jury of eminent personalities. The first Award took place in Istanbul on June 4, 1996 as part of the HAPITAT II Conference's main events.

Dubai Municipality is pleased to be associated with the international effort in responding positively to the immense challenges of human settlements issues in the 21st century. The Dubai Declaration will give a momentum to this effort and galvanize the achievement of meaningful exchange of expertise and co-operation among governments, local authorities, NGOs and CBOs for the common good of humanity.

The Dubai International Conference for Habitat II on Best Practices in Improving the Living Environment, having brought together over 900 delegates from governments, United Nations Agencies, international organizations, local authorities, non-governmental organizations (NGOs), community-based organizations (CBOs), professional associations and the private sector, from 19th to 22nd November, 1995 and having reviewed a selection of 28 Best Practices documented for the Habitat II Conference.

BACKGROUND AND GUIDELINE PRINCIPLES

1. Recalling Agenda 21 adopted by the United Nations Conference on Environment and Development (Rio de Janeiro, 1992) and particularly its Chapters 7 and 28 which highlight the essential linkages between human settlements and sustainable development.

2. Also recalling the United Nations Conferences on the Rights of the Child (New York, 1991), Population and Development (Cairo, 1994), Social Development (Copenhagen, 1995) and Women and Development (Beijing, 1995) which highlighted major human development issues: unsafe and unhealthy environment, violence and the differentiated effects each has on men and women.

3. Desirous to explore the full implications of the recommendations of these conferences for sustainable urban development.

4. Recognizing the importance of the call of the General Assembly to forge a positive vision of an urbanizing world and the goals of Habitat

II – "The City Summit": adequate shelter for all and sustainable human settlements development in an urbanizing world.

5. Recognizing that human settlements are where sectorial issues addressed at previous conferences intersect in daily life and that Habitat II represents the convergence of on-going local and global concerns as well as an opportunity for the confirmation and consolidation of earlier plans of actions.

6. Recognizing the recommendations and decisions of the Preparatory Committee for Habitat II calling upon all national committees and the Secretariat to identify and disseminate best practices as an integral part of the preparatory process and establishing guidelines and criteria for this purpose.

7. Concerned with finding practical and sustainable solutions to the social, economic and environmental challenges facing an urbanizing world, including: management of development, employment creation and poverty elimination, access to land and security of tenure, management, protection and rehabilitation of the environment, efficient use of resources, prevention of crime and all forms of violence, rehabilitation of refugees and displaced persons, equality for all men and women, social integration and equality for children, the elderly and the disabled, empowerment of local communities, and access to shelter, basic services and finance.

8. Equally concerned with the need for the Habitat Agenda resulting from the "City Summit" to guide and inspire concrete actions in solving shelter and human settlements problems in an integrated and sustainable way for the first two decades of the 21st century.

9. Recognizing that special attention has to be given to the situation of poor countries in assuring balance between urban and rural development and the continuing need for international cooperation for shelter and basic infrastructure.

10. Believing that the worldwide promotion of effective mechanisms for extending the exchange of best practices will significantly contribute towards empowering local communities to shape their futures.

11. Acknowledging the various institutional, financial and human resources constraints may limit local capacity to take full advantage of and contribute to such best practice exchanges and that these constraints particularly the need for human resources development and adaptation, also be addressed in this context.

12. Expressing appreciation for the invaluable contribution of Dubai Municipality, United Arab Emirates, in sponsoring and hosting that International Conference on Best Practices in Improving the Living Environment and providing assistance to partners in developing countries to facilitate the documentation of their case studies.

13. Commending the leadership of UNCHS (Habitat) in providing technical assistance and disseminating guidelines, nomination criteria and unified format to facilitate the compilation and exchange of best practices, including the innovative methodology adopted to analyze and document their gender impact, as a major component of the Habitat II process.

14. Taking note of the efforts underway by UNCHS (Habitat) and its partners to disseminate the best practices through electronic, printed and audio-visual media to the largest possible audience, updated electronic catalogue of best practices.

15. Believing that ready access in all parts of the world to such information will contribute to more effective and meaningful partnerships between and among governments, local authorities NGOs/CBOs, and the professional, academic and private sectors in addressing the challenges of sustainable human settlements development.

RECOMMENDTIONS AND FOLLOW-UP ACTIONS

1. Call for a coordinated strategy to be implemented by UNCHS (Habitat II) in collaboration with other United Nations agencies and all appropriate stakeholders, designed to empower action, influence policy at the local level, and promote real synergy between local, national and international development initiatives, and, to strengthen communication between national and local authorities and their constituencies.

2. Stress that any international effort for collecting and exchanging best practice information on human settlements development must be transparently designed and implemented with the organizations representing local authorities and other stakeholders, building upon their extensive international and national networks and expertise.

3. Recommend to the Preparatory Committee and the "City Summit" that the following considerations be added to complement the already adopted criteria of tangible impact, partnerships and sustainability for selecting those practices worthy of global dissemination:

a. Leadership in inspiring action and change, including change in public policy;
b. Promotion of accountability and transparency;
c. Empowerment of people, neighbor-hoods and communities and incorporation of their contributions;
d. Acceptance of and responsiveness to social and cultural diversity;
e. Potential for transferability, adaptability and replicability;
f. Appropriateness to local conditions and levels of development;
g. Promotion of social equality and equity.

4. Further suggest that the following be incorporated to strengthen the unified reporting process to enhance best practice dissemination:

   a. Formation of international networks to assess innovation, creativity and transferability of pr at various levels of development;
   b. Formation of international networks to assess innovation, creativity and transferability of pr at various levels of development;
   c. Establishment with the international associations of local authorities and other stakeholders national and regional focal points to advice on the usefulness and on-going refinement of the system;
   d. Formation of international network to access the extent to which participatory processes are diverse interests and needs, particularly those related to gender differences are assessed;
   e. Development and use of indicators for participatory planning, implementation, monitoring, evaluation, disaggregated by gender and age.

5. Welcome the steps being taken by UNCH (Habitat) in developing a global electronic catalogue on best practices, in its various forms including the Internet, CD-ROM, diskette and printed forms, as well as other practical means of facilitating access by policy makers and practitioners to the experience of their counterparts in addressing common problems.

6. Encourage all governments, United Nations Agencies, local authorities and their associations, NGOs/CBOs and professional associations to work toward common reporting formats and processes and to establish direct and cross referencing links with each other systems

and with the UNCHS (Habitat) electronic catalogue of best practices in order to greatly enhance and facilitate the transmission of information, experience and expertise to their respective end-users.

7. Call upon UNCHS (Habitat), in partnership with governments, other United Nations agencies, associations representing local authorities, the private, public, non-governmental, professional and voluntary sectors to explore mechanisms for compilation, systematic analysis and assessment of best practices as an integral part of the follow-up process beyond Habitat II, for the purpose of:

    a. Developing best practice initiatives as sites of learning for sharing their experiences and knowledge base with the global community;
    b. Using and disseminating best practice case studies as training, management and organization development materials;
    c. Further developing the best practices catalogue as a means of matching supply and demand technical co-operation at all levels;
    d. Compiling and disseminating an international roster of experience, expertise and knowledge on those persons, institutions and organizations directly responsible for implementing the best practices;
    e. Promoting the transfer and adaptation of environmentally sound, socially-responsive, economy viable technologies, products and services;
    f. Furthering the transfer and adaptation of practical solutions for capacity-building, including exchange programmes, at the international, regional, national and local levels.

8. Welcome, with appreciation, the establishment by Dubai Municipality of the Dubai Award for Best Practices which will be administered in collaboration with UNCHS (Habitat).
9. Call upon UNCHS (Habitat) to make the presentation of the Dubai Declaration a part of the official events of the Istanbul Conference.

Annex 4

List of Partners of the Dubai International Award for Best Practices to Improve the Living Environment:

The Best practices and Local Leadership Programme works with a decentralized network of organizations committed to the identification, analysis and dissemination of lessons learned from Best Practices.

Each partner brings its own expertise and georgraphic coverage to the programme, creating a world-wide network of organizations. Partners incorporate Best Practices into their on-going activities such as education, research, training, capacity-building and advocacy. These partners include:

THE SECRETARIAT
UN-HABITAT
Best Practices Programme
United Nations Avenue, NOF Block 4 South Wing - Level 2
P.O BOX 30030 - 00100
Nairobi, Kenya
Tel: (254 20) 7624981/7623342
Fax: (254 20) 7623080/ 7624266/ 7624267
Email: bestpractices@unhabitat.org
Web: http://www.unhabitat.org http://www.bestpractices.org
Contact Person: Wandia Seaforth

AFRICA
Environmental Development Action in the Third World (ENDA Tiers Monde)
4 -5 Rue Kleber
Dakar BP 3370 / Senegal
Phone : +221 8 21 60 27 / + 221 8 22 42 29
Email : rup@enda.sn
Web : www.enda.sn
Contact Person : Malick Gaye
Centre for French speaking Africa

ARAB STATES
Dubai Municipality
P. O. Box: 67
Dubai

UAE

Tel: (971 4) 2064450/2215555
Fax: (971 4) 2063673/2246666
Email: dubaiaward@dm.gov.ae
Web: www.dubaiaward.ae
Contact Person: Obaid Salem Al Shamsi - Assistant Director-General
Dubai Municipality is the sponsor of the Dubai International Award for Best Practices, a biennial award which recognizes 12 best practices which result in the Improvement of the Living Environment

ASIA

IAARA
International Art & Architecture Research Association (IAARA)
Unit 1, 12th floor, Iran Trade Center (ITC Tower)
Afrigha Blvd
Tehran / Iran
Phone: +98 21 26212516 +98 21 26212537
Fax: +98 21 26212522
E-Mail: office@iaara.org.ir
Web: www.iaara.org.ir
Contact Person: Reza Pourvaziry M. Arch - President

EUROPE

UN-HABITAT Best Practices Hub
Vienna
TINA Vienna
Urban Technologies & Strategies GmbH
Anschützgasse 1
1150 Vienna / Austria
Phone: +43 1 4000 84260
Fax: +43 1 4000 7997
E-Mail: office@bestpractices.at
Web: www.bestpractices.at
Contact Person: Ariane Müller Co-ordinator; D.I. Alexandra Vogl, Director
The Best Practices Hub - Vienna is a cooperation between UN-HABITAT and the City of Vienna. It is the UN-HABITAT BLP regional center for Central and Eastern Europe and the thematic center for Urban Environmental Technologies. It is managed by TINA Vienna - Urban Technologies & Strate-

gies GmbH
Ministerio de Fomento
Secretaría de Estado de Vivienda y Actuaciones Urbanas.
Dirección General de Urbanismo y Política de Suelo
Paseo de la Castellana, 112
Madrid 28071 / Spain
Phone: +34917284091
Fax: +34 91 728 48 61
E-Mail: jlnicolas@fomento.es
Web: http://www.fomento.es
http://habitat.aq.upm.es
Contact Person: Jose Luis Nicolas

The government of Spain represented by the Secretary of State for Housing and Urban Policies, by the General Directorate on Urbanism and Land-policies, and as head of the Spanish National delegation to UN-HABITAT is partner of the BLP, sponsor of the Ibero American Forum for Best Practices and holds a national Best Practices competition in Spain.

UN-HABITAT Office for city-to-city co-operation
Diputació de Barcelona
Relacions Internacionals
Diana A. Lopez Caramazana
C/ Corsega 273 - 2 planta
Barcelona, Catalunya 08008 / Spain
Phone: +34.93.404.94.73
Fax: +34.93.402.24.73
E-Mail: diana.lopez@unhabitat.org
Web: http://www.unhabitat.org/categories.asp?catid=508
The Best Practice Office in Barcelona is the BLP partner in Barcelona. The office helps to identify and assess best practices, public policies and enabling legislation; facilitate exchange of technical expertise and best practices; and promote capacity building for local and regional authorities.
University of Naples 'Federico II'
Department of Conservation of Environmental and Architectural Assets
Via Roma, 402
Naples 80132 / Italy
Phone: +39 081 25 38650

Fax: +39 081 253 86 49
E-Mail: girard@unina.it / cerreta@unina.it
Web: www.unina.it
www.conservazione.unina.it
Contact Person: Luigi Fusco Girard - Professor
LATIN AMERICA
Ibero-american and Caribbean Forum on Best Practices
Rua Rumânia, 20 Cosme Velho
Rio de Janeiro 22240-140 / RJ Brazil
Phone: +55 21 32358550
Fax: +5521 2515-1701
E-Mail: secretariado@mejorespracticas.org
Web: http://www.mejorespracticas.org

The Foro Iberoamericano y del Caribe sobre Mejores Prácticas was founded in 1997, one year after the start of the Best Practices Programme of UN-HABITAT with the help of the Government of Spain. It is an information network with four subregional nodes and four national focal points.

Brazilian Institute for Municipal Administration (IBAM)
1-Humaita
22271 070, Rio de Janeiro, Brazil.
Tel: +55 21 25369703,
Fax: (55 21) 2537 1262, 25381613
Email: ibam@ibam.org.br , marlene.fernandes@ibam.org.br
Web: http://www.ibam.org.br
Contact Person: Marlene Fernandes.
Centro de Vivienda y Estudios Urbanos (CENVI)
Luis Cabrera # 68
Col. San Jerónimo Aculco, c.p.
Mexico City 4340 / Mexico
Phone: +52 55 568 333 45 +52 55 568 198 34
E-Mail: infocenvi@prodigy.net.mx
Web: http://www.cenvi.org.mx

CENVI is the sub-regional node for Mexico, Central America and the Spanish speaking Caribbean.
El Agora

Jimenez de Lorca 4229 CP 5009
Cordoba, Argentina
Tel: (549 351) 5132881
Fax: (54 351) 4812570
Email: claudiacristina.laub@gmail.com / elagora@arnet.com.ar
Web: www.elagora.org.ar
Contact Person: Claudia Laub
El Agora is the Southern sub-node of the Foro Iberoamericano and member
of the BLP.
Fundacion Habitat Colombia
Bogotá D.C., Calle 127C #6A40
Telefax: + 571-2163606,
Phone: + 57 - 3165284268.
Email: direccion@fundacionhabitatcolombia.org
Web: http:///www.fundacionhabitatcolombia.org
Contact Person: Ms. Lucelena Betancur Salazar - Director
La Fundación Hábitat Colombia - FHC is the node for the Andean countries
of the Foro Iberoamericano and member of the BLP.

NORTH AMERICA

IIUD-Institute for International Urban Development
2235 Massachusetts Avenue, Second Floor
Cambridge, MA 02140 / United States of America
Phone: +617-492-0077
Fax: ++617-492-0046
E-Mail: serageldin@i2ud.org / leith@i2ud.org
Web: www.i2ud.org
Contact Person: Mona Serageldin
The Institute for International Urban Development (IIUD) is member of the
Steering Committee of the Best Practices and Local Leadership Program
(BLP). It is committed to identifying, documenting, analyzing and dissemi-
nating Best Practices. This information is used in international executive ed-
ucation programs for which short case studies geared to executive level
participants are prepared.
Joslyn Castle Institute for Sustainable Communities (JCI)
1004 Farnam Street, Suite 101
Omaha, Nebraska 68131 / United States
Phone: +1 402 472 0087

Fax: +1 402 933 0082
E-Mail: csteward@unlnotes.unl.edu / info@sustainabledesign.org
Web: www.ecospheres.com
Contact Person: Cecil Steward
INTERNATIONAL NETWORKS
Practical Action
The Schumacher Centre for Technology & Development
Bourton Hall
Bourton-on-Dunsmore
Rugby CV23 9QZ / Great Britain
Phone: +44 01926 634400
Fax: +44 01926 634401
E-Mail: theo.schilderman@practicalaction.org.uk
Web: www.practicalaction.org.uk
Contact Person: Theo Schilderman

Practical action is a BLP partner which helps to identify best practices focusing on the use of technology to challenge poverty at an international level.

International Council for Local Environmental Initiatives (ICLEI)
100 Queen St. W., City Hall, 16th Fl. West Tower,
Toronto, Ontario, M5H 2N2, Canada
Fax: (415) 392-1478.
Email: Monika.Zimmermann@iclei.org,
Web: http://www.iclei.org
Contact Person: Monika Zimmermann
Global Urban Development
1050 K Street, NW, Suite 400
Washington, DC 2001 / USA
Phone: +1 202 554 5891
E-Mail: info@globalurban.org
Web: www.globalurban.org
Contact Person: Marc A. Weiss
Huairou Commission
249 Manhattan Avenue
Brooklyn, NY 11211, USA
Fax: (1-718) 388 -0285
Email: info@huairou.org ; jan.peterson@huairou.org ; bpfound@gmail.com

Web: www.huairoucommission.org
Contact Persons: Jan Peterson / Dr. Sangeetha Purushothaman

PART 2

THE HORN OF AFRICA

CHAPTER 6: Horn of Africa's History and Challenge

This part focuses on the Horn of Africa Region which is known to have historic roots and substantial natural resources but suffers from abject poverty and instability. An attempt is made here to provide the region's historic context as well as its challenges for peace and development. My vision for the region requires a paradigm shift on the part of the governments in the region and the international community. An attempt is also made here to recommend a new and vital initiative: the establishment of a Red Sea Cooperative Council comprising all the countries around the Red Sea including Ethiopia.

The Horn of Africa and Its Historic Perspective

During most of the first millennium in the Common Era (C.E.), the Horn of Africa, constituted a region that was a superpower in the affairs of northeastern Africa and southern Arabia. Its influence and, at times, its authority extended from Egypt to the Indian Ocean and across the Red Sea all the way to Mecca. The capital for its overseas territory in south Arabia was Sanaa in Yemen. It was a major partner with the other superpowers of the time: Persia, Byzantium, and India on matters of trade, politics, and military issues. Like the United States of America (USA) today, the Horn of Africa was the place of refuge for people escaping various forms of oppression. The first followers of Islam survived the onslaughts by Meccan authorities by escaping to Axum, Ethiopia's capital at that time, and residing there for 15 years before returning to Mecca, their homeland.(Sergew Hable Sellassie: "Ancient and Medieval Ethiopian History to 1270")

During the second millennium C.E., the Horn of Africa suffered a severe decline due to internal and external conflicts and diminished trade. Not only did it lose its overseas territories, it also fell victim to the avarice of colonialists who bit off all the peripheral parts along its borders at the Red Sea, the Gulf of Aden and the Indian Ocean. By the end of the second millennium, the Horn of Africa comprised a number of fragmented countries (Djibouti, Eritrea, Ethiopia and Somalia), largely known for their crippling poverty, insecurity, lack of democracy, severe environmental degradation, a prevalence of pandemic diseases including malaria and HIV/AIDS, illiteracy, and continued tension. It is amazing that during this period not only has Ethiopian independence survived, but the region has also seen the decolonization of Djibouti, Eritrea and Somalia. Eritrea's subsequent federation with and cessation from Ethiopia was another occurrence that took place during this period. Somalia's internal fragmentation continues to cause instability and a serious strain to the region's peace and development.

At the beginning of the third millennium C.E., the Horn of Africa is still fraught with major ills and scars that have afflicted it during the previous millennium. The issue now is whether this region will continue with its socio-economic and political conditions of misery or transform itself into being, if not a superpower, a self-reliant, peaceful, and democratic entity. Today, the human population of the Horn of Africa is about 115 million, which is expected to increase to 145 million by 2025. Given this and taking into account its substantial natural resources including water, agricultural, and mineral, along with a more positive role by the international community as well as civic organizations and the private sector, it is my considered view that there are good prospects for hope in this beleaguered part of Africa. Such a hope, however, presupposes a more vigorous effort by all internal and external stakeholders including governments, non-governmental and international organizations as well as academic institutions in the formulation, promotion and achievement of appropriate socio-economic and political development strategies for the benefit of the region and the international community. It is also suggested that the strategic interests of the United States and its allies in the Horn of Africa would be predicated on the long-term intrinsic values of the region and not, as has been the case so far, for the mere protection of the oil lanes/sources, Israel's survival and the fight against international terrorism.

Introduction

In his book entitled: "The Horn of Africa: Conflict and Poverty", Mesfin Wolde-Mariam uses "common boundary", as an indicator for determining those countries that constitute the Horn of Africa. Accordingly, he suggests that the "PRINCIPAL" Horn of Africa countries are Djibouti, Eritrea, Ethiopia, Somalia, and Somaliland.[1] He also includes what he calls "PERIPH-ERAL" countries i.e. Kenya and the Sudan because they share boundaries with the "core country", namely, Ethiopia. A statement in the German foreign pol-icy strategy on the Horn of Africa, refers to Djibouti, Eritrea, Ethiopia and Somalia as the countries that constitute the region.[2] Using terms such as "The Greater Horn of Africa", other sources include a wider range of countries, namely, Uganda, Rwanda, and Burundi.

For the purposes of this book, the countries that constitute the Horn of Africa region are Djibouti, Eritrea, Ethiopia, and Somalia. These four have been chosen based on their relatively higher level of mutual cultural and so-cial affinity, shared history and interdependence. Somaliland has been omit-ted because it has yet to be recognized by the United Nations as an independent country[3]. While this paper may appear mainly ethio-centric—due to the propensity of Ethiopia's recorded history, it is by no means in-tended to diminish the historical evolution and importance of the other Horn of Africa nations.

Many publications on the Horn of Africa for the most part, tend to dwell on the huge constraints encountered in the region and very little on its glorious past or the specific strategies for its development. It appears, at times, as if col-laboration and integration in the Horn of Africa are a totally new phenome-non. One need only have a closer look at the region's history during the first millennium to discover the level of strength and respect it had at that time. This chapter attempts to fill that gap. This is not to glorify colonialism by any means rather simply to underline the importance of unity and collaboration. It is also important for the current and future generations in the Horn of Africa and the Diaspora to be aware of their legacy in order to aspire for higher goals and objectives. This chapter further attempts to draw attention to the chal-lenges and risks being faced by the Horn as well as the opportunities and ben-efits available to all the stakeholders and interested parties from the region's vast human and natural resources.

Although there are substantial resources for information on the Horn of Africa, for the purposes of this book, a few carefully selected materials have been utilized mainly aimed at triggering more intensive and practical discus-sion and action by concerned individuals, institutions, organizations, govern-ments and the private sector.

Horn of Africa's Glorious Millennium
Horn of Africa as a Superpower in Eastern Africa and the Middle East

The Horn of Africa used to be known by a variety of names including Punt, Ethiopia/Nubia and Ethiopia. The area extended from today's eastern parts of the Sudan to the Indian Ocean including modern day Djibouti, Eritrea, Ethiopia and Somalia (See Figure 1: "Trade Routes to the Land of PUNT" and Figure 2: "The Empire of Ethiopia According to Monumentum Adulitanum"). Richard Pankhurst states: "The coastal areas of Ethiopia in Pharonic times formed part of what the ancient Egyptians termed the land of Punt, and sometimes God's Land."[4] According to E. Naville, Punt "....must have begun near Suakim or Massawah and stretched to the south, perhaps even beyond the straits of Bab el-Mandeb and the Cape of Gardafui to the coast of Somalis"[5]. Sergew Hable Selassie states: "No doubt that the present (1972) Ethiopian Empire was included within the region of Punt".[6]

During the early parts of the first millennium C.E. the Horn of Africa's (i.e. Ethiopia's) authority extended to South Arabia.[7, 8] H. von Wissman states: "....the first Ethiopian occupation in Arabia lasted over one and a half centuries, from 80 or 90 C.E. to 265 C.E."[9] By the 6th century, Ethiopian territory in the Arabian peninsula included not only "the Kingdom of Himyar and Saba but extended further to the north as far as Nagran...." Ethiopian garrisons were present in "key positions" such as Zafar and Nagran.[10]

As the major power in the Horn of Africa and with territories in South Arabia; Ethiopia was treated with the respect and deference due a superpower. The Emperor of Constantinople "....dispatched an ambassador to Axum (Ethiopia) to negotiate a treaty of alliance with the Negoos and to bring about his friendly attachment to the Roman Empire...."[11] Renowned sociologist, Donald Levine, states: "In the latter part of the third century Mani wrote that Axum (Ethiopia) ranked third among the great powers of the world.....To many Byzantine emperors Ethiopia appeared a most desirable ally...."[12] Quoting Antonio Gramsci, Daniel Kendie states: "Having controlled the Red Sea-Indian Ocean trade,.....Axum carved out an empire that extended from Nubia to Somalia, and from South Arabia to Southern Ethiopia".[13]

Among the numerous occurrences of those times that clearly illustrate the might of the Horn of Africa's Ethiopia was an event that took place in Nagran and Zafar. An Arab prince by the name of Dhu Nuwas converted to the Jewish faith. In his effort to convert the residents of the two settlements to Judaism, 3000 people, including Ethiopians were massacred. Although the Ethiopian king of the time, Emperor Caleb, was already in the process of taking punitive

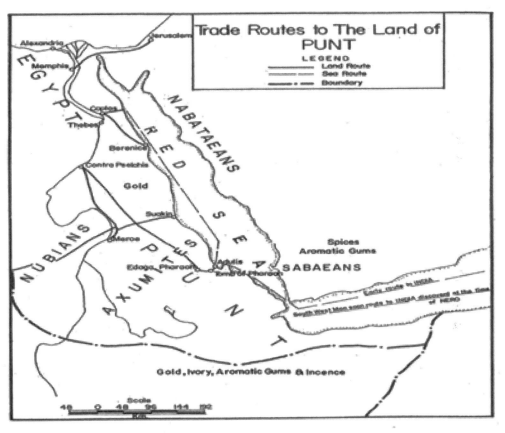

Figure 1: Trade Routes to the Land of PUNT[7]

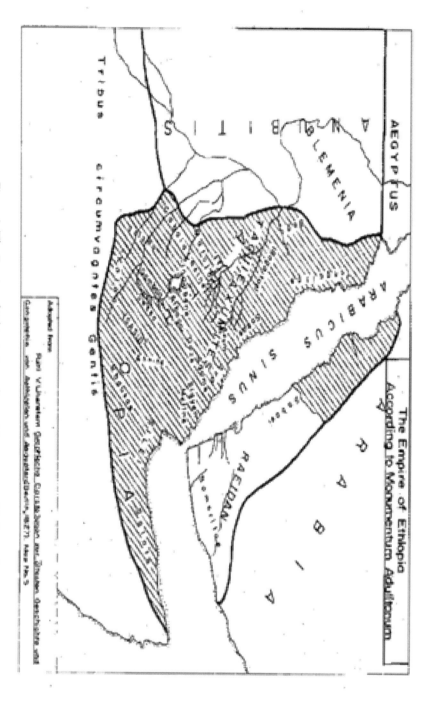

Figure 2: The Empire of Ethiopia According to Monumentum Adulitanum[8]

measures, the head of the Roman Empire, Justin I (518-27) attempted to per-suade" …the Aksumite (Ethiopian) King, Kaleb to go to the rescue of a group of Christians attacked by a South Arabian prince who had adopted the Jewish faith….."[14] Emperor Caleb launched a counter attack using 70 large and 100 small ships built at Adulis in Ethiopia and 60 additional ships obtained from elsewhere, along with an army that was reported to range from 70,000 to 120,000. He undertook two military expeditions into Southern Arabia in 523 and 525 which resulted in a complete victory and the restoration of Ethiopian authority over its territory across the Red Sea.[15] "The success of the Abyssinian expedition in 525 C.E., led to the founding of a new and powerful dynasty at Sanaa, the capital of Yemen"[16]

Another, even more renowned event is the expedition to Mecca in 570 C.E. by the Ethiopian Emperor's representative in South Arabia, Abraha and his army which was accompanied by elephants. According to Ethiopian histo-rians, the main purpose of the expedition was to divert trade from Mecca to Sanaa, and to destroy the Kabba which was at the time a place for worshipping idols. On his way to Mecca, Abraha's forces defeated two resisting armies. The story as to what transpired once the army reached Mecca varies. The Arab ver-sion—which is related to this day—is that the sky was filled with birds each of which was carrying three pebbles of stone, one in its bill and the other two in its feet. The birds dropped the pebbles on the Ethiopian army which suffered death and defeat. This episode is referred to in the Quran as "Um al-Fil" meaning the Year of the Elephant. The Ethiopian version, is that the Ethiopian Army was affected by an incidence of smallpox causing it to retreat. In any case, Abreha returned with his army to Sanaa and continued his reign until he died and was replaced successively by his sons Yaksum and Masruk. [17]

The Ethiopian occupation of South Arabia ended as a result of several fac-tors including the waning strength of the Axumite Empire, the harsh rule by Abreha's sons, and the intervention by the Persian Empire at the request of the then Arabian prince, Sayf b. Dhu Yazan.[18]

Nevertheless, the Horn of Africa continued, through Ethiopia, to be a force to be reckoned with in Middle Eastern affairs. This is illustrated by its strong and positive support during the advent of Islam in the 7th century when its first followers suffered persecution and the Prophet Mohammed advised them to take refuge in Ethiopia. He is quoted to have stated that Ethiopia had "….a king under whom none are persecuted. It is a land of righteousness where God will give you relief from what you are suffering."[19] It is interesting to note that the Prophet chose Ethiopia as a place of refuge over Persia and the Byzantine Empire. He was wise in doing so as soon after the first migration took place in 615, the Meccan officials (the Quraysh) followed them to Axum and tried, unsuccessfully, to have them repatriated to South Arabia. The refugees numbering over 100 and including the Prophet's daughter Rockeya and her husband Othman, stayed in Ethiopia for some 15 years and those who wished to do so eventually returned to their country safely.[20]

Other examples of the continued prowess of Horn of Africa's Ethiopia was its invasions of Jeddah in 702 and 768 C.E. and its attempt, again, to march to Mecca. However, both attacks were repulsed.[21]

During the first millennium C.E., the Horn of Africa was reputed for its civilization and commerce. It had its own written language, an active trade with Egypt, Persia, the Arab Peninsula, and India in valuable products including gold, spices, cassia, calamus, animals, and animal products.[22] The Horn of Africa also accepted Christianity[23] and Islam peacefully without any military duress.

With the increasing expansion of the Ottoman and Arab hegemony, Ethiopia and the rest of the Horn of Africa became isolated and the region's decline set in during the ninth and early tenth centuries. In addition, internal conflicts intensified thereby finally ending the glorious reign of the Axumite Empire.

Horn of Africa's Millennium of Misery and Struggle for Survival

The decline of the Axumite Empire was precipitated by external attacks such as the one by the Bejan invasion as well as the devastating impact of Gudit's attacks which resulted in the destruction of churches and monuments. The fall of the Axumite Empire was finally made definite when the Zagwe Dynasty took over during 1030-1050 C.E. which lasted up to 1268 or 1270.[24] Nevertheless, as correctly observed by Bahru Zewde, Emeritus Professor of History at Addis Ababa University, there were periods during this millennium when the Ethiopian empire extended over a much wider area. In his book entitled "Church and State in Ethiopia 1270-1527", Taddesse Tamrat states: "For a period of just over a century and a half after the establishment of the new dynasty in 1270, the Christian kingdom underwent an intensive process of expansion throughout the Ethiopian region. In the south, with the early conquest of Damot and Hadya....the presence of the kingdom was felt ....in the basins of Gibe, Gojeb, and Omo rivers ....The Falasha country was gradually brought under Christian control. King Yishaq (1413-30) probably sent his troops into the country of the so-called Shanqilla west of Agaw-Midir in Gojjam."[25] Tadesse Tamrat further states: "More reliable sources indicate that King Dawit (1380-1412) took the offensive against Egypt much further than his father ever did. Maqrizi reports that in 1381 news arrived in Cairo that 'an army sent by Dawit, son of Sayfa-Arad, king of Ethiopia, had entered in the territory of Aswan, had defeated the Arabs......King Dawit had in fact led his troops beyond the northern frontiers of his kingdom..."[26]

In reaction to the persecution of Christian Egyptian Copts by the Mamluke sultans of Egypt, the Ethiopian King, Zara-Yaiqob (1434-68) "also made a reference to the Nile, which, he said, rose in his realms, and it was within his power to divert its course. He desisted from doing it, only for the fear of God, and in consideration of the human sufferings that would result from it."[27]

Though such aggressions may not be condoned even in an historical context, these episodes nonetheless clearly indicated the extent of regional power exerted by the Horn of Africa during that period. In any case, subsequent periods of internal conflict coupled with colonial interventions effectively ended the region's military and economic predominance.

As far as the interests of the Horn of Africa were concerned, this millennium ended with its decline and fragmentation making it vulnerable to its age old enemies which forever remained bent on weakening the region and attacking it at its moment of disunity and weakness. For instance, the Egyptian ruler, Khedive Ismail was pursuing his dream of establishing a huge African empire in order to make the Nile an Egyptian river and to annex the whole geographical area of its basin.[28] No wonder Egyptians had such ambitions as their country depended, and continues to depend, on Horn of Africa's Nile River for 86% of their water supply. While the Mahdists of the Sudan were prosecuting their incursions into Ethiopia, Egypt was also trying to encircle it occupying its border on the Red Sea and going far inland up to and including Harar. The Egyptians waged two wars against Ethiopia at Gundet and Gura in 1875 and 1876 assisted by American mercenaries including General Loring who was Chief-of-staff and second in command of their army. The Ethiopians defeated the Egyptian army in both instances [29].

By the middle of the 19th century, European colonialism was at its height and had its sight on the Horn of Africa. The British and the French were competing for the control of the Horn of Africa while the Ottomans and their Egyptian vassals were weakening. When an Egyptian garrison, a British surrogate, was under attack by the Mahdists, the British requested the assistance of the Ethiopian Emperor Yohannes to rescue it. This was undertaken successfully under the infamous Hewett Treaty between Ethiopia and Britain in June 1884.[30] Under the Hewett Treaty, "country called Bogos" was to be restored to Ethiopia. The British, however, committed one of their worst betrayals against Ethiopia and the Horn of Africa. "The problem for Britain was what to do with Massawa. So on October 20, three months after the ratification of the treaty, Lord Granville sounded Rome's ambassador in London about eventual Italian occupation of Massawa, which he allegedly did not want to leave to the barbarians (read Abyssinia) or to a rival power (read France)... ..On 5 February 1885 the Italians landed at Massawa."[31] Thus, the British seed of betrayal subsequently resulted in the establishment of a colony within the Horn of Africa's Ethiopia, which the Italians named Eritrea. The French leased Djibouti from Emperor Minelik while the British and Italians colonized Somaliland and Somalia respectively. The Italian attempt at colonizing the rest of the Horn of Africa i.e. Ethiopia suffered an ignominious defeat at Adowa in 1896. Although the Italians tried again during the Second World War, they were booted out after a short period of occupation.

The survival of Ethiopian independence was the beacon of hope from the Horn of Africa that ignited the yearning and struggle for independence by colonized people in Africa and throughout the rest of the world.

From mid-19th century onwards, successive Ethiopian Emperors particularly Tewodros, Yohannes, Minelik II and Haile Selassie I were largely engaged in uniting the country and resisting foreign domination. Emperor Tewodros was fully aware of what the colonialists were up to when he stated: "I know... ..the tactics of European governments when they want to seize a country. First they send missionaries, then consuls to support the missionaries, then battalions to sustain the consuls. I am not a raja from Hindustan to be made a fool of like that: I prefer to engage the battalions at once."[32]

During the 20th century, the last period of the 2nd millennium C.E. the Horn of Africa comprised of four independent countries most of which have been at war with each other: two wars between Ethiopia and Somalia, and one between Ethiopia and Eritrea. Somalia has become a failed state as a result of its fragmentation, internal conflict, and the endangerment of neighboring countries resulting in the deployment of peace-making armed forces from Burundi, Ethiopia, Kenya and Uganda. The millennium of misery has left the countries and people of the Horn of Africa destitute with the highest levels of poverty, environmental degradation, illiteracy, absence of democracy, and prevalence of pandemic diseases. Tribalism and corruption are rampant. The Governments in the region are in the most not even on talking terms let alone engaging in matters of common interest. Instead of being a place of refuge, the Horn of Africa has become a region of emigrants subject to a continuous brain drain.

As a failed state, Somalia has to host AMISOM (African Union Mission in Somalia). As declared in the Mission's website: http://amisom-au.org:

> "As per UN Security Council Resolution, 2124, AMISOM is authorised to deploy 21, 586 soldiers into Somalia in addition to 540 police officers. Currently the military component is comprised of troops drawn from Uganda, Burundi, Djibouti, Sierra Leone, Kenya and Ethiopia who are deployed in six sectors covering south and central Somalia." It should be noted that three of Somalia's neighbors have deployed their armed forces in Somalia in the framework of AMISOM. Whether such an action would have a salutary consequence in the future is yet to be seen."

On the positive side, it is reported that Ethiopia has been, in recent years, registering double digit economic growths as well as a significant development of its road infrastructure. However, on the other hand, based on well recognized indices such as the UNDP human development index, Ethiopia remains among the poorest countries in the world despite its abundant natural resources. Its investment is mainly driven by the public sector. Its budget is provided for mainly by donor assistance as well as the US $3-5 billion annual inflow from the Ethiopian diaspora. Above all, the economic progress registered has, so far, not trickled down to the majority of Ethiopians especially the 85% living in the rural areas.

Horn of Africa's Millennium of Hope?

At the start of the 3rd millennium C.E. the Horn of Africa finds itself facing extremely serious socio-economic and political challenges and opportunities. The big question at this stage is which direction the countries in the region as well as the international community should take for their long-term mutual benefits. There are options: at least two. One that is unacceptable is to continue with the legacy of the misery that afflicted the region during the 2nd millennium C.E. Regrettably, current trends seem to indicate that this option is being pursued. The second option is to systematically do away with the fundamental causes that brought about the region's current predicaments and make a concerted effort in achieving peace and development in the Horn of Africa. The following aspects deserve a special consideration:

Need for a Positive Vision and a Comprehensive Development Strategy

The most fundamental challenge facing the Horn today is the abject poverty that its people are suffering under. This is mainly due to poor governance and underutilization of the region's huge natural and human resources. At the international conference on the Horn of Africa in Florida in November 2002, it had been resolved to recommend, inter alia, the formulation of a comprehensive development strategy for the region.[33] A series of international consultative meetings are to take place the first one of which has been conducted by the Africa Program at the University of Texas (Arlington) and the Horn of Africa Peace and Development Center in Dallas, Texas during October 20-22, 2006. For details, please visit www.hafrica.com. There is no doubt that a carefully formulated and practical development strategy will be a catalyst for achieving an enhanced collaboration leading to an enduring peace and prosperity in the region.

Need for Democracy and Rule of Law

The need to enhance democracy and rule of law is one other fundamental requirement in the Horn. Tribalism, corruption, arbitrary arrests and trampling on human rights are rampant. These are the realities that fuel the grinding poverty in the region. These are the breeding grounds for international terrorism. Meaningful changes for improvement can be achieved only if internal efforts are strengthened by concrete support from the international community which is capable of taking effective steps to inhibit dictatorship and create suitable incentives for positive change. Horn of Africa people living in the Diaspora could also play a pivotal role by working together for achieving a meaningful change in the region. In his book: "Yekihedet Qulqulet" (approximate translation: The slippery slope of Betrayal), Mesfin Wolde-Mariam states: "When those who have the responsibility for ensuring the respect of law trample on it irresponsibly, they are leaving the door open for others to do the same." He goes on to state: "We should learn from the sad conditions in Somalia how harmful and endless tribal conflicts are."[34]

Horn of Africa's Potential and Its Strategic Value

In this age of globalization and the pursuit of direct and narrow interests, it is essential to determine the extent to which there is a positive internal and external perception about the importance of the Horn of Africa.

Internal Perception

Among the governments in the Horn, it is evident that they give scant regard to the strategic interests of the region as a whole bent as they are on internal conflicts and their mutual tensions. This trait makes them part of the basic problem facing the Horn. On the individual level, some have been known to ask what, for instance, Ethiopia would benefit from collaboration in the Horn context. It would not be surprising if the same query is raised by individuals in the other Horn countries. The answer to such questions is that no enduring peace and development can be achieved in the Horn without mutual collaboration in the region based on democracy and mutual respect. The absence of collaboration will only mean the continuation of conflicts, tension and heavy spending on defense and security instead of investing the scarce resources for the benefit of the poorest people on earth. Loud words of bravado notwithstanding, the Horn of Africa ports on the Red Sea and the Indian Ocean are important to Ethiopia and the huge natural resources in Ethiopia are essential for the other Horn countries. Above all, what bind the people in the Horn of Africa are their common history, culture, shared values and geography.

Ironic as it may seem, the Horn of Africa which is at the bottom of any scale of economic development, does have substantial human, agricultural, water and mineral resources which, with good management and governance, would extricate it from the grips of the stifling poverty. In his excellent work expounding the potential for economic cooperation, Daniel Kendie has identified specific and practical development schemes that could transform the Horn of Africa into a self-sustaining and stable region which would not be vulnerable to international terrorists. The schemes he refers to include the establishment of a transport and communication system to link the various countries, the development of the Wabi Shebelle and Juba River basins, the exploitation of the natural gas and oil resources discovered in the Ogaden region, and the full utilization of the substantial agricultural and water resources.[35] The accelerated development of such a huge potential ought to be of direct interest to the people of the Horn as well as to the international community. A more judicious utilization of the Nile River could benefit the countries in the region including Sudan and Egypt from its vast water, energy and soil resources. The Ethiopian Nile dam is a worthy project.

For their own selfish agenda, some so called leaders and intellectuals betray their legacy by alleging, for instance, that Ethiopia's history is only a century old. For a fascinating discussion of this subject, please refer to Mesfin Wolde-Mariam's book: "Yekehedet Qulqulet". Horn of Africa's rich history over several millennia is a matter of an established record not subject to whimsical manipulations based on narrow and myopic objectives of tribalism and thirst for power.

Importance of the Horn of Africa to USA Interests

According to Jeffrey A. Lefebvre, Ethiopia (including Eritrea at the time of his writing) was of interest to the USA only in terms of "its location across the Red Sea from Saudi Arabia, (and) was of no direct strategic value."[36] He goes on to state that US interests in the Horn were for the purposes of:

    a.   Protecting the sea lines of communication or oil lanes;

    b.   "Supporting Egypt's efforts to protect its southern flank and the Nile waters;" and

    c.   Blunting destabilization activities aimed at Saudi Arabia and other pro-Western States.[37]

Mesfin Wolde-Mariam states: "For the United States, none of the countries of the Horn have any significance outside its material interests on the Arabian Peninsula, and the prosperity and military strength of Israel."[38] He adds: "No country in the Horn or the Middle East has any strategic importance in a modern global and military sense. Their importance is purely regional and can be assessed only in terms of their capacities to affect each other. Beyond that they were of very little use to the superpowers, and they have very little use to the US today."[39]

It would appear, from the above that the Horn of Africa is sadly of no strategic interest to the international community and to the current regimes themselves. It would also seem that the USA and French forces present in the Horn of Africa in Djibouti are there, arguably, as preventive measures of containment in the Horn. Be that as it may, in the opinion of this writer, the strategic importance of the Horn would be in direct correlation with the extent to which there is unity, peace and development in the region. A divided house commands no respect or as per an Ethiopian saying: "Salt, be tasteful for your own sake."

Arab Interests in the Horn of Africa

It has often been stated that Egypt is "the gift of the Nile" in view of its almost total dependence on the Horn of Africa for its water supply. As stated above, 86% of the water that cascades to Egypt originates from Ethiopia. Mesfin Woldemariam states: "The Horn of Africa constitutes, for the Arab Peninsula, the gateway to the heart of Africa" [40]. The relationship between the Horn of Africa and the Arabs in general over the last two millennia has not been one of a sustained collaboration and mutual respect. As has been presented above, the Horn had the upper hand during the first millennium while the Arabs have been having a negative impact on the region's internal affairs during the second millennium. This, again, is the result of the Horn's own internal fragmentation and disunity. The best option for both the people of the Horn and the Arabs is to take new and positive initiatives for the mutual benefit of both regions as well as the international community. Specific examples of such measures include: (a) The Nile Basin Initiative being promoted by the World Bank as long as the interests of the upstream states are duly protected; and (b) the proposal to establish a Red Sea Co-operative Council comprising all the countries surrounding the Red Sea including Ethiopia.[41] Such an institutional capacity would enable the 400 million people living in the wider region to take advantage of their complementary resources: human, agricultural, water, and mineral on the part of the Horn, and oil as well as investment resources on the Arab side, and technology from the Israelis. The enhanced peace and development that could ensue from such initiatives would no doubt be of great benefit locally as well as internationally moving away from two millennia of conflict and distrust to an enduring partnership based on mutual respect.

Horn of Africa's Importance to Africa

As the only region that had a part i.e. Ethiopia that successfully survived the onslaught of Arab and European colonialism, the Horn of Africa certainly contributed positively to the continent's renaissance and achievement of independence in the 20th century. No wonder that all the most important regional institutions concerning Africa i.e. the African Union, the UN Economic Commission for Africa, and the Inter-Governmental Agency for African Development (IGAAD) are all located in the Horn of Africa. The Horn of Africa has been an active participant in African and UN affairs. Peacekeeping forces were sent to Korea, the Congo, Liberia, Burundi and South Sudan from the Horn. The challenge in the 3rd millennium is how the regional institutions based in the Horn of Africa could make effective contributions to bring about concrete improvements in terms of socio-economic and political developments. Collaboration within the Horn of Africa would facilitate and enhance the achievement of the objectives of African unity development efforts through the New Partnership for Africa's Development (NEPAD), The Common Market of Eastern and Southern Africa (COMESA), IGAAD, etc.

China and India in the Horn of Africa

A new paradigm shift has occurred in the Horn with the increasing heavy presence of China, to a greater extent, and also India. It is becoming increasingly evident that the "cold war" which had involved a struggle between the Soviet Union and the West in general is being replaced in the Horn by the competition between China and India on the one side and the West on the other. Although the Horn's partnership in security and military matters is still anchored in its relations with the West, it is the Chinese that are increasingly taking the lead in infrastructural development projects.

Land Grab in the Horn of Africa

Another new development in the Horn of Africa, especially, Ethiopia is the advent of land grabs by various countries. Large tracts of land, comprising millions of hectares, have been ceded to countries such as India, Saudi Arabia, Djibouti and Egypt at nominal prices. A huge controversy has arisen over this occurrence as, on the one side, it is alleged that such leasing of fertile land could result in an increased investment for an accelerated development as well as higher employment while on the other hand, it is stated that it would engender the dislocation of the indigenous people as well as the denial of the benefits of agricultural development to the affected people. In any case, according to Aklog Birara, in his recent book: "Ethiopia: The Great Land Give Away", the benefits of the recent land grab policy in Ethiopia are most likely to be in favour of the grabbers and those who facilitate the grabbing rather than the affected Ethiopian people.

Need to Emphasize Horn of Africa's Mutual Interests and Reduce Animosities

In his farewell address on September 17, 1796, George Washington stated: "The nation which indulges toward another an habitual hatred or an habitual fondness is in some degree a slave. It is a slave to its animosity or to its affection, either of which is sufficient to lead it astray from its duty and its interest."[42]

In 1993, Tesfatsion Medhanie had urged Eritrea and Ethiopia "….to work for a process whereby the two states would be reunited within a framework of confederation."[43] His prophecy that the alternative would be war turned out to be regrettably quite correct. The ill-conceived policy of dismantling the federation without the full commitment of the Eritrean population as well as the secession that occurred after a 30-year conflict brought about disastrous consequences including a war between Eritrea and Ethiopia in which 70,000 people lost their lives. The tension between the two nations remains strong. Somalia's previous attacks, though repulsed many years ago, continue to cause rancor like an open wound, mainly because the chaotic and fragmented Somali nation has yet to abandon its claim on a huge part of Ethiopia's territory. Ethiopia's incursion into Somalia, albeit at the request of the current Somali regime, and the continued negative statements by certain Somali religious fundamentalists continue to poison Ethio-Somali relations.

Consequently, animosities are still rampant even among certain so called intellectuals in the Diaspora. Instead of being preoccupied with finding solutions to the ongoing problems, they prefer to give vent to their jingoistic zeal by attacking any initiative aimed at achieving peace and development in the Horn. This was certainly the case during the preparations for and arrangement of the international conference on prospects for a confederation in the Horn of Africa in Tampa, Florida during November 14-15, 2002 (www.hafrica.com).

The fundamental causes of such extreme animosities vary but they could be ascribed to the highly controversial and negative policy of secession and ethnicity adopted in the Ethiopian constitution and the lack of focus on opportunities for the common benefit of the region's population. It is surprising to note, for instance, that certain political entities try to use Horn of Africa wide efforts for the promotion of their narrow minded ethnic oriented agenda instead of promoting visions of unity and integration. They care little for the dire consequences of pitting tribe against tribe. Others are engaging in religious fundamentalism. The article in the Reporter on January 1, 2004 about the attempt by the Wahabists to influence the election of officers for the National Ethiopian Majlis for Islamic Affairs using four million Saudi Riyals is very revealing. For more details, please see Hibret Selamu's article: "Proof of Wahabi Activities in Ethiopia", on Ben's News Page. It would seem that external elements with latent motives intend, hopefully in vain, to arouse religious conflicts in Ethiopia.

It is incumbent on all interested parties, especially those in the Diaspora to seek all ways and means of responding to the divisive issues afflicting the Horn in a positive manner having regard to the interests of the poor people and not for the mere perpetuation of power.

Need to Establish Mechanisms for an Effective Dialogue

As stated above, governments in the Horn of Africa are not engaged in any move towards collaboration, let alone integration. This would benefit only those countries which wish to keep the region fragmented and weak. Therefore, urgent and meaningful initiatives need to be taken especially in the Diaspora in order to facilitate practical discussions and awareness of the challenges facing the Horn and the international community. An example of such an initiative is the recent establishment of the Horn of Africa Peace and Development Centre. The Centre's mission is to facilitate dialogues and research on the Horn's socio-economic and political issues. The institutional arrangement of the Centre is such that while its headquarter will, at least for the time being, remain in USA, its branches will eventually be established in each of the four Horn countries.

A major international conference was undertaken by the Center in collaboration with the Southern Methodist University in Dallas on November 11, 2011 on the subject of Conflict Prevention and Resolution in the Horn of Africa. The conference was attended by renowned diplomats, scholars and experts in the Horn of Africa. The conference resolution can be seen at www.hafrica.com.

Another important shortcoming is the lack of focus by Horn political parties on the region's issues. It is time that they recognize the fact that they need to widen their perspective to regional and international issues if they do intend to strengthen peace and development in their own respective countries.

The active participation of political, civic, community based and non-governmental organizations including associations, churches, mosques, academic institutions, the media, the private sector, etc. in the important quest for peace and development in the Horn within a democratic and equitable framework could go a long way to achieving the eventual objective of a united, strong and self-reliant Horn of Africa.

ConclusionThe main lesson to be learned from the Horn of Africa's experience during the 1st millennium A.D. is that it was a world power when the people were at peace and united. When they were able to devote energies to the defense and development of their region, they achieved a high rate of success both at home and abroad.

The Horn fell to bad times during the 2nd millennium C.E. There are lessons that should be learned from the negative causes that brought the region to such depths of utter poverty and insecurity. Quite aside from external factors such as colonialism, the main factors that had devastating effects on the Horn were and continue to be internal. These include the highly devastating effects of myopic tribalism or ethnicism, lack of democracy and good governance, corruption, and the absence of a cohesive vision and strategy that could bind the people of the Horn together for the common good.

There is now a fresh opportunity to learn the right lessons from the successes and failures of the past two millennia and proceed positively on the path of peace, unity, democracy, and sustainable development during the 3rd millennium C.E.

Will there be hope for the Horn of Africa?

CHAPTER 7

VISION FOR HORN OF AFRICA'S PEACE AND DEVELOPMENT

My focus on the Horn of Africa commenced soon after my retirement in 2000 from my job with the United Nations as a Senior Management Expert/Chief Technical Advisor (CTA) at Dubai Municipality in the United Arab Emirates. My concern with the Horn of Africa was in my mind for many years, although I was unable to do much due to pressure of work. Therefore, my retirement in good health enabled me to pay a special attention to the region which suffered from the ailments of poor governance, abject poverty, and incessant conflict while it also possessed immense wealth in terms of a hard working population, huge agricultural, water, energy, mineral, and other natural resources as well as an excellent geographic location.

It was, for me, extremely sad to note that a region that was, in its historic past, a superpower by any standards, relegated itself, mainly because of poor leadership, to the worst conditions by any international standards. Conditions were deteriorating from bad to worse as instead of forging reconciliation and unity among the Horn of African countries, they were in fact disintegrating as Eritrea seceded from Ethiopia in 1993.

Eritrea's cessation was, according to the wishes of those who fought for it, meant to usher in an era of an accelerated development that was supposed to transform itself into another Singapore in the region. Instead, what materialized was an increased tension and conflict that resulted into a devastating war between Eritrea and Ethiopia in which some 70,000 people lost their lives. Eritrea, Ethiopia and Somalia continued with their mutual animosities and occasional conflicts.

In 2001, I wrote a small article in which I presented the constraints encountered in the region as well as the main avenue for achieving peace and prosperity i.e. a confederation among the Horn of African countries. I had thought that the article would receive very little attention but to my pleasant surprise, one of my friends, Fasil Gabremariam, suggested to me the idea of arranging an international conference on the issue.

His important status in Florida as a member of the Board of Trustees of the University of South Florida (USF), and his being a member of the Board of Directors of the Federal Reserve Bank as well as being the President of the US-Africa Free Enterprise Education Foundation, greatly facilitated the support for the University to host the International Conference on Prospects of a Horn of Africa Confederation.

The key individuals who hosted the conference on behalf of the University of South Florida were Dr. JoAnn McCarthy, Dean, Office of International Affairs, and Dr. O. Geoffrey Okogbaa, Director, Institute on Black Life. I recall, with great appreciation, the support provided by the Hillsborough Country of Florida as well as the students of the University of South Florida (USF).

The international conference which had presenters from important organizations such as the US President's Office, the US Department of State, the United Nations, the Common Market for Eastern and Southern Africa, numerous universities and institutions took place at USF in Tampa, Florida (USA) during November 14-15, 2002.

One of the guest speakers was the renowned Ethiopian poet laureate, Tsegaye Gabre-Medhin who presented the following poem as part of his speech at the conference:

> "When our fathers gave us the cradle of the First World,
> At the beginning there was KA, the first God of Earth and Sky,
> On this birth land of our first ancestors.
> They raised for us the sacred shrine
> On the glowing head piece of the Horn of Africa,
> Where the sun first touched the body of the Earth.
> But, alas, now, look at us!
> The generation who has forgotten how to unite.
> The rotten link that has lost the scale of self-respect.
> Look at us!"

By Poet Laureate Tsegaye Gabre-Medhin: "Yes. We betrayed our ancestors"

The conference was a great success as presenters included important personalities such as former President of Zambia, H.E. Dr. Kenneth Kaunda, Mr. Tsegaye Gabre-Medhin, poet/laureate, Mr. Zachary Teich, Deputy Director, Office of Eastern Africa Affairs, U.S. State Department, Mr. Michael Wales, of the UN Food & Agricultural Organization (UNFAO), Mr. Tegegnework Gettu, UN Development Program (UNDP), Dr. Elizabeth Onjoro, U.S. Preseident's Advisory Council for HIV/AIDS (PACHA) Mr. Fassil Gabremariam, President, U.S. Africa Free Enterprise Education Foundation, Mr. Brian Chigawa, Common Market for Eastern and Southern Africa (COMESA), Mr. Sam Smoots, Overseas Private Investment Corporation (OPIC), Dr. Kopano Mukelabai, UNICEF, Dr. Jama & Dr. Abdulahi Mohamed, World Health Organization (WHO), and Dr. JoAnn McCarthy, Dean, Office of International Affairs, University of South Florida. Keynote addresses and presentations were also made by various scholars regarding political, social, economic, health, and a business forum, under various chairmen and co-chairmen, from various universities including Princeton, Henderson, Missouri-Rolla, Oakland, New York (CUNY), South Florida, Michigan State, Spellman College, Howard, as well as other institutes and centers.

The conference covered the various aspects of importance to the Horn of Africa organized in four panels: (a) political and social issues; (b) economic issues; (c) health issues; and (d) a business forum. The outcome of the conference was presented in a resolution entitled: "Tampa Initiative On The Horn of Africa"(please see Annex 1). My speech at the conference is presented as Annex 2.

The main conclusions and recommendations of the conference included the acceptance, in principle, of a confederation among the Horn of African countries, namely, Djibouti, Eritrea, Ethiopia, and Somalia as "a noble objective" subject to the prevalence of the required preconditions including good governance with full accountability and transparence as well as improvements in fundamental aspects such as education, gender equality, inter-faith understanding and peace, conflict prevention and resolution, resolving cross-border issues, etc.

In the conference resolution (please see Annex 1), item 4.1.2.2, it was recommended that an institution be established to facilitate collaborative efforts in the Horn of Africa. Although the declaration had recommended that the region should be referred to as " Northeast Africa" comprising Djibouti, Kenya, Eritrea, Ethiopia, Somalia, Sudan, and Uganda, later reviews continued with the usual, Mesfin Woldemariam's definition of the Horn of Africa to include Djibouti, Eritrea, Ethiopia, and Somalia.

Formation of the Horn of Africa Peace and Development Center

Although the principle of establishing an organizational entity was clearly enunciated in the 2002 resolution adopted in Tampa, it took a considerable time to find individuals with interest and time to devote the required energy and to proceed with additional studies on issues of importance to the Horn of Africa. In 2003, the Center's by-laws were established in 2004, the Horn of Africa Peace and Development Center could be established as a legal entity in Tampa, Florida with this author as the founder. Later, the legal registration was changed to Texas mainly as a result of my residence transfer to Dallas.

The members of the Center's Board of Directors gradually increased in number as well as participation from the four countries in the Horn of Africa. The Center's bylaws were established. I continued to serve as the Center's Founding President and Chairman up to 2008 when Yusuf Kleib (from Somalia) took over followed by Ismail (from Somalia) who led the Center up to 2011 when Semere Habtermariam (from Eritrea) took over. In 2013, the Board of Directors of the Center comprised:

Semere Habtermariam (from Eritrea), Chairman
Yussuf Kaleb (from Somalia), Member
Betru Gebremariam (from Ethiopia), Member
Loala Isman (from Djibouti), Member
Lili Gebru (from Ethiopia/Eritrea), Member
Ismail Mahmoud (from Somalia), Member
Dr. Ahmed Nasser (from Somalia), Member
Harun Musa (from Ethiopia), Member
Sarah Fara (from Somalia), Member
Kidane Alemayehu (from Ethiopia), Member.

The Center managed to undertake, despite being run by people who are extremely busy with their respective other commitments and serving on voluntary basis, two important international conferences as well as weighing in on vital issues of concern to the Horn of Africa region. For more details, please see: www.hafrica.com.

It was decided that, initially, it was important to focus on the region's development needs. Therefore, the International Conference on a Development Strategy for the Horn of Africa took place in Texas in collaboration between the Center and the University of Texas at Arlington (UTA) during October 20-22, 2006. The main partners from UTA were Dr. Alusine Jalloh, the

Founding Director of the Africa Program and Dr. Dana Dunn, Provost and Vice President for Academic Affairs. The Center was led by this author as the Founding President. The co-sponsor of the conference was the Amoud Foundation. The keynote address was delivered by Dr. Mulu Ketsela, the Alternate Executive Director of the World Bank.

The main agenda items were:

a. Macro-economic development and globalization;
b. Agricultural and rural development;
c. Infrastructure and water development;
d. Education, science, and technology;
e. Health care;
f. Women and social development.

The above subjects were chaired and presented by various institutions i.e. the United Nations, National Science Foundation, USAID, The World Bank, and the Hurley Medical Center, as well as numerous universities including Okalahoma State, Missouri at Rolla, Western Michigan, Oregon State, Prairie View A&M, Minnesota, UTA, Princeton, Howard, Buffalo, York, and the University of Dallas.

The conference proceedings can be seen at: http://hafrica.org/docs/HOA-ConferenceProceedings_2006.pdf

My address to the conference covered the objectives and reasons for arranging the conference. It exposed the main challenges being encountered in the Horn of Africa including problems of poor governance and the consequent issues of lack of democracy, absence of collaboration, poverty, poor health conditions, and the international community's inadequate responses to the region's needs. Please see Annex 2 for details.

INTERNATIONAL CONFERENCE ON CONFLICT PREVENTION AND RESOLUTION

The Center's next major agenda was the convening of an international conference on conflict prevention and resolution in the Horn of Africa, which was convened at the Southern Methodist University (SMU) in Dallas on November 11, 2011. This conference brought together academics and experts in conflict prevention and resolution from various renowned organizations and universities including SMU, Oklahoma State, Davidson College, North Carolina at Chapel Hill, Old Dominion, and Macalester

College. In addition, US Ambassador to Djibouti, Lange Schermerhorn; former US ambassador to Ethiopia, Tibor P. Nagy; Semhar Araia, Diaspora African Women's Network; and Yussuf Kaleb, representing the Horn of Africa Peace and Development Center addressed the conference. Finally, the conference declaration was presented to the conference by this author and approved by acclamation.

The conference agenda comprised a review of the prevailing conditions in the Horn of Africa followed by detailed presentations on the appropriate measures required for the prevention and resolution of conflicts in the region.

In general, the conference's deliberations included:

- A review of the Horn of Africa's potential including its significant agricultural, water, hydropower, and human resources as well as its geo-political importance in international affairs including trade;
- The challenges facing the region such as the abject poverty, absence of good governance, prevalence of pandemic diseases, continued conflicts including the unabated anarchy in Somalia, the perennial drought as well as the increasing migration from the region;
- The serious challenges facing the international community including the incidences of piracy, the spread of terrorism, the economic burden arising from the continued need for aid by all the four countries;
- Recommendations for conflict prevention and resolution including:
    ° To the people and government of the region "to transcend ethnic, tribal, clan, and narrow nationalistic enclaves" and achieve unity, peace, democracy and a sustainable socio-economic development through an integrated confederal framework;
    ° To the international community including USA, EU (European Union), the BRIC nations (Brazil, Russia, India, and China), Japan and Arab countries "to pursue policies that foster partnership, collaboration and long-term mutual benefits";
    ° To international organizations: UN, EU, AU (African Union), IGAAD (Inter-African Agency for African Development), etc. "to exert their influence to achieve unity, socio-economic development, including gender equality, democracy as well as the prevention of conflict in the Horn of Africa and, for this purpose, establish special task forces of envoys to address the region's issues in an integrated and sustainable manner";
    ° To the Horn of Africa Diaspora to transform itself from being di-

visive and ineffective to a constructive, cohesive and an integrated force for the achievement of unity, democracy and socio-economic development in the Horn of Africa and, for this purpose, utilize its substantial advocacy as well as its human and financial resources for the benefit of the people of the Horn of Africa."

The conference declaration can be viewed in the following link: http://hafrica.org/docs/HAPDC_Conf_declaration_Nov2011.pdf

CONCLUSION

The Horn of Africa is blessed with a total population of 115 million as well as huge natural resources including agricultural, water, energy, and mineral resources as well as being important in terms of international geo-political interests.

On the other hand, it is facing severe challenges from poor governance, excessive corruption, a debilitating level of poverty, health and deteriorating environmental conditions. Added to these immense constraints is the generally highly myopic, if not negative, role of the international community regarding the Horn of Africa. Whether it is the Western, Middle Eastern, or the Far Eastern countries, they are all bent on their immediate interests. A far sighted approach to the political and socio-economic development of the Horn of Africa could have a much greater benefit for all sides.

The region's as well as USA's interests need to go beyond the resolution of global conflicts related to international terrorism. President Barack Obama's statement in support of protecting civic interests and economic development needed to be translated into a meaningful action. Countries such as China, India and Saudi Arabia as well as the concerned European nations should, in their own interests, exert mutually beneficial efforts for the long-term instead of merely short-term objectives.

It is interesting to note that the UN Secretary General, Mr. Ban Ki Moon visited Ethiopia in the context of the organization's encouraging policy for the development of the Horn of Africa. It is hoped that the UN would express the initiative in terms of a positive vision, strategy, action plan and program for the region's stability and development.

The big question is what strategic measures should be taken to lift the Horn of Africa from the depth of poverty, unabated conflict, and poor governance. As indicated in the declaration of the international conference on conflict prevention and resolution, it is essential for all stakeholders, namely, the people and governments of the region, the international community, and the diaspora residents from the region to take a full stock of the challenges and opportunities in the region and apply a strategy and action plan that are based on long-term mutual interests including a democratic framework with an accountable and transparent governance, and a socio-economic development that makes a judicious use of the region's huge natural resources for the benefit of all stakeholders.

Annex 1

International Conference on Prospects of a Horn of Africa Confederation

November 14-15, 2002

Tampa Initiative On The Horn Of Africa

1. Preamble

1.1 Taking note of the extensive deliberations undertaken at the international conference that was convened in Tampa, Florida, during Nov. 14-15, 2002, to explore Prospects for a Horn of Africa Confederation;

1.2 Recognizing the diverse stakeholders at the conference representing international, national, and local organizations in the public and private sectors, as well as individuals from the Horn of Africa and other countries in Africa, thus facilitating objective and thorough considerations of all significant issues;

1.3 Having scrutinized carefully the historical developments in the Horn of Africa, as well as the current and future challenges facing the concerned countries and the international community;

1.4 Recognizing that consideration of a possible confederation in the Horn of Africa is essentially a matter that requires a vision for a future in that region, a future that would, hopefully, be characterized by peace, stability and sustainable development;

2. Appreciation

2.1 The conference expresses its fullest appreciation to the organizers, namely, the University of South Florida and the U.S.-Africa Free Enterprise Education Foundation for their initiative and excellent accommodations and hospitality.

2.2 The conference wishes to express its particular appreciation and gratitude to Hillsborough County, as well as the USF Students Government, for their financial contributions—without which the conference would have not taken place.

2.3 The conference expresses its utmost appreciation to all the organizations and individuals for their participation in the conference and for their interest in the future of the Horn of Africa which is home to over 75 million people.

2.4 The conference further expresses its appreciation of the satisfactory Contributions and inspiring leadership of the keynote speaker, H.E. Dr. Kenneth Kaunda, Former President of Zambia and Poet Laureate Tsegaye Gebre Medhin.

2.5 The conference expresses its appreciation for the outstanding contributions of Mr. Zachary Teich, Deputy Director for East African Affairs, U.S. Department of State; Dr. Elizabeth Kearly Onjara from Presidential Advisory Council on HIV/AIDS; Dr. Judy Genshaft, USF President; and His Excellency Abdel Bagi H. Kaber , Deputy Chief of Mission, Embassy of the Republic of the Sudan as observer.

2.6 The conference appreciates the position and scientific papers presented by various speakers from international and national organizations, such as Enterprise Florida, OPIC, the UNDP, WHO, FAO, UNICEF, and COMESA.

2.7 The conference appreciates the scholarly works, position papers, and discussions of the conference theme by distinguished African and American scholars and experts on the Horn of Africa from Howard University, Michigan State University, Western Michigan University, Henderson University, Spelman College, City University of New York, University of California (Los Angeles), Princeton University, the University of Missouri, and the University of South Florida.

3. Observations

3.1 Horn of Africa's Major Resources

3.1.1 The conference recognizes that the Horn of Africa possesses significant resources:

3.1.1.1 It has a population of 75 million, which is expected to increase to more than 140 million within the first quarter of this century.

3.1.1.2 It has abundant agricultural, water, energy, and other resources. Ninety percent of the available water and arable land resources remain virtually unexploited.

3.1.1.3 Being adjacent to the Red Sea, the Gulf of Aden, and the Indian Ocean, the Horn of Africa is located at one of the most important regions with a potential for immense positive implications for world trade.

3.1.1.4 The ports of Masawa, Asseb, Djibouti, Berbera, Mogadisho, and others could promote viable links to local, regional, and international trade if improved and utilized more efficiently.3.1.1.5 The Horn of Africa, being the seat of international organizations such as the African Union and the Economic Commission for Africa, plays an extremely important role in the economic and political affairs of the African continent.

3.1.1.6 Archaeological and anthropological studies have proven that the Horn of Africa was the cradle of humanity and civilization.

3.2 Challenges Facing the Horn of Africa and the International Community Despite the above resources, the Horn of Africa continues to face significant challenges in its current and future economic and political circumstances:

3.2.1 As a result of past colonial interventions, the Horn of Africa consists of four independent countries—Djibouti, Eritrea, Ethiopia and Somalia—that have, to a large extent, suffered from mutual conflicts, rendering collaboration in the sub-region extremely difficult.

3.2.2 On the basis of the major socio-economic indices, the Horn of Africa is recognized to be among the poorest regions in the world, dependant on international technical assistance and subject to perennial natural disasters and repetitive famine. Fifteen million people in Ethiopia and 50 percent of Eritrea's population are currently facing starvation due to the advent of drought in the two countries.

3.2.3 The Horn of Africa continues to be caught in a vicious cycle of underdevelopment, consequent low productivity, and high unemployment, leading to political and social tensions.

3.2.4 The absence of an effective collaboration in the Horn of Africa continues to create tension among the neighboring countries, thereby making it difficult to take full advantage of the resources available in the region.

3.2.5 Among the stark examples that dramatically illustrate the suffering of the people in the region is the proliferation of pandemic diseases such as HIV/AIDS and malaria, which are so rampant that only national and international emergency measures would result in an effective response.

3.2.6 The very low level of technology prevailing in the Horn of Africa is another major impediment adversely affecting the socio-economic development of the region.

4. Conclusions and Recommendations The conference considered the above challenges in the Horn of Africa by focusing on three themes, namely, (a) political and social issues, (b) economic issues, and (c) health issues, and arrived at the following conclusions and recommendations:

4.1 Political and Social Issues

4.1.1 Conclusions

4.1.1.1 The Tampa Initiative on the Horn of Africa is the product of deliberations by concerned individuals in collaboration with academics and representatives of international agencies interested in developing greater regional cooperation, development, and peace for the peoples of Northeast Africa. The initiative represents a private civic effort unaffiliated with any government or political faction.

4.1.1.2 The goals of the initiative include greater democratization, guaranteed basic human rights and the rule of law, government accountability, and greater transparency. The process must foster good governance, strengthen civil society, gender equality, and the concurrent encouragement of women's groups as a major goal of the initiative.

4.1.1.3 The conference considers a confederation among the Horn of Africa countries to be a noble objective. However, due to current tensions and governance issues, a confederation would be feasible only if the preconditions or prerequisites are developed step by step as indicated in the list of recommendations stated hereunder.

4.1.1.4 The people of Horn of Africa are afflicted with poverty, social and economic upheaval, inadequate shelter and health care facilities, droughts, displacement, political injustice, fear, and uncertainty. The Tampa Initiative is directed toward their interests and not for the purpose of increasing the power of governments.

4.1.1.5 The Tampa Initiative should not be viewed as a political threat by any national leadership or organization, but rather as a positive catalyst for stability and accelerated development in the Horn of Africa.

4.1.1.6 The conference debated fundamentalism and extremism and was unable to agree on a conclusion. This area requires more extensive study and research, which may be appropriate for an Institute of East African Studies to undertake.

4.1.2 Recommendations

4.1.2.1 Solutions to the many problems of the Horn of Africa will require time; in our view, advances toward regional cooperation will be achieved only in a gradual process. The conference recognizes that fundamental to the success of the Tampa Initiative is good governance that is transparent and has the confidence and trust of the people in each country. The conference encourages various political parties, civic leaders, the media, and the international community to promote collaborative actions that would lead to such a transition.

4.1.2.2 Utilizing the natural economies of scale in a region of 75 million inhabitants, these steps can best be achieved by the development of crosscutting institutions that will facilitate cooperation across frontiers. We suggest that these institutions may include the following:

a. Education - through the development of an integrated regional education plan, sharing specialized facilities throughout the Horn of Africa;

b. Media - by encouraging the development of regionally-based TV, radio, and print media resources;

c. Creative arts - through the creation of theater, art, musical centers of learning for interested students of the region;

d. Women - through encouragement of women's associations across borders to deal with common gender, health, and children's issues;

e. Sports - by facilitating regional sporting competitions;

f. Religious understanding - by fostering regional meetings of religious and lay leaders to develop greater inter-faith understanding;

g. Elders - by promoting dialogue and meetings among influential elder community leaders;

h. Environment - by working with international and regional environmental groups to achieve greater environmental sensitivity, including the introduction of alternative energy sources;

i. Democratization - by enhancing the democratization process through the strengthening of accountability, transparency, rule of law, and procedures;

j. Conflict mitigation and avoidance - development of regional non-governmental organizations to foster mitigation and avoidance of conflicts at the local level;

k. Cross-border issues - citizens of the region should be able to travel without visa or other administrative impediments to travel;

1. Organizational recommendations:

i. The region referred to as the "Horn of Africa" should be changed to "Northeast Africa" and including the following countries: Djibouti, Kenya, Eritrea, Ethiopia, Somalia, Sudan, and Uganda.

ii. Arrange future meetings on the Northeast Africa, the next of which should occur within the next two years;

iii. Establish an institute for further studies and research on Northeast Africa;

iv. Establish a Web site to facilitate further consultations, information, and communication on Northeast Africa issues.

4.2 Economic Issues

4.2.1 Conclusions

4.2.1.1 The challenges facing the Horn of Africa with regard to economic issues include:

a. Inadequate commitment from political leaders;

b. Difficulty securing a consensus among elites in the Diaspora on Horn of Africa issues;

c. Difficulties in accepting unequal benefits accruing from integration;

d. Dependence on cash crops primarily for exports;

e. Excessive pre-occupation with national sovereignty;

4.2.1.2 The advantages of a confederation or integration would be as follows:

a. Peace and security (removal of incidences of border conflicts);

b. Shared struggle against poverty;

c. Reduced vulnerability to food insecurity;

d. Market integration (larger market share, economies of scale);

e. Increased cross border as well as international trade;

f. Improvement of conditions for a common market based industrialization;

g. Improvement of regional infrastructure (telecommunications, power, electronics, and others);

h. Conservation of natural resources/water management (early warning systems);

i. Development and trade of regional mineral resources (strategic minerals, oil and gas potential);

j. Harmonization of trade and investment policies;

k. Improvement in science and technology, standardization, language policy, and communication (facilitate research and development, and enhance innovation/minimize obsolescence);

l. Enhancement of higher education (human capital development and centers of excellence);

m. Achievement of macroeconomic stability (fiscal and monetary policies);

n. Enhancement of credit worthiness (investor confidence);

o. Improvement of environment for private investment/foreign direct investment;

p. Encouragement of small business development;

q. Encouragement of complementarities within the countries (low land and high land interactions);

r. Fostering efficient use of the port facilities of the region.

4.2.1.3 The barriers that mitigate against the above advantages are considered to be the following:

a. Internal conflicts and class struggles, including ethnic control; b. Inter/intra-ethnic conflicts (ethno-phobia);

b. Lack of effective secular institutions such as sub-regional dialogue, and conflict resolution mechanisms;

c. Ineffective administrative boundaries based on ethnic criteria alone such as "Killils";

d. Enforcement of ethnically based proprietary rights based on ethnic criteria such as "Killils";

e. Political party ownership of economic resources;

f. Lack of economic welfare for the poor;

g. Lack of democratic rights that encourage mass participation;

4.2.2 Recommendations

4.2.2.1 Establish a discussion forum that would embrace all constituencies, both in the region and the Diaspora, to achieve a consensus on economic issues concerning the Horn of Africa;

4.2.2.2 Collaborate with existing organizations such as IGAD, COMESA, etc;

4.2.2.3 Open channels of communication with all interested stakeholders including those in political power;

4.2.2.4 Develop a vision plan for political and economic development;

4.2.2.5 General recommendations:

a. Call upon the international community, as well as international organizations, to allocate increased resources to alleviate the poverty afflicting the region;

b. Reduce the debt burden for the countries in this region;

c. Accelerate the assistance of food aid in light of the imminent food insecurity crisis afflicting more than 15 million people;

d. Create an enabling environment for developing communication technology and information dissemination (bridge the digital divide).

4.3 Health Issues

4.3.1 Conclusion

4.3.1.1 It is important to promote an environment of sustainable health, peace, and development within and among the nations in the Horn of Africa to eradicate epidemic endemic diseases, famine, ignorance, conflicts, and violence. The mechanisms to achieve these goals in the Horn of Africa should be based on mutual interests and collaborative public-private partnerships. These relationships will instill confidence building for peace and dialogues both regionally and globally.

4.3.1.2 The region has a history of collaboration among the involved countries in malaria, pest control, famine, and drought assistance under the WHO, UNICEF and other UN agencies, bilateral and multilateral arrangements. These successful paradigms must be revisited in order to facilitate and build capacity for strategic management of the diverse health care delivery systems. In so doing, the region will be able to effectively utilize shared resources to eradicate diseases that are common to the area.

4.3.1.3 The epidemiology of HIV/AIDS demonstrates the intensity of this new disease in Africa. As significant a number of people affected by HIV/AIDS and other opportunistic diseases, such as malaria and TB, live in the most populous areas in the Horn of Africa, conditions are aggravated by a lack of political will, poor surveillance systems, and a lack of collaboration among the countries at risk in the region.

4.3.1.4 The synergistic relationships between armed conflicts, civil disorders, border disputes, and the disintegration of health care infrastructure have affected access to primary care. This can be evidenced by the resurgence of malaria, TB, and HIV/AIDS in the population of the region. Moreover, military mobilization use of mass destruction weapons, and mines have had negative psychological and physical effects on sustainable development.

4.3.1.5 The demobilized military personnel are one of the major carriers of sexually transmitted infections and other communicable diseases into the civilian populations. Military, commercial truckers, and sex workers are at risk because they are sexually active and the least protected population. Regional and national priority must be given to develop effective preventive strategies to protect the youth and work forces and control the spread of HIV/AIDS, malaria and TB to the rest of the population.

4.3.1.6 The WHO Horn of Africa Initiative, endorsed by the regional Ministers of Health as a Bridge for Peace, is a new paradigm established to strengthen health care delivery services across internal borders and protect internally and externally displaced populations affected by violence and wars. This Initiative must be sustained and encouraged as a model of relationships in the future.

4.3.1.7 The state of wars, drought, famine and newly emerging diseases has overburdened the health care delivery service capacity. Conflict resolution may ameliorate the massive influx of displaced rural populations and urban migration in search of security and employment. These groups are the most vulnerable populations, suffering from mental health, psychosocial, and communicable diseases. Regional and national priority must be given to the neglected mental and psychosocial services in order restore normal and stable environment and quality of life.

4.3.1.8 It is therefore recognized that:

a. Physical and mental health statistics identified in the country-by-country case studies are strongly associated with poverty, violence, and economic underdevelopment;

b. HIV/AIDS is a major threat to the survival, security, nutrition, and health development of all peoples of the region;

c. Malaria is the number one killer in the region, especially among children. It was noted that malaria was better controlled under conditions of peace and economic development in the region. Armed conflicts and expenditures for war efforts take away the gains achieved in the state of peace within each country and the region in general;

d. Distribution of anti-malaria drugs and anti-retroviral drugs to interrupt mother-to-child transmission of HIV requires capacity building of the health infrastructure, outreach and home based services in the community, trained human resources, and mobilization of grassroots community resources. To achieve these goals, multilateral and bilateral assistance for indebted and resource poor region of the Horn of Africa are prerequisite for sustainable development.

4.3.2 Recommendations

4.3.2.1 Implement successful strategies applied in the eradication of polio, and other preventable, opportunistic diseases impacting HIV/AIDS with global collaboration and mobilization of financial and public-private partnership.

4.3.2.2 Encourage the UNDP, UNAIDS, WHO, UNICEF, World Bank and bilateral organizations to a play a more active role in sustainable health development. They can use resources available in the Millennium Initiatives, Global Funds and New Partnership for Africa's Development, and Hope for African Children's Initiative. These funds will assist the Horn of Africa in developing common strategies to provide drugs and ensure appropriate medical technologies in these resource-poor countries.

4.3.2.3 Establish inter-country early warning system network on disease, drought, and famine surveillance initiatives, such as US CDC and WHO, for disease surveillance and FAO World Food Programs for drought and famine to enhance planning, detecting and implementing effective management of technological, human, and physical resources.

4.3.2.4 Priority must be given to public - private partnerships within the region to increase voluntary counseling and testing (VCT) supported by multilateral technical assistance. These partnerships can assist in establishing laboratories, testing centers and other community based home care and distribution networks for anti-retroviral and malarial drugs, especially for mothers and children at risk.

4.3.2.5 Strengthen border health facilities, improve referral systems, and control infectious and communicable diseases such as HIV/AIDS, TB, and malaria resulting from the uncontrollable influx of two-way migrations, nomadic and pastoral sick populations; in addition provide direct observed treatments.

Annex 2

Keynote Speech by Kidane Alemayehu, President of the Horn of Africa Peace and Development Center

International Conference on a Development Strategy for the Horn of Africa

October 20th at 7:00pm
By Kidane Alemayehu
Founding President
Horn of Africa Peace and Development Center

Mr. Chairman

Ladies and Gentlemen

My address will focus on the background, reasons for having the conference, its expected outcome and future prospects.

But first, please allow me to welcome you, on behalf of the Horn of Africa Peace and Development Center, to this historic, unprecedented conference and to acknowledge the important contributions of certain organizations and individuals without whom this conference would have not been possible.

1. The Africa Program of the University of Texas at Arlington led by Dr. Jalloh who exerted a huge effort as chairman of the organizing committee along with his excellent secretary, Ms. Lois Lettini.

2. Amoud Foundation represented by Mr. Yussuf Kalib whose dedication and extraordinary support made this conference possible.

3. My thanks are also due to the other members of the organizing committee:

   Dr. Habte Woldu,
   Dr. Dereje Agonafer,
   Mrs. Safia Ismail
   Mr. Betru Gebre-Egziabher
   Mr. Semere Habtermariam
   Ms. Martha Melaku
   Mr. Solomon Haile

4. May I also express, on behalf of the Horn of Africa Peace and Development Center, our gratitude to Dr. Mulu Ketsela, Alternate Executive Director and, through her, to the World Bank for her support to this civic initiative and hope that our mutual collaboration will continue.

5. I would like further to express my appreciation and thanks to all the

speakers at this conference. As per the conference program, the six workshops will conduct concurrent sessions the whole day, and night if necessary, tomorrow (Saturday) to discuss the issues and to formulate the respective development strategies for the Horn of Africa. On Sunday, we are scheduled to have our second plenary session at which each chairperson will present his/her proposed development strategy for the Horn of Africa. This will be followed by a general discussion after which the chairpersons will have a joint meeting to formulate the final resolution which will be presented to the third and final plenary session.

BACKGROUND

The idea of organizing a conference on a development strategy for the HOA was initiated at the international conference on prospects of a confederation in the Horn of Africa held in Tampa, Florida in November 2002. The outcome of that conference is contained in a document entitled the Tampa Declaration and can be seen in the website: www.hafrica.com.

Shortly thereafter, the Horn of Africa Peace and Development Center was established in Tampa, Florida. The Center's vision is to achieve a sub-region where genuine democracy, peace and stability will prevail and where the evils of poverty and deadly diseases will have been eliminated.

The Center's main mission is to initiate research and studies on HOA issues and to generate practical ideas and strategies and action plans for implementation by the concerned countries with the support of regional, international and civic organizations as well as bilateral assistance. For more information, please visit the Center's website: www.hafrica.com.

The members of the Center's Board include Mr. Yussuf Kalib, Mr. Semere Habtemariam, Mr Harun Musa and myself.

The Center's first major outcome is this conference which was organized, as stated earlier, in collaboration with UTA's Africa Program and the Amoud Foundation.

INTERNATIONAL CONFERENCE ON A DEVELOPMENT STRATEGY FOR THE HORN OF AFRICA

This historic and unprecedented conference is to focus on all the major socio-economic aspects needed for the formulation of a development strategy, namely, macro-economic development and globalization; agricultural and rural development; infrastructure and water; education, science and technology; public health; as well as women and social development. Scholars from 13 universities, 8 institutions, and 3 UN organizations including the World Bank are meeting here in Dallas for the purpose of formulating the development strategy which will be the first of its kind in the history of the Horn of Africa Region.

It should be noted that the Horn of Africa Peace and Development Center will collaborate with interested partners such as COMESA and, hopefully the World Bank and the UN, in promoting the outcome of this conference as well as in conducting further detailed studies for the implementation of the Development Strategy.

REASONS FOR HAVING THE CONFERENCE

There was an international hue and cry when the Tsunamis hit Indonesia recently. However, not much is said and done about persistent disasters of Tsunami proportions that afflict the Horn of Africa resulting in the perennial death of hundreds of thousands including women and children. The main ones are the following:

Tsunami #1: Poverty

The HOA is among the very poorest regions in the world. The GNP per capita income is about $100.00 per annum. The policy of land ownership by the state has relegated 85% of Ethiopia's population which depends on agriculture, to a status of serfs. According to the UN Development Index: out of 177 countries:

Djibouti	150th
Eritrea	161st
Ethiopia	170th
Somalia	unknown

Tsunami #2: Problems of Health and Environmental Degradation

The people of the HOA suffer from the blight of diseases such as malaria, TB, and HIV/Aids from which hundreds of thousands die every year. The devastation of the environment is progressing at an alarming rate. Life expectancy in the Horn of Africa is 40 years.

Tsunami #3: Mutually Antagonistic Leadership

The current leadership in the HOA countries is incapable of initiating an integrated development strategy. They are not even on talking terms let alone initiating any regional development.

Governance in the HOA is characterized by lack of democracy and abuse of human rights. A heavy cloud is looming over the HOA with signs of impending conflagration: a Jihad proclaimed by Somali militants, and the worsening tension between Eritrea and Ethiopia.

Tsunami #4: Disunity

Thanks to the British, French and Italian colonial legacy, the HOA is torn into four desperately poor countries.

There were times when most of the HOA was a united entity whether known as Punt or Ethiopia. In the words of Donald Levine: "In the latter part of the 3rd century Mani wrote that Axum (Ethiopia) ranked among the great powers of the world." For at least half of the First millennium, the powers that be in the Middle East and the Horn of Africa were Byzantium, Persia, and Ethiopia. For more details, please refer to my paper entitled: "Horn of Africa: From Glory to Misery, and Hope?"

Let me quote a poem by the famous Poet-Laureate Tsegaye Gebremedhin entitled: "Yes, We betrayed our ancestors":

> "When our fathers gave us the cradle of the First World,
> At the beginning there was KA, the first God of Earth and Sky,
> On this birth land of our first ancestors.
> They raised for us the sacred shrine
> On the glowing head piece of the Horn of Africa,
> Where the sun first touched the body of the Earth
> But, alas, now, look at us!
> The generation who has forgotten how to unite.
> The rotten link that has lost the scale of self-respect.
> Look at us!"

Tsunami #5: An Indifferent International Community

The international community is pursuing a policy of containment in the HOA and does very little for the region's socio-economic development for mutual benefit.

There are three foreign armies located in the HOA: two belonging to USA and France are there to protect others from the HOA including the so-called "international terrorism". The UN force is simply an observer.

In his book entitled: "Arms for the Horn", Jeffrey A. Lefebvre states that the HOA has no strategic value to USA except "its location across the Red Sea from Saudi Arabia". According to him, USA interests in the HOA are for:

(1) Protecting the sea lines of communication or oil lanes;
(2) "Supporting Egypt's efforts to protect its southern flank and the Nile waters"; and
(3) Blunting destabilization activities aimed at Saudi Arabia and other pro-western states.

In his book "The Horn of Africa – Conflict and Poverty", Mesfin Woldemariam states:

> "For the US, none of the countries of the Horn have any significance outside its material interests on the Arabian Peninsula, and the prosperity and military strength of Israel."

WHY SHOULD THE INTERNATIONAL COMMUNITY BE INTERESTED IN THE HOA?

The international community should be interested in the HOA for the following mutual benefits:

1. With its current population of nearly 100 million, increasing to 145 million by 2025, the HOA has a tremendous trade potential;
2. The HOA has substantial water, energy, agricultural, and mineral resources. 86% of the water flowing to Egypt originates in Ethiopia;
3. The HOA possesses a significant cultural, historic and environmental tourism potential;
4. The HOA is situated at a sensitive strategic location with ports on the Red Sea, the Gulf of Aden and the Indian Ocean;
5. The HOA plays a highly significant role in international affairs as it hosts three important organizations: the African Union headquarters (AU), the Economic Commission for Africa (ECA), and the Inter-Governmental Agency for African Development (IGAAD);
6. Countries surrounding the Red Sea could form a Cooperative Council which could bring together an area which has a population of 200 million, increasing to 400 million in 20 years. These countries have mutually complimentary resources: agricultural, labour and water re-

sources on the Horn of Africa side and investment and oil on the side of the Arab Peninsula. Such a Council could contribute immensely to international peace and development.

FOCUS ON POLITICAL AND ECONOMIC DEVELOPMENT

Before I conclude, let me address two points that are raised regarding this conference and the previous one held at Tampa:

1. Those whose perspective of history spans only a century or so give scant regard to earlier times when the Horn of Africa was a united entity. I obviously disagree. We ignore history at our own peril. As indicated already, the Horn of Africa was prosperous and strong when it was united and weak as well as poor when, as at present, it is divided.
2. With the exception of few far-sighted scholars such as Dr. Sisay Assefa of West Michigan University, current wisdom among Horn of Africa activists holds that politics should be the sole focus of attention. While the struggle for democracy and human rights should be supported, ignoring socio-economic development needs is, in my opinion, a folly of gigantic proportions. In Clinton's campaign words: "It is the economy, stupid!"

CONCLUSION

1. An integrated development strategy is essential for the Horn of Africa as no such instrument has ever been devised so far. Because of leadership problems in the region, such a strategy can only be formulated through civic initiatives such as ours.
2. An appropriately formulated development strategy would facilitate a meaningful response by the international community to the desperate plight of instability, poverty and disease afflicting the Horn of Africa region.
3. In order to promote an accelerated development in the region, it is essential for the international community to encourage the governments and people of the region to strive for unity, democracy and respect for human rights.
4. It is also essential for the international community to reassess its strategy and role in the Horn of Africa so that it will, for its own interests,

contribute to the region's accelerated economic development.

5. For all the above reasons, the conference is extremely beneficial for the people of the Horn of Africa and humanity at large. The Center is confident that all the scholars gathered here today will contribute effectively to the formulation of an appropriate development strategy for the Horn of Africa. It is anticipated that the chair of each conference workshop will come up with a concise identification of the issues and strategies aimed at enabling the 90 million people of the Horn of Africa to finally defeat the grinding poverty and associated diseases from which they have been suffering for so long.

In the words of Senator Barak Obama, our effort is an expression of "An Audacity for Hope."

CHAPTER 8: Red Sea Cooperative Council

Utilization of the Red Sea for the benefit of adjacent countries as well as the international community.

As indicated in Chapter 7, the Red Sea is currently utilized, in the most, for the benefit of transporting goods in the context of the East/West trade. The Red Sea is hardly used for the benefit of the adjacent countries. There is no regional institutional framework so far to facilitate regional collaboration for socio-economic and political interests of the adjacent countries.

The countries adjacent to the Red Sea as well as in close proximity in the region are: Djibouti, Egypt, Eritrea, Ethiopia, Israel, Jordan, Saudi Arabia, Somalia, Sudan, and Yemen. The Gulf of Aqaba and the Gulf of Aden are included in the Red Sea region. Although Ethiopia is not directly adjacent to the Red Sea, it is included in the region because it is heavily dependent on the Red Sea. Djibouti is in fact Ethiopia's main port of trade. If peace were to prevail between Eritrea and Somalia on the one hand and Ethiopia on the other hand, Assab, Berbera, and Mogadishu could be other important ports for Ethiopia.

The population and GDP of the countries adjacent and in close proximity to the Red Sea are the following:

Country	Population* (in million)		GDP** (in billion $)
	2013	2050	
Djibouti	0.9	1	2.4
Egypt	82	113	543
Eritrea	6	10	3.4

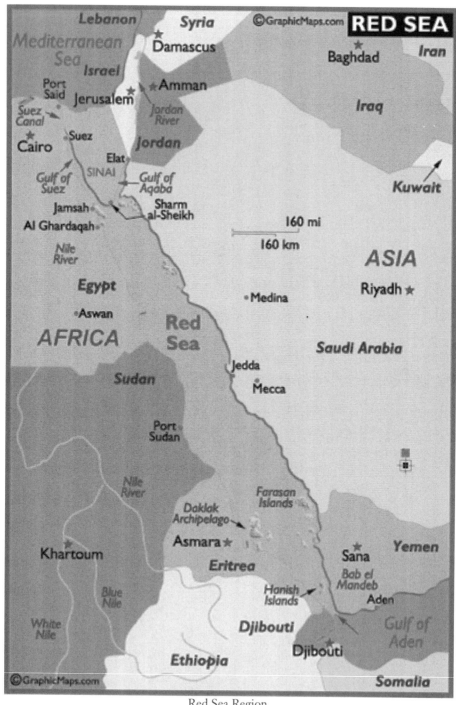

Red Sea Region

Ethiopia	94	186	105
Israel	8	10	252
Jordan	6.5	12	31
Saudi Arabia	29	60	682
Somalia	10	38	5.9 (CIA)
Sudan	38	64	59
Yemen	24	102	59
Total	298.4	596	1,742.7

Sources: * United Nations: July, 2013; ** World Bank: 2012

COMPATIBILITY OF THE RED SEA REGION'S RESOURCES

With regard to resources, the countries surrounding the Red Sea could be grouped in three sectors: (a) on the African side: human, water, hydropower, agricultural, and mineral resources; (b) on the other side of the Red Sea (Saudi Arabia and Yemen): oil and financial/investment resources as well as employment opportunities; and (c) on the Israeli side: technology resources. In particular, two of the region's countries, namely, Ethiopia and Saudi Arabia, possess very compatible and abundant resources i.e. water and oil respectively that could contribute substantially to each other's as well as the region's development.

RED SEA AS A REGION OF PEACE AND DEVELOPMENT

Even a cursory look at the Red Sea region's history, and current status, will reveal that it is marked with conflict, continued tension, and the absence of any mechanism or institutional framework for collaboration. Egypt and Ethiopia have engaged in over ten wars against each other. They had occupied each other's territories. Ethiopia had occupied parts of Saudi Arabia as well as Yemen for centuries at the beginning of the first millennium. Ethiopia and Somalia have engaged in devastating wars. Over 70,000 people have died as a result of the recent war between Eritrea and Ethiopia. Religious fundamentalists supported by Arab sources have caused huge conflicts within Ethiopia and Somalia.

On the other hand, there are also positive aspects that could be considered a harbinger of peace and development in the region. Examples of these include the first Muslim refugees from Mecca to Ethiopia when they were persecuted there and directed by Prophet Mohammed himself to flee to Ethiopia where they would find adequate protection. Over 100 of the Muslim refugees including Prophet Mohammed's daughter, Rockeya and her husband, stayed in Ethiopia and returned to Mecca when peace prevailed there. Another important example is the fact that 86% of the water that cascades to Egypt in the form of the Nile River emanates from Ethiopia. In addition, Ethiopia is currently engaged in the development of hydropower and wind energy that would be of benefit to the region. Taking into account the huge water quantity that evaporates from the Nile River and the water that flows out of the Nile Delta into the Mediterranean Sea, it is reasonable to consider the possibility that even if part of this resource could be saved, it could be utilized by those nations such as Israel and Saudi Arabia whose needs for water are bound to increase in the future.

Despite the above positive examples, however, the extent of collaboration and mutual benefit from the region's huge natural and potential resources is unfortunately highly limited. What reigns supreme in the region is mutual animosity, suspicion, tension, intolerance instead of collaboration for mutual benefits.

NEED FOR A RED SEA DEVELOPMENT COUNCIL (RSDC)

It is, therefore, time for the governments and people of the region to consider forming a mechanism for a full collaboration among themselves. This could be in the form of a Red Sea Development Council (RSDC) with a vision for peace and an accelerated development in the region. RSDC could formulate the region's policy, strategy, and action plan (short-, medium, and long-term) focused on the achievement of the fullest stability, democracy, and an accelerated socio-economic development.

In order to achieve a practical meaning to the fundamental concept behind the principles of RSDC, arrangements could be made whereby regional frameworks of collaboration could be established on issues of mutual interest such as research, trade, industrial activities, social services including regional sports programs, intellectual services, communication such as joint television, radio, internet, and other media operations.

In order to avoid any semblance of hegemony on the part of any country within the RSDC, it would be essential to ensure that institutional mechanisms are established including internationally agreed legislations, policy declarations and institutional arrangements so that all member countries are treated in an equitable manner. This should include the establishment of RSDC Centers in all member countries, chairmanships of RSDC annual conferences on a rotating basis by heads of the various member governments.

The establishment of a Red Sea Region with a leadership having a clear vision, strategy, and an action plan (short- medium-, and long-term), in a democratic context could engender a lasting peace and an accelerated development that could place the region among the major partners on the global level. The region would thus finally extricate itself from being one of the areas of tension, poverty and under-development (on the African side), and exporter of fundamentalism (on Saudi Arabian side), to an era of a lasting and sustainable peace and an accelerated development.

PART 3

JUSTICE FOR ETHIOPIA

CHAPTER 9: A Cry for Justice

JUSTICE DENIED

If there is any country that can be clearly identified as a nation that has been the victim of huge war crimes and destruction, despite its membership of the League of Nations, but continues to this day to be denied the justice it deserves for over 75 years, it is Ethiopia. It is a historic fact that during 1935-41, Fascist Italy perpetrated, with the complicit support of the Vatican, unimaginable war crimes in Ethiopia that, as a result, brought about devastating losses in terms of the massacre of one million men, women, and children as well as the destruction and looting of vast quantities of Ethiopian properties.

To this day, the war crime remains unattended. Not one Italian has been brought to a tribunal to answer for the war crimes committed against Ethiopia. It is truly amazing to note that the United Nations has not even placed the war crime in its records. It is as if all that devastating war crime never happened. The world continues to turn a blind eye to the huge Fascist war crimes undertaken by a European power in an African country, Ethiopia, the only nation from the continent that was, at the time, a member of the League of Nations.

The continued cry for justice is met with a stunning silence on the part of the main perpetrators: Italy and the Vatican. The major European powers, namely, France and Great Britain as well as the USA which all supported Fascist Italy by applying a policy of utter negligence or neutrality and the supply of war materials to the Fascists, continue to pursue a similar policy of silence in the face of a case that cries for justice to this day. Italy was supplied with oil; and the gateway to the Red Sea which was then under British control was left open for the Fascist transportation of its huge army and war material to Ethiopia which suffered, during the same time, a debilitating international

Fascist atrocity in Ethiopia

A Vatican priest blessing the Fascist army

boycott that made it impossible for Ethiopia to obtain the required war material to defend itself. Thus, the unprovoked attack on, arms wise, defenseless Ethiopia, a member country of the League of Nations, by another member nation, Italy, was facilitated through a deliberate action of a negligent support by major powers countries including France, Britain and USA.

ITALY'S FIRST WAR AND DEFEAT AT ADOWA, ETHIOPIA

Aside from relatively minor earlier clashes between the forces of Ethiopia and Italy, the first main war between the two countries occurred in March, 1896 in which Italy suffered a humiliating defeat at Adowa. Ethiopia's Emperor Minelik as well as the heroic forces are remembered with pride by all Ethiopians as well as people who believe in freedom, for having succeeded to thwart Italy's attempted colonization objective.

The defeat, at the hands of Ethiopia, an African nation, of a European power, Italy, had international significance, a harbinger of freedom and independence by colonized nations throughout the world including Africa, Asia and Latin America.

Prior to the 1896 war between Ethiopia and Italy, there was an attempt, at least on the part of Ethiopia, to engage in friendly relations between the two nations. At the beginning of May, 1889, six months prior to King Minelik's elevation to being emperor of Ethiopia, the Wuchale Treaty between Ethiopia and Italy was signed by Minelik and Italy's representative, Pietro Antoneli.

An Ethiopian delegation headed by *Dejazmach* (later Ras) Mekonnen, Emperor Haile Selassie's father, soon headed for Italy accompanied by Antoneli, for the ratification of the treaty in Italy as well as to obtain financial assistance.

Among the members of the Ethiopian delegation was one of my forefathers Qegnazmach (title) Abba Nada (nom de guerre; actual Dilnessahu Tenfu) who was a close relative of Dejazmach Mekonnen. The other important members of the delegation were: [1]

1. Abba Woldemikael, Dejazmach Mekonnen's confessor (priest);
2. Fitawrari Biratu;
3. Grazmach Yoseph, translator;
4. Grazmach Dessalegn, later Fitawrari;
5. Belamberas Negemae, later Qegnazmach;
6. Basha Qolech, later Fitawrari

There were also other members of the delegation. A picture of the Ethiopian delegation taken at Napoli, Italy can be seen on the facing page.

The delegation stayed in Italy for a period of three months during which the Wuchale Treaty was duly ratified and Ras Mekonnen was able to obtain a loan of 4 million Lire from the Italian Government part of which funds he used to purchase 28 70-mili-meter guns, 28,000 regular guns, and 2,500,000 bullets.

Later, a serious controversy arose between Ethiopia and Italy as a result of Article 17 of the Wuchale Treaty, which gave differing meanings in the Amharic and Italian texts. Whereas in the Amharic text, the article provided, simply as a choice, for the Ethiopian government to use the Italian government to contact other states, the Italian version, made it necessary for the Ethiopian government to communicate with other governments only through the Italian government. Thus the Italian version made Ethiopia a virtual colony which was totally unacceptable to the Ethiopian government then led by Emperor Minelik.

The above controversy led to the war of Adowa as instigated by Italy but ended in its utter defeat in March, 1896. However, after 40 years, Italy perpetrated its second aggression against Ethiopia in 1935.

MY MEMORY OF THE FASCIST AGGRESSION

The war crimes committed by Italy, with the support of the Vatican as well as the absence of justice on the part of the international community was always present in my mind throughout my life. This was the case especially because my family had also been victimized by the Fascist war crimes. My grandfather, Grazmach Gessesse Fanta lost his life in the Ogaden, Eastern Ethiopia while fighting against the Italian invasion there. My father, Alemayehu Gebremichael, and my uncle, Merid Gessesse, had also fought in the same war.

When recounting his experience about some of the events during and after the war, my father explained to me the heroic resistance by the Ethiopian fighters who were overwhelmed by the superior, modern Fascist armaments including tanks and airplanes which the Ethiopians lacked. Nevertheless, they used ingenious methods for disabling some of the tanks. My father told me that they used to dig holes in the areas where the Italian tanks were likely to proceed. They then covered the holes on top of which some grass and soil were scattered to make the place look similar to the adjacent area. My father and his co-fighters then waited hidden in front and when the tanks got bogged down in the holes, and the tank's driver opened the hood and looked up, that

Ethiopian Delegation in Italy in 1889 for the Ratification of the Wuchale Treaty: (seated on chairs in the middle from left: Qegazmach "Abba Nada"; the priest, Aba Wolde Michael, Dejazmach (later Ras) Mekonnen and Fitawrari Biratu

Ras Mekonnen Woldemichael, Emperor Haile Selassie I's father

Qegnazmach Abba Nada (nom de guerre; actual: Qegnazmach Dilnessahu Tenfu)

was his end with some bullets straight to his head. Unfortunately, the Ethiopian patriots could not make use of the tanks.

My grandfather was among the victims of the Fascist war crime. My father survived the war but after returning to his dwelling area, he was captured by the Fascists who claimed that he had killed some Italians in the war and that he had some guns in his possession. He was tied to a tree and beaten severely by some Libyan soldiers used by the Italian Fascists. He remembered seeing the blood jutting out from his nose. He told the Italian officer that he had fought against the Fascist invaders in the Ogaden and that, obviously, he had shot some bullets but that he could not tell whether his bullets killed anyone or not.

The search for weapons at my father's house did not yield any result. My father had hidden the guns by burying them right under the entrance to the house. The Italians and their soldiers were, therefore, stepping over the hidden guns and never thought of digging for them. Eventually, my father was released and thus survived the Italian Fascist invasion.

Grazmach Gessesse Fanta

In this connection, it should be stated that according to Professor Theodore Vestal, the number of Libyan soldiers deployed by Fascist Italy during its invasion of Ethiopia was 30,000. Please see his note, www.globalalliansforethiopia.org.

I was born a year prior to the Italian invasion. Therefore, my recollections of the war were some aspects of the final days of the Italian aggression. My experience was related to the Somali soldiers of the Italian army fleeing from Ethiopia through villages in the rural areas including the locality where my parents were living. As my father was away for the war, I recall my mother and other neighbours some times taking us to a wooded area hiding from marauding Somalis. One particular incident etched in my mind was the sudden appearance of two armed Somalis who pushed me aside and went into our house to steal whatever they could find. My father walked into the compound and one of our helpers rushed and informed him about what was happening. He immediately turned back and started running when I heard a gunshot from outside our fence where, apparently, a third armed Somali was waiting. The two Somali soldiers inside the house rushed out when they heard the gunshot and ran away from the house, to a child's great relief. I remember that one of them had my father's wallet in his hand.

FASCIST ITALY'S AGGRESSION AND ITS CONSEQUENCES

As stated above, Fascist Italy's invasion of Ethiopia during 1935-41 was motivated by two fundamental factors: a revenge for its humiliating loss at the war of Adowa between the two countries in 1896 and, secondly, the colonization of Ethiopia for resettling Italians as well as the consequent economic benefits. Therefore, the then leader of Fascist Italy, Benito Mussolini, concocted a pretext and initiated his aggression against Ethiopia at Walwal in 1934 followed by an invasion of Ethiopia from the east and north using numerous airplanes, the internationally forbidden poison gas, light and heavy war materials, and thousands of Italian and other soldiers some of whom were from the then Italian colonies: Eritrea, Libya, and Somalia.

The Italian aggression was, in terms of formality, opposed by the League of Nations. Richard Pankhurst states:

> "The invasion was duly condemned by the League, on 10 October 1935, by fifty votes against one (Italy), with three abstentions (Albania, Austria and Hungary, all three in the

Italian orbit). The international organization decided, however, to impose only mild Economic sanctions – and excluded from them the ban on petrol, without which the invader's airforce could not have flown, and armoured vehicles would have come to a halt. Nor was any action to close to Italy the largely British-owned Suez Canal, through which Italian soldiers, military equipment – and poison-gas – continued to pass."2

Nevertheless, Italy's invasion went ahead as Mussolini was sure that the League of Nations was not serious about its condemnation of his aggressive action. It has to be noted here that although Ethiopia was a member of the League of Nations and was, therefore, entitled to a united defense by the organization, it was abandoned and Fascist Italy was given a field day to do as it wished. Countries such as Britain and France did not initially raise a finger in support of Ethiopia. USA adopted the immoral excuse of being neutral in a case where Italy committed war crimes against an independent country, namely, Ethiopia. Ethiopia was in fact condemned and denied the acquisition of the required arms to defend itself. It must be stated, however, that once Fascist Italy sided with Nazi Germany in the Second World War, Britain played an unforgettable commendable role in the liberation of Ethiopia from Italian occupation.

The details of the comparative military capacity were as follows:

a. On the Italian side:
    1,300,000 Italian soldiers plus indigenous regiments (askaris) from Eritrea, Libya, and Somalia;
    9,300 machine guns;
    2,275 pieces of artillery;
    795 tanks;
    595 aircraft;
    Logistics including thousands of transport vehicles; and
    200 Italian journalists.
b. On the Ethiopian side:
    500,000 men only few of whom were trained as soldiers;
    400,000 outdated rifles;
    50 light and heavy anti-aircraft guns;
    200 antiquated pieces of artillery;

Benito Mussolini 1883-1945

Few vehicles; and

13 outmoded "Potez 25 biplanes" 3

Eventually, Mussolini was executed by the Italian patriots. The following link has the video showing the execution:
http://www.youtube.com/watch?v=Vel-OeI_bgk

FASCIST WAR CRIMES IN ETHIOPIA

The consequences of the Fascist war crimes in Ethiopia during 1935-41 were devastating. The huge losses that were incurred by Ethiopia included:

1. One million Ethiopians killed of whom 30,000 were massacred in only three days in Addis Ababa in 1937;
2. Huge quantities of Ethiopian properties were looted by the Italians; some of these properties are currently still in the possession of the Vatican and the Italian Governments;
3. 2,000 churches and 525,000 homes as well as 14 million animals were destroyed as a result of the bombing, fire, and the use of the mustard poison gas;
4. The use of the internationally forbidden poison gas also had a devastating effect on the environment.

In her book entitled: "Italy's War Crimes in Ethiopia 1935-1941", Imani Kali-Nyah provides the following details [4]:

> "Provisional estimates of the slaughter of Ethiopians compiled by the Ethiopian Government in 1946 from the evidence thus far investigated (these figures are not final) and there are in addition a large number of persons rendered permanent invalids, including victims of poison-gas(*):

> (*) The above report was compiled eleven years after Mussolini's mass extermination campaign first began in 1935. A more conservative estimate of civilian and military casualties would probably be no less than one million."

Killed in action	275,000
Patriots killed in battle during five years	

of fascist occupation	78,500
Children, women, old and infirm people killed by bombing during the occupation	17,800
Massacre of February, 1937	30,000
Patriots condemned to death by "Court Martial"	24,000
Persons of both sexes who died in concentration camps from privation and maltreatment	35,000
People who died of privations owing to destruction of their villages during the five years' occupation	300,000
PROVISIONAL ESTIMATES OF CASUALTIES	**760,000**

In his book entitled: "YeEthiopianna yeItalia Tornnet" (translation: The Italo-Ethiopian War), p. 225, Paulos Gnogno presented other claims by the Ethiopian Government in 1946 as follows[5]:

Destruction of:

2,000 churches;
525,000 homes; and
13,700,000 animals.

In his book entitled: "Hiywotenna yeEthiopia Ermeja" (translation: My Life and Ethiopia's Progress), Emperor Haile Selassie I stated [6]:

"Italian airplanes came in drones of 9, 15, and 18 to drop rains of poison gas on people, animals, rivers and streams as well as pastures."

His Imperial Majesty further stated [7]:

"The picture of many thousands of soldiers as well as rural people including women and children who were burned to death by the poison gas used by the enemy (Fascist Italy) is still etched in our mind."

The genocide that was inflicted on the people of Ethiopia was not limited to the use of bombs, bullets, and poison gas. The Italian Fascists used every weapon they could think of to wage their horrendous crimes against Ethiopia including hanging, burning people up in their own homes, chopping heads off, and, amazingly, throwing people off airplanes. For example, Abune Mikael,

Ethiopian patriots hanged by Fascist Italian soldiers

Abune (Bishop) Petros

one of the Bishops of the Ethiopian Orthodox Tewahedo Church, was killed by being thrown off from a Fascist airplane.

Abune Petros, another famous Ethiopian Orthodox Tewahedo Church patriot and thousands of other people were simply shot by the Fascists.

Looting by the Fascist Italians

In addition to the huge devastation that was inflicted on Ethiopia in terms of loss of life and destruction of properties, the Fascists also engaged in the looting of vast quantities of Ethiopian properties. The following sources are presented merely as examples:

1. Alberto Sbacchi states:

    a. Badoglio, the first Viceroy of Ethiopia (under Fascist occupation), "...requested to be given all the money in the Bank of Ethiopia in Addis Ababa....The amount found in the Bank of Ethiopia was 1,700,000 Maria Teresa dollars half of which went to Badoglio. With this money he built himself a villa in Rome and furnished it with 300 cases of war booty and gifts flown from Ethiopia by the air force."

    b. Graziani who took over as Viceroy from Badoglio as of June 1, 1936 had a luggage of 79 suitcases when he returned to Italy[8].

2. Ian Campbell provides evidence of Fascist Italian lootings from certain Ethiopian churches and monasteries, especially the renowned Debre Libanos Monastery including the following:

    A very large prayer book given by Emperor Ghelawdewos;

    A very large Geez manuscript decorated with gold;

    A gold bound bible;

    Innumerable prayer books;

    Many illustrated religious manuscripts;

    Large drums decorated with gold;

    Crowns of Emperors Yohannes IV, Minelik II, and Haile Selassie I;

    Ecclesiastical ornaments of high quality;

    Golden crosses;

    12 gold-embroidered gowns including one given by Emperor Fasiladas;

    4,000 Maria Theresa Thalers[9].

ETHIOPIAN RESISTANCE AND THE 2ND ITALIAN DEFEAT

Despite the Fascists' overwhelming modern arms, Ethiopian military resistance continued throughout the five years of Italian occupation. Organized guerilla fighters led by the renowned leaders such as Ras Abebe Aregay, Belay Zelleke, Hailemariam Mammo, Abebe Shenkut (later Dejazmach) continued with their effective struggle with a result that the Italian occupation was prevalent, in the main, only in urban centers and some surroundings. Therefore, Italian occupation in Ethiopia during 1935-41 never achieved the status of a full colonization of the country, characterized by peaceful and orderly governance. The Fascist Italians were always harassed and constantly on the alert expecting the continued attack by the Ethiopian patriots.

The Fascist atrocities inflicted on Ethiopian patriots were unimaginable. Here below is an account about the barbaric and brutal measures taken by the Fascists: [10]

> "An important patriot known as Abba Retta had been encircled by the enemy force but had managed to keep it off by fighting for eight days. In this fight, they killed numerous Bandas (African soldiers of the Fascist army) and Italians but surrendered as they were unable to escape as well as the fact that their bullets were finished. The Italians chopped off the heads of about 13 patriots and showed them off at Debre Berhan town. The renowned patriot, Abba Retta's 12-year old son was also captured as he was also firing along with his father. When they wanted to pardon him in view of his youthful age, he responded with courage: "I do not want you to spare me when my father sacrificed his life for the love of his country." The Italians who were enraged by his statement shot and killed him as well as chopping off his head."

It was thanks to these and thousands of other great Ethiopian patriots that Ethiopia continued with its independence for over 3,000 years. On the other hand, it should be noted that the Fascist Italians who were claiming to bring civilization to Ethiopia were obviously perpetrating crimes against humanity.

In the mean-time, Emperor Haile Selassie I had gone to Europe to appeal to the League of Nations at Geneva, Switzerland in June 1936, to come to Ethiopia's aid which never materialized. The Emperor informed the league:

> "I ask the fifty-two nations not to forget today the policy upon which they embarked eight months ago, and on faith

of which I directed the resistance of my people against the aggressor whom they had denounced to the world. Despite the inferiority of my weapons, the complete lack of aircraft, artillery, munitions, hospital services, my confidence in the League was absolute. I thought it to be impossible that fifty-two nations, including the most powerful in the world, should be successfully opposed by a single aggressor. Counting on the faith due to treaties, I had made no preparation for war, and that is the case with certain small countries in Europe."

The Emperor's further prophetic statement resonates to all nations to this day:
"I ask the fifty-two nations, who have given the Ethiopian people a promise to help them in their resistance to the aggressor, what are they willing to do for Ethiopia? And the great Powers who have promised the guarantee of collective security to small States on whom weighs the threat that they may one day suffer the fate of Ethiopia, I ask what measures do you intend to take?

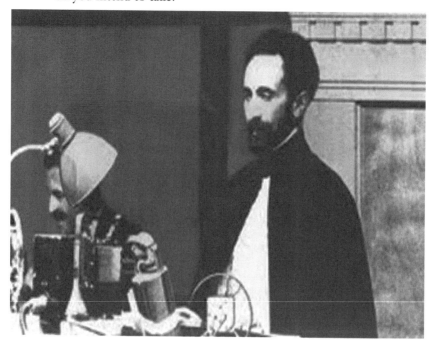

Emperor Haile Selassie I delivering his historic appeal to the League of Nations

Representatives of the World I have come to Geneva to discharge in your midst the most painful of the duties of the head of a State. What reply shall I have to take back to my people?"

Ras Abebe Aregai

The Emperor's prophecy did materialize as Fascist Italy eventually joined with Nazi Germany in their attack on the Allied Forces. This resulted in Ethiopia obtaining the support of the United Kingdom in ousting Fascist Italy from Ethiopia with the partnership of the valiant Ethiopian patriots who, as stated above, were always prosecuting their resistance against the Italian occupation during 1935-41.

Other Non-Ethiopian Patriots Who Fought Against the Fascist Invasion
Although, as stated above, the big powers turned a blind eye to Fascist Italy's invasion of Ethiopia, this had provoked the outrage and active opposition of many people in Europe and the United States of America. The following are merely examples of individuals who stood, heroically, for justice on behalf of Ethiopia.

SYLVIA PANKHURST
Sylvia Pankhurst was among the prime fighters against the Fascist invasion of Ethiopia. She waged an unrelenting struggle against the unjust policies of the League of Nations and exerted the maximum possible pressure to bring about

Sylvia Pankhurst

the required change in the British attitude towards Fascist Italy. [11]

Sylvia was born in Britain in 1882 and passed away in 1960. She was buried at the Trinity Cathdral in Addis Ababa, an event attended by several prominent Ethiopian dignitaries and heroes including HIM Haile Selassie I as well as the then Crown Prince, HH Prince Asfa Wossen.

Sylvia served the Ethiopian cause for 20 years in various important aspects including her highly significant struggle against the Fascist aggression, her support for the rights of Ethiopian women, and the establishment of the Princess Tsehay Hospital which initially served as a school for nursing.

Among the numerous huge efforts she exerted on behalf of Ethiopia:[12]

1. She travelled to Geneva repeatedly to appeal to the members of the League of Nations to support Ethiopia at her moment of need due to the Fascist invasion and war crimes;

2. She established a newspaper in 1936 entitled: "Addis Times and Ethiopian News" and contributed substantially to the enhancement of awareness about Ethiopia's plight;

3. She submitted letters of appeal to various important Government leaders of the time including the British Prime Minister, Winston Churchill, USA President Roosevelt and others calling for justice on behalf of Ethiopia;

4. She contributed effectively to the struggle against the Fascist invasion of Ethiopia by human rights activists including intellectuals such as F. L. Lucas, members of parliament e.g. Phillip Noel, anti-colonialist fighters such as Kenya's Jomo Kenyatta, Jamaica's Amy Ashwood, church leaders, and anti-Fascist Italians;

5. She collaborated effectively with the then Ethiopian envoy to Britain, Dr. Workneh Martin as well as corresponded with Empress Menen (wife of Emperor Haile Selassie I) about the Ethiopian cause;

6. HIM Haile Selassie I's diplomatic struggle coupled with the valiant Ethiopian patriots' fight against the Italian Fascists had Sylvia's significant support which, in sum, eventually brought about a change in British policy that resulted in a joint war of liberation of Ethiopia from the Fascist invasion;

7. Once the Italian Fascists were ousted from Ethiopia, a new challenge presented itself in Ethiopia due to the British interest in making Ethiopia a protectorate or annexing parts of Ethiopia to its colonies in East Africa. Here again Sylvia fought valiantly against the unjust British policy by taking the following steps:

   a. She expressed her opposition in the form of letters of appeal to the British Prime Minister, members of parliament, the British Foreign Minister, and others. Her strong actions brought about criticisms against Sylvia by various key individuals including Col. Gilbert McBeret but she persisted in her struggle despite all the pressures against her;

   b. Despite the opposition to her efforts, she travelled as far as Eritrea as part of her effort to facilitate the rejoining of that former Italian colony to the motherland, Ethiopia;

   c. It took 14 years of unrelenting struggle by the Ethiopian Government with the support of the international community and Sylvia's sustained effort for the British to finally leave Eritrea.

Sylvia's contribution was definitely immense in the struggle against Fascist Italy's invasion as well as the latent motives of the British Government. After victory over the European challenges was fully achieved, Sylvia moved to live in Addis Ababa, Ethiopia in 1956 along with her son, Richard Pankhurst who is one of the most respected academics on Ethiopia today. After her move to

Addis Ababa, Sylvia's service to Ethiopia did not abate:

a. She strived hard for the improvement of the Ethiopian parliament and women's rights;

b. She wrote extensively about Ethiopian culture, civilization, and history;

c. She established a newspaper entitled: "Ethiopia Observer", her former newspaper having been discontinued earlier;

d. She contributed significantly to the establishment of the Princess Tsehay Hospital which also served as the first nursing school in Ethiopia.

Sylvia Pankhurst passed away on September 27, 1960. The 50th anniversary of her death was commemorated, with the initiative of this author and the support of numerous individuals including Mrs. Elleni Mocria, Dr. Girma Alemayehu, etc. in Addis Ababa as well as various cities in USA, and Britain. Ethiopians will be forever beholden to Sylvia Pankhurst for her heroic support of the fight against the Fascist invasion of Ethiopia.

AFRICAN-AMERICAN PARTICIPATION

There was also a great deal of interest on the part of African-Americans in the Fascist Italian invasion of Ethiopia. This was expressed, despite the prevailing policy of neutrality on the part of the United States Government, in terms of volunteering to fight for Ethiopia, recruitment campaigns in several cities including the city of Fort Worth in Texas, military drills in New York, and fundraising efforts. However, due to economic and diplomatic constraints, the extent to which the African-American interest could be translated into action was eventually limited.

Nevertheless, the case of the so-called "Brown Condor", John C. Robinson deserves a special mention as he managed to join the Ethiopian war against the Fascist Italians as a pilot. It was reported that he participated not only in the war, and also in the reconstruction of Ethiopia after its liberation from the Italian invasion.[13]

Another person worthy of mention was Dr. Melaku Beyan who was, at the time a resident in New York and exerted a great deal of effort in raising awareness among African-Americans regarding the Fascist Italian invasion of Ethiopia.[14] He was the one who introduced John C. Robinson to HIM Haile Selassie I. Dr. Melaku established the "Ethiopian World Federation" in 1937 in order to spearhead the campaign for mobilizing support to the Ethiopian cause.

John C. Robinson

Dr. Melaku Beyan

Ras Getachew and his entourage with Mussolini

Eritreans are another group worth mentioning and remembering their contributions to the fight against the Fascist invasion of Ethiopia. Some of these Eritreans were trained as Bandas by Fascist Italy but they abandoned them and joined the Ethiopian fighters.

Of particular mention are, of course, Abrham Deboch and Mogus Asgedom, the two Eritreans who had, in February 1937, thrown bombs and injured General Rodolfo Graziani, the supreme ruler of Ethiopia at the time, resulting in a three-day Fascist rampage in Addis Ababa during which 30,000 Ethiopians were massacred. [15]

Non-Italians Who Fought for the Fascists

Those who fought with the Fascists in the invasion of Ethiopia were mainly Eritreans, Libyans and Somalis. Later, some Ethiopians also sided with the Fascists. Of the latter, the most famous one is *Dejazmach* Haile Selassie Gugsa who was the son-in-law of Emperor Haile Selassie I but eventually abandoned the Ethiopian forces and joined the Fascists.

Libyan Soldiers with the Fascists

According to Ted Vestal, Professor at the State University of Oklahoma, Fascist Italy had deployed 30,000 Libyan soldiers in its invasion of Ethiopia.[16]

Eritreans, Ethiopians, and Somalis with the Fascists

The number of Ethiopians, Eritreans, and Somalis who had fought alongside the Fascists is not known but the estimate is in the thousands.

Some of the more renowned Ethiopian personalities who sided with the Fascists include Ras Hailu Teklehaimanot, Ras Seyum Mengesha, and, of course, Ras Haile Selassie Gugsa who had all submitted to Graziani. Ras Hailu was decorated with the "Star of Italy" as well as the "Order of Saints Maurice and Lazarus".[17]

The Fascists' Divide and Rule Policy

The Fascist Italians had applied policies that would sow division among Ethiopians based on ethnicity and religious differences. Graziani had a particular dislike for the Amharas who he must have thought were the main source of the Ethiopian resistance to the Fascist invasion:

"Taking advantage of the presence of many notables and officials of the former government, he (Graziani) went on to launch a diatribe against what he characterized as Amhara rule, announcing that Amharas presently residing in non-Amhara regions such as Harar and Sidama would be resettled in "their land of origin." "This supremacy", the Viceroy announced, "is over for ever." [18]

Ras Hailu Teklehaimanot

The divide and rule Fascist policy did not, however, take root in Ethiopia and the extent to which there were engagements, in remote and limited areas, based on religious considerations was limited. In any case, the Fascist brutality, including the massacres that took place in Addis Ababa, Debre Libanos, etc. characterized, to the Ethiopian people, the brutal nature of the invaders. On top of all that the application of the Fascists' apartheid policy of separating the whites from the local population was met with utter rejection.

The Role of Britain

The British role regarding Ethiopia was contradictory. On the one hand, as stated in detail under the part dealing with the Horn of Africa, it was the British who facilitated Italy's taking foot in Eritrea, contrary to the provisions of the Hewitt Treaty between Britain and Ethiopia (then under Emperor Yohannes) in which there was an agreement that the Bogos area (including Massawa) revert to Ethiopia. Italy extended its hold from the peripheries to

General Orde Wingate (on right) with Emperor Haile Selassie I (seated)

the annexation of the whole of Eritrea. Italy continued, later, with its first attempt to grab the whole of Ethiopia in the war of Adowa in 1896 and its second disastrous invasion by Mussolini during 1935-41.

On the other hand, it was the British who provided the major military support led by General Wingate that together with the Ethiopian patriots, threw the Fascists out of Ethiopia. It should be stated here that the army deployed by Britain for the liberation of Ethiopia, in collaboration with Ethiopian patriots, included forces from Kenya, India, Nigeria, South Africa, and Sudan.[19]

However, another twist in British policy occurred again. After the defeat and departure of the Fascists, the British tried to colonize Ethiopia or, at least, annex parts of its territories including Sidamo, and Ogaden as well as Eritrea which was a protectorate at the time. Fortunately, with the steadfast struggle by the Ethiopian government led by Emperor Haile Selassie I and the unforgettable support of people like Sylvia Pankhurst the British attempt failed miserably. Nevertheless, the British military and diplomatic support for Ethiopia's liberation from Fascist Italy's invasion of Ethiopia deserves appreciation.

2nd Italian Defeat and the Ethiopian Magnanimity

Finally, in 1941 the Italian invasion came to its dismal end and Ethiopia continued as an independent nation. Thus the Italians were defeated by Ethiopians for the second time in its attempted colonization of Ethiopia; the first one being the war of Adowa in 1896.

Emperor Haile Selassie I returned to power and one of the important measures taken by the Ethiopian government for which it deserved the highest compliments was to forbid any reprisals against the remaining Fascist Italians and their supporters. With few exceptions, the Fascist Italians and their Ethiopian supporters (Bandas) were not subjected to any attack.

Injustice Against Ethiopia:
1. No Tribunal for the Fascist War Criminals

It is important to note that none of the Fascist war criminals were brought to justice in an international tribunal similar to the Nazis. Therefore, the major Fascist leaders such as Badoglio and Graziani escaped justice for their huge war crimes in Ethiopia. That does not, however, mean that they and the other Fascist criminals, post-mortem or the living are free from prosecution as there is no statute of limitation for such war crimes.

The related sad situation that has recently occurred is the installation of a mausoleum for the "Butcher of Ethiopia", the Fascist criminal, Rodolfo

Benito Mussolini and his mistress Clara Petacci hanged by partisans

Graziani, at a small town south-east of Rome, called Affile on August 11, 2012, with some funding by the Italian Government. Objections to this inappropriate action have been expressed through public demonstrations and written appeals by various anti-Fascist groups as well as the activist entity: Global Alliance for Justice – The Ethiopian Cause (www.globalallianceforethiopia.org).

Mausoleum for the Fascist "Butcher of Ethiopia", Rodolfo Graziani, being inaugurated at Afile, Italy in the presence of Italian officials and a representative of the Vatican. For a full report on the event, a reference to a BBC news item of August 15th would be useful.

2. Highly Inadequate Reparations and Restitution

In terms for the Fascist war crimes which resulted in one million Ethiopian victims, and other devastations, Italy managed to pay a miniscule amount of US$25 million whereas it agreed to pay $125 million to Yugoslavia, $105 million to Greece, and $100 million to the Soviet Union as well as, recently, $5 billion to Libya. The only restitution that has occurred so far is Italy's return of the Axum Obelisk to Ethiopia. The properties looted by the Fascists and currently in the possession of Italy and the Vatican have yet to be returned to the Ethiopian people. These include an airplane known as "Tsehay" looted from Ethiopia being shown at the Italian Air Force museum and the over 500 manuscripts found at the Vatican library.

It is obvious that the blood of Ethiopian martyrs is still crying for justice from the international community including the United Nations, Italy and the Vatican.

With regard to the major Fascist criminal, Benito Mussolini, he was subjected to a form of justice by Italian partisans and was hanged upside down along with his mistress, Glara Petacci, at Mazzegra, Italy on April 28, 1945.

CHAPTER 10: Vatican's Complicity with the Facists

The Trigger

My concern with the Fascist war crimes in Ethiopia and the Vatican's complicity dates back to my younger days when I was told stories by my father about the war he participated in Eastern Ethiopia, the Ogaden. My recent engagement with the Ethiopian cause for justice was triggered by an event that occurred soon after the accession to the throne by Pope Benedict XVI who, immediately after his election as the prelate of the Catholic Church, made it his primary duty to travel to his home country, Germany, and visit a synagogue in Nuremburg where he was reported to have stated that the Nazi holocaust against the Jews was an unimaginable crime. This created, in my mind, an irresistible urge to submit a letter of appeal dated August 18, 2005 to His Holiness reminding him about one other issue that has been awaiting justice for a long time and that the Ethiopian people deserved a Vatican apology. Please see Annex 1. Unfortunately, I never received a response and Pope Benedict XVI is in retirement as I write this book.

Vatican's Complicity with the Fascists

It is always a source of wonder as to how it was possible for the most populous Christian entity i.e. the Catholic Church could form a partnership with a highly criminal political organization, the Fascist Party applying an inhuman political system in Italy as well as the nation it had invaded, namely, Ethiopia and its colonial empire i.e. Libya, Eritrea, and Somalia. Although there are some who deny this fact such as the journalist/author, Zewdie Retta, in his

Pope Pius XI

book entitled: "Ye Haile Selassie Mengist" (translation: The Government of Haile Selassie), the fact on the basis of the abundant evidence, remains that the Vatican was definitely complicit with Mussolini and his Fascist Party.

The Vatican's complicity with the Fascists commenced in 1922 when Pope Pius XI and Mussolini started moves towards laying down concrete steps for collaboration in a mutually beneficial manner. There are numerous sources of evidence proving beyond any reasonable doubt as to Pope Pius XI's and the Vatican's complicity with the Fascists. The following are provided as examples:

1. Avro Manhattan, "The Vatican in World Politics",[1]:

   a. Cardinal Ratti was elected as Pope Pius XI in 1922.

   b. After his coronation, Pope Pius XI..."who had no love for democracy.....steered the political helm unhesitatingly towards the new (Fascist) Party, making overtures by rendering it a great service....." On October 2, 1922, the Vatican issued a circular letter.... bidding the clergy not to identify themselves with the Catholic Party thereby paving the way for a national recognition of Fascism. Following the dissolution of its own Catholic Party, the Vatican, under the leadership of Pope Pius XI, joined hands with Mussolini's Fascist party in finally getting rid of the Socialist, and Liberal parties in Italy. By 1926, "....The Fascist Government became what it had wanted to be – the First Fascist totalitarian dictatorship."

   c. "The negotiations which significantly enough, were started with the dissolution of the Catholic Party in 1926 were concluded in 1929 with the signing of what has since been known as the Lateran Agreement by which the Vatican was recognized as an independent sovereign state, and the Fascists Government undertook to pay a vast sum of money as compensation." The Agreement was acclaimed by the Catholic Church and Catholics throughout the world, and the prestige of Fascism was greatly enhanced. The Lateran Agreement, therefore, provided the foundation for the close collaboration between Pope Pius XI and Mussolini paving the way for the Fascist dictatorship in Italy as well as its unbridled subsequent international adventures including its invasion of Ethiopia.

   d. Mussolini's response was to arrange the payment of 1,500,000,000 lire to the Bank of Rome which was on the brink of bankruptcy at the time. The Bank of Rome was under the control of the Catholics, and the funds of the Vatican's High Prelates and the Holy See itself were entrusted to it.

e. "It was the alliance of these two men, Pius XI and Mussolini, that influenced so greatly the social and political pattern, not only of Italy, but also of the rest of Europe in the years between the two world wars."

f. Once the Lateran Agreement was signed and the Vatican achieved its financial and political objectives with the Fascists, it vigorously undertook its share of promoting the Fascists within Italy as well as internationally:

i. Cardinal Vannutelli, Head of the Sacred College of Cardinals paid a public homage to Mussolini by stating: "….that the Duce (Mussolini) had been chosen (by God) to save the nation and to restore her fortune."

ii. On February 13, 1929, Pope Pius XI "proclaimed to the world that Mussolini was "the man whom Divine Providence" had allowed him to meet…."

iii. All priests were ordered to pray daily for the King and the Duce ("Pro Rege et Duce").

iv. "….children had to say grace before each meal: a typical example: "Duce, I thank you for what you give me to make me grow healthy and strong. O Lord God, protect the Duce so that he may be long preserved for Fascist Italy".

v. "Thus the Church became the religious weapon of the Facist State, while the Fascist State became the secular arm of the Church. The Vatican had at last gathered the fruit of its new policy—annihilation of its great enemies (Secularism, Liberalism, Freemasonry, Socialism, Communism, Democracy); and restoration of the Catholic Church as the predominant spiritual power in the land."

g. "He (Mussolini) had a plan for the success of which the help of the Catholic church was needed. And in 1935 the first of a series of successive Fascist aggressions which finally led to the outbreak of the Second World War was ruthlessly carried out: Fascist Italy attacked and occupied Abyssinia."

h. "After the conquest of Abyssinia, the Pope expressed his joy in his speech of May 12, 1936 by stating: "……the triumphant joy of an entire, great and good people over a peace which, it is hoped and in-

The Lateran Treaty being signed by Benito Mussolini and Cardinal Gasparri

tended, will be an effective contribution and prelude to the true peace in Europe and the world."

i. Catholic countries' representatives at the League of Nations were directed not to vote against Fascist Italy.

j. The Italian Papal Legate, Cardinal Gasparri, the Bishops of San Minato, Nocera Umlara, Civita Castellana, Milan, and Naples blessed the Fascist invasion of Ethiopia.

k. The Archbishop of Tarano declared: " The war against Ethiopia should be considered as a holy war, a crusade" because the Italian victory would "open Ethiopia, a country of infidels and schismatics, to the expansion of the Catholic faith."*

l. "Many bishops and priests led the offering by giving to the Fascists the jewelry and gold belonging to their churches."

m. "Fascist armies were immediately followed by priests, missionaries, nuns, and Catholic organizations."

2. *It is surprising that the Archbishop of Tarano alleged Ethiopians to be "infidels and schismatics". He should have known that according to the bible, The Acts, chapter 8 vs 26-39, it was an Ethiopian that was christened so soon after the resurrection of Jesus Christ (in the year 34 AD according to the traditions of the Ethiopian Orthodox Tewahedo Church). What were the ancestors of the Archbishop doing in those days? Was it not the Romans who inflicted so much suffering and finally hanged Jesus Christ. Did Pilate's (the then Roman Governor of Israel) washing his hands absolve him from causing the historic injustice? On top of all that was it not the Romans that, for a number of years, persecuted and killed Christians including some of the highly renowned disciples?

3. T.L Gardini[2]

Cardinal Schuster of Milan stated: "The Italian (Fascist) flag is at the moment bringing in triumph the Cross of Christ in Ethiopia, to free the road for the emancipation of the slaves, opening it at the same time to our missionary and propaganda."

4. Teeling,[3]

"Practically without exception the whole world condemned Mussolini, all except the Pope (Pius XI)."

5. Slavembini[4] 7 Italian Cardinals, 29 Archbishops, and 61 bishops gave immediate support to the aggression (against Ethiopia).

6. Corriere della Sera, January 10, 1938

In his address to archbishops, bishops and priests, Mussolini admired: "the efficient cooperation given by the clergy during the war against the Abyssinians…remembering with particular sympathy the example of patriotism shown by Italian bishops, who brought their gold to the local office of the Fascist Party…"[5]

7. Manchester Guardian, February 12, 1929: "Pope Pius XI is credited with much admiration for Mussolini. That the Italian clergy as a whole are pro-Fascist is easy to understand, seeing that Fascism is antinationalist, authoritarian, anti-liberal, and anti-Socialist force."[6]

8. Martindale, the Jesuit scholar representing the Pope, confirmed that the secretary of state at the Vatican, Eugenio Cardinal Pacelli (later Pope Pius XII), offered Haile Selassie 1 million (Sterling Pounds) on behalf of Italy in return for his abdication."[7]

9. Sbacchi continued to state: "Bishop Andre Marie Elie Jarosseau, Haile Selassie's former tutor and a man who had influence over him, also invited the exiled ruler to recognize Italian sovereignty over Ethiopia. By submitting to Italy he could rule with Italian consent." P. 124 (Sbacchi's sources: "Times (London), 29 April 1938; Le Petit Parisien, 22 August 1939; La Garonne, 22 August 1939; Bernoville, Monseigneur Jarosseau et la Mission des Gallas, p. 360" p. 127)[8]

10. New York Times, February 13, 1937: "Earlier today the Pontiff (Pope Pius XI) had given his recognition of Italian sovereignty over Ethiopia by bestowing his apostolic benediction upon Victor Emmanuel as "King of Italy and Emperor of Ethiopia."[9]

11. Statement by an eye-witness, Dr. Syoum Gebregziabher, author of "Symphony of my Life", 2012:

"From my book you can note, how one of the Catholic priests took the personal responsibility to entice me to be a priest! How we the seminarians marched outside Harar in a heavily Moslem country protected by Fashist military to attend church every week! Picture P. 63. This was a clear policy of the Catholic Church in support of Fascism. The establishment of "Collegio Ethiopico" within the Vatican compound was to train and indoctrinate Ethiopian seminarians. We were then told that if we become good potential priests, we will be eligible to go to Rome for further education (indoctrination). There was a definite crusade to propagate Catholicism in Ethiopia with the help of fascism based on Aparthaid policy I had faced on my way to priesthood!"

In addition, Dr. Syoum Gebregziabher stated in his letter to me dated July 19, 2012:

> "...In 1948 my uncle Gebremeskel Habtemariam (Dejasmach) mentioned in the book; not only protested the Vatican collaboration with Mussolini; but officially dropped his Catholicism and joined and embraced the Ethiopian Orthodox Church!"

12. Contrary to the abundance of evidence proving Pope Pius XI's complicity with Mussolini and the Fascists, Zewdie Retta claims,[10] that the Pope, in his speech to graduating nurses, expressed, as an aside to his formal speech a statement to the effect that he objected to Italy's invasion of Ethiopia. However, in addition to the evidence provided above, Rev Dr. Mikre-Sellassie G/Ammanuel quotes Gaetano Salvemini, in his book:

> "To anyone reading without close attention, Pius XI's address to the nurses gives an impression of condemning not only war but also this particular war as an abominable crime. In actual fact it does not condemn the imminent war. It condones it as a war of self-defense. In addition it puts in a plea for indulgence and leniency should Mussolini, in the exercise of his rights of self-defense, exceed the limits of moderation."[11]

13. In his book: "Church and Mission in Ethiopia During The Italian Occupation", 2014, p.149, Rev. Dr. Mikre-Sellassie G/Amanuel states further:

> "...the Pope very clearly expressed his love and wholehearted support to Italy and the Fascist Government"[12]

14. Another eyewitness account by the 97-year old, General Lema Gabremariam, a participant in the war at Maichew in 1936 states, in his open letter to Pope Francis I:

> " ... the battle of Maichew, 1936... was my first experience

of war. I witnessed the deadly poison gas, yperite raining from aircrafts, which was a routine of the Fascist warfare. As a result of the acidic-rain, my eyes were affected and I was nearly blinded and made unconscious.

…When I regained my consciousness, I found myself in the middle of heaps of dead bodies of humans and pack animals…..

There are proofs that some (Vatican) Cardinals and clergy rallied behind fascism, among them the Cardinal of Milan, Alfredo Ildefons Schucter. In addition to his anti Ethiopia campaign, the Cardinal was photographed with war generals and others next to tanks, machineguns, and the army, which were on their way to invade Ethiopia.

15. Karlheinz Deschner, "God and the Fascists", 2013, p. 44:

   "Even Catholic papers flatly admitted that Pisus XI had permitted colonial war. The conscience of the world condemned Italy's vigorous approach." Gert Buchheit also wrote in 1938: "What did the Papacy do? ….The Church demanded that the bishops hand in their gold crosses and chains…..Yes, the Pope even gave the Duce (Mussolini) the frozen assets in Germany so that Italy could purchase the necessary raw materials…"

16. David I Kertzer, "The Pope and Mussolini", 2014, pp405/6:

   "The Vatican (Pope Pius XI) played a central role both in making the Fascist regime possible and in keeping it in power…..The central player in the effort to keep Pope Pius XI (in check) was Cardinal Eugenio Pacelli – later Pope Pius XII."

17. Jeff Pearce, "Prevail", 2014, pp117/8:

   "…By mid-September (1935), Eugenio Pacelli, Cardinal Secretary of State (and later Pius XII) sent word to Musolini that the Pope (Pius XI) would not stand in the way of an invasion

(of Ethiopia). As Professor Christopher Duggan noted in
Fascist Voices, "The Church provided overwhelming backing for the war, with seven cardinals, twenty-nine archbishops, and seventy-five bishops offering public endorsements
to the press."

From the preponderance of the evidence provided above, there should be
no doubt whatsoever that Pope Pius XI and the Fascist Mussolini were in
league in the Fascist aggressions including the invasion and the war crimes in
Ethiopia. Therefore, the campaign for a formal and public Vatican apology as
well as the restitution of properties such as 500 documents presently in its custody to the Ethiopian people is fully justified. For more details, please see:
www.globalallianceforethiopia.org.

It should be recalled here that the evidence listed above was used by me
for the letter by the Global Alliance for Justice – The Ethiopian Cause addressed to His Holiness Pope Francis I dated July 10, 2015 appealing for the
Vatican's apology to the Ethiopian people. The letter was submitted following
His Holiness' apology to the Latin American people on July 9, 2015 during
his visit to the continent.

The Vatican has also apologized to the Jewish people repeatedly. It has
also recognized the Turkish genocide on the Armenian people. With its recent
apology to the Latin American people, the question arises as to when the Vatican would apologize to the African people in Ethiopia.

Annex 1

4002 Blacksmith Drive
Garland, TX 75044.
August 18, 2005.

Open Letter to His Holiness Pope Benedict XVI
The Vatican.

Your Holiness,

These days, the news is replete with Your Holiness' admirable owning up to your country, Germany's previous crimes against humanity during the Nazi period. It is remarkable that you have taken such a courageous step so early in your leadership of the most populated Christian organization on earth. Your Holiness deserves every accolade for the step you have taken as it exemplifies the true role of a spiritual leader. I pray that current leaders will learn from your example.

The fact that Your Holiness has seen fit to promote the important concept of taking responsibility for crimes committed even in historic contexts gives hope to other peoples throughout the world who were victims of such atrocious acts. Here I am referring to heinous crimes committed by Fascist Italy which, as Your Holiness is aware, was responsible for the murder of thousands of Ethiopians on the eve of and during the Second World War. Of the thousands of Ethiopians murdered by the Fascists were my grandfather, Grazmach (Ethiopian title) Gessesse Fanta, and my uncle, Merid Gessesse.

The relevance of the above tragic episode to Your Holiness now is the fact that when the Fascist army was about to set sail on its murderous voyage to Ethiopia, the then head of the Catholic Church, His Holiness Pope Pius XI gave them his blessing to go forth and commit their inhuman crimes. His Holiness declared, on December 20, 1926 that "Mussolini (was) the man sent by Providence." On August 27, 1935, His Holiness declared that the fascist aggression against Ethiopia was a "defensive war"! (Manhattan, Avro, The Vatican in World Politics, 1949) It is ironic that the Pope was blessing his seemingly Christian army to go and commit crimes against innocent Ethiopian Christians. Ethiopians including myself have been waiting, in vain, for the type of apology that Your Holiness and the German people and government have so magnanimously expressed to the Nazi victims.

I feel sure that Your Holiness would not differentiate between the crimes committed by the Nazis and Fascists and their respective victims especially in the context of His Holiness Pope Pius XI's direct responsibility for the tragic episode. Therefore, I plead with Your Holiness to finally enable Ethiopians to put the matter to rest by offering a full and formal apology to our nation for the unholy blessing given by Pope Pius XI to the Fascist Army which perpetrated heinous crimes against Ethiopians including the use of poison gas.

"Ethiopia shall raise its hands unto God." (Psalm 68:31)

Yours respectfully,

Kidane Alemayehu
A Christian

CHAPTER 11: Global Alliance for Justice— The Ethiopian Cause (GAJEC)

(www.globalallianceforethiopia.org)
Establishment of the Alliance (GAJEC)

Soon after the dissemination, through various Ethiopia related websites, of my open letter to Pope Benedict XVI, in 2005, I was invited to be one of the speakers at an event held in Washington, DC, during March, 2006, concerning the Adowa War in 1896 between Ethiopia and Italy. My speech was focused on the second Ethiopian-Italian war during 1935-41, perpetrated by the Fascists partly as a revenge for Italy's devastating defeat by Ethiopia during the Adowa war. It was fortunate that one of the other speakers was HH Prince Ermias Sahle Selassie, the grandson of Emperor Haile Selassie I, with whom I had subsequent discussions and, to my greatest delight, I discovered that he had an abiding interest in achieving justice for Ethiopia with regard to the Fascist Italian war crimes.

We, therefore, agreed to establish an organization in collaboration with other interested individuals to fight for justice on behalf of Ethiopia. It was, in fact, HH Prince Ermias that came up with a name for the organization i.e. Global Alliance for Justice – The Ethiopian Cause. It was eventually agreed to adopt the website name, www.globalallianceforethiopia.org. Wolette Selassie, helped in the design of the following logo:

In 2014, GAJEC's leadership comprised:

HH Prince Ermias Sahle Selassie, Chairman
Dr. Aklilu Habte, Member

H.H. Prince Ermias Sahle Selassie, President of the Ethiopian Crown Council And Chairman of the Global Alliance for Justice – The Ethiopian Cause

Dr. Getatchew Haile, Member
Dr. Jon Levy, Member
Dr. Girma Abebe, Member
Dr. Astair Gebremariam, Member
Dr. Mikael Wossen, Member
Mr. Nicola DeMarco, Member
Dr. Steve Delamarter, Member
Kidane Alemayehu, Executive Diretor

N.B. Ms. Imani Kali-Nyah was also a participant during the Alliance's formative years.

GAJEC's Objectives
GAJEC's main objectives were the following:

1. Adequate reparations by the Italian Government to the Ethiopian people for the war crimes it committed in Ethiopia;
2. A Vatican apology to the Ethiopian people for its complicity with Fascist Italy;
3. Restitution of Ethiopian properties looted from Ethiopia and currently in the custody of both the Vatican and the Italian Governments;
4. The inclusion of the Fascist war crimes in the historic records of the United Nations; and
5. The removal of the Graziani monument established at Affile, southeast of Rome.

GAJEC's Main Activities
Since its establishment in 2006, GAJEC has been engaged in various activities, the main ones of which were the following:

1. Diplomatic advocacy efforts. Efforts have been exerted, through high level diplomatic, advocacy efforts in order to achieve GAJEC's objectives.
2. International Campaigns:
   GAJEC has been campaigning internationally, in various forms, in commemoration of the "Yekatit 12" (February 19th) event when Fascist Italy, led by Mussolini and Rodolfo Graziani, massacred 30,000 Ethiopians within only three days in Addis Ababa, in 1937. The com-

memoration event has been taking place annually in collaboration with supporters in numerous countries, through public demonstrations, meetings, and/or prayers. The campaign in February, 2014 was undertaken in 30 cities throughout the world: Addis Ababa, Amsterdam, Atlanta, Aurora, Boston, Chicago, Cologn, Dallas, Denver, Dubai, Houston, Jamaica Jerusalem, Kingston, Las Vegas, London, Los Angeles, Miami, Minnesotta, Munich, New York, Rome, Seattle, Sidney, Stockholm, Tampa, Tel Aviv, The Hague, Vancouver, Washington, DC. In cities such as Atlanata, Washington, DC, and New York public demonstrations took place in front of the Italian Embassy or Consulate. In Addis Ababa, two types of public demonstrations took place in February, 2013: one organized by the Ethiopian Patriots Association in front of the statue commemorating the victims of the Fascist massacre, commonly known as "Sedest Kilo", whereas a public demonstration that was organized by the "Semayawi" Party to take place in front of the Italian Embassy was cut short after the detention of the participants by the Ethiopian Government's security forces. The detainees were released the following day but the controversy as to the justification of the detention is still not resolved.

Another development that has given rise to a great deal of hope is a documentary film, "If only I Were that Warrior" that has been produced by Valerio Ciriaci, an Italian, and his partners relating to the historic as well as the current situation concerning the Fascist war crimes in Ethiopia. It is anticipated that the dissemination of the film on a global basis will enhance awareness about the Ethiopian cause.

3. Prospects for collaboration with Armenian Activists

Initiatives for collaboration with Armenian activists such as the Armenian American Committee have commenced. It is recalled that the Ottoman Empire had committed a crime of genocide on 1.5 million Armenians during 1915-23.

A century later, the Armenians have achieved effective results. The European Union (EU) Parliament and the Vatican have accorded a formal recognition to the crime of genocide committed by the Turks against the Armenians. In addition, the Armenian Church has launched a legal action in Turkey against the Turkish government for the restitution of its church and monastery located in southern Turkey's region of Adana. Furthermore, Armenian professionals have initiated a comprehensive study on the reparations they consider are due to the Armenian people and have submitted a report in which it is claimed that US$3 Trillion is owed to Armenia by Turkey, Germany, Italy, US, France, England, Russia, Kurds, Austro-Hungary, and Israel. For details, the reader is advised to check the following link: http://armeniangenocidelosses.am/

4. Letter to the European Parliament
A letter of petition by GAJEC, through its legal representative, Dr. Jonathan Levy, to the European Parliament, (Annex 1) had a response from the parliament in a letter dated March 27, 2013 stating "the petition has been entered in the general register under number 0265/2013;" that it has been forwarded to the Committee on Petitions; and that it will be considered if it will be found admissible." Annex 2. The Alliance has been awaiting a response.

5. Collaboration with the Ethiopian Patriots Association (EPA)
GAJEC has been in communication with the EPA for over five years although intermittently. In general, it can be stated that on the basis of its demonstrated activities so far, EPA is restrained to deal with merely some aid to a few patriots as well as focusing on historic issues such as the annual commemoration of February 19, 1937 Fascist massacre of 30,000 people in Addis Ababa. However, under the new leadership in 2014, it is hoped that EPA would engage in all aspects of the quest for justices for Ethiopia.

6. The Institute of Ethiopian Studies
The Institute of Ethiopian Studies used to conduct symposia on the February 19th memorial day. In the February 19th, 2012 event, I was invited to participate as one of the speakers. It was not without some surprise that the other speakers presented, again, the historic facts about the Fascist invasion and atrocities that took place in Ethiopia but not any demand for justice for the Ethiopian people. I was allowed to present GAJEC's usual demands for the justice still owing to the Ethiopian people from Italy, the Vatican, and the United Nations. It was interesting to note that soon after the 2012 symposium, the head of the Institute was dismissed. I have not had a confirmation as to whether his dismissal had anything to do with my presentation at the symposium. Another interesting development was the fact that the Institute did not conduct its usual symposium during 2013, 2014 and 2015.

7. Ethiopian Orthodox Tewahedo Church (EOTC)
The other Ethiopian entity that had been victimized by the Fascists

and should, therefore, be in the forefront of the international struggle for justice on behalf of Ethiopia is the EOTC. It is well known that the Fascists' destructive policy had singled out EOTC among the ones to destroy in Ethiopia in order to facilitate its colonial policy as well as the Vatican's objective of converting Ethiopians to the Catholic faith. As a result, 2,000 churches were destroyed; over 2000 monks and parishioners were massacred at the famous Debre Libanos monastery; numerous EOTC properties were looted of which 500 documents can still be seen in the custody of the Vatican; etc. It is known that EOTC Bishops Petros and Michael were killed by the Fascists. GAJEC has attempted to encourage EOTC to act in the pursuit of the justice that has been outstanding for so long. It is hoped that the EOTC will act on behalf of the justice that is still owing to the church which is estimated to have over 40 million adherents in 2013.

8. Other Relevant Ethiopian Organizations and Institutions
    It is a source of great encouragement and hope that Dr. Yacob Haile-mariam, a renowned activist as well as a popular political party, namely, Semayawi had risen to the occasion and paid the sacrifice in the campaign for justice for Ethiopia. Their attempt to demonstrate in front of the Italian Embassy in Addis Ababa was cut short due to their one-day detention. On the other hand, relevant political and civic organizations and institutions need to exert an enhanced effort to campaign against the Fascist war crimes that continue to cry for justice on behalf of Ethiopia. Some personal expressions by members of opposition entities are to the effect that their efforts should be merely focused on the current challenges. Such a policy or an attitude is, to say the least, quite sad and myopic as ignoring past crimes such as the Fascist genocide in Ethiopia that has no statute of limitations, is tantamount to absolving the criminal without paying the dues and even inviting subsequent attacks. It should not be forgotten that in the case of Ethiopia, it was attacked by Italy twice so far: in 1896 when it was defeated at the war of Adwa; and, later, its occupation of Ethiopia during 1935-41. The international community including Italy, the Vatican, and the United Nations are absolutely quiet about the second war crimes in Ethiopia. The silence on the part of Ethiopian political and civic organizations with regard to the Fascist

war crimes in Ethiopia is a highly questionable policy that should be reconsidered and corrected as a matter of urgency.

9. Other letters of appeal:

Letters of appeal have been submitted to world leaders and appropriate institutions:

a. To Pope Benedict XVI and Pope Francis I; (Annex 3)

b. To the Italian President and Prime Minister; (Annex 4)

c. To the Italian Foreign Minister; (Annex 5)

Additional letters of appeal were also submitted to:

d. To all supporters of human rights; (Annex 6)

e. To the Prime Minister of Great Britain; (Annex 7) and

f. To the Governor of Lazio, the region in which the town of Affile is located and where the monument for the Fascist Graziani was inaugurated, in the presence of a Vatican representative, on August 11, 2012. (Annex 8)

Responses were obtained from the European Union Parliament, the Vatican Embassy, in Washington, DC as well as Cardinal Berhaneyesus in Ethiopia and the Italian Embassy, in Washington, DC all promising to consider our appeal and respond but none were forthcoming by the time this book was published.

10. International Petition for a Vatican apology to the Ethiopian people: An international petition has been launched through GAJEC's website: www.globalallianceforethiopia.org demanding a public apology by the Vatican to the Ethiopian people. Over 4,500 people from over 30 countries have signed the petition. One of the petition signers, Mr. John Polifronio (No. 60 in the website's list of petition signers), a person of Italian origin, and currently residing in California, USA, has submitted the following remarks:

"I'm an Italian, born during this atrocity, and wish to express my profoundest horror that this was done by members of the government, who were from the country of my origins. No apology can possibly begin to deal with this inhumanity directed at the Ethiopian people. I'm filled with revulsion and sorrow at discovering the extent of the Italian government's involvement during the period 1935-41 in these hideously inhuman actions."

11. Media Campaigns

A substantial effort was exerted in order to enhance awareness about the Alliance's objectives and efforts. These were undertaken not only through its website but also in collaboration with important radio services such as VOA, DWelle, SBS (Australia), Hiber (Las Vegas), Dallas, Denver, etc; other Ethiopia related websites such as ECAD Forum, Zehabesha, Addisvoice, Quatero, Abugida, Ethiopia.org and others as well as other media including Ethsat. Nevertheless the need for a more exerted campaign effort still prevails especially to create awareness among the youth.

12. Strategy and Action Plan

GAJEC has established task forces for the formulation and implementation of strategies and action plans as well as task forces for the achievement of its major objectives:

a. Reparations and restitutions;

b. Vatican apology to the Ethiopian people;

c. United Nations Affairs;

d. Removal of the Graziani monument; and

e. International campaigns for February 19th Memorial Day.

13. GAJEC's Registration with UN ECOSOC

GAJEC registered (Annex 9) with the United Nations Organization called ECOSOC in 2014, in order to enable the Alliance to promote its objectives on a global basis.

14. Removal of the Graziani Mausoleum and Park

As indicated above, one of GAJEC's objectives is the removal of Graziani Mausoleum and park installed in his honour at Affile, Italy. It is important to note that, in addition to the GAJEC's own efforts, the effort by the activist support group led by Mrs. Muluwork, President of the Ethiopian Community in Rome and Mr. Carmelo Crescenti, head of the Ras Taferian group in Rome has achieved concrete results:

(a) Based on media reports, the Governor of Lazio, Mr. Nicola Zingeratti has withdrawn the financial budget from the mausoleum;

(b) Affile's mayor has been indicted for the installation of a mausoleum for Fascist Graziani.

(c) The name Graziani has apparently been withdrawn from the adjacent street.

Exodus – Ethiopian Cultural Service - Associazione della Comunità Etiopica in Italia & F.A.R.I. (Federazione delle Assemblee Rastafariane in Italia) con il patrocinio di Roma Capitale

Vi invitano a partecipare al

"GIORNO DEI MARTIRI"

SABATO 22 FEBBRAIO 2014

dalle ore 16:00 alle19:00 presso la Sala del Carroccio in Piazza del Campidoglio

In memoria del sacrificio e della lotta del popolo Etiope contro
l'aggressione dell'Italia fascista.
Interverranno:

Rev. Abba Selama *(Parroco della Chiesa Ortodossa Etiopica)*
Carmelo Crescenti *(Presidente EXODUS - E. C. S. e F.A.R.I.)*
Muluwork Ayele *(Pres. dell'Ass. della Comunità Etiopica in Italia)*
Belay Mesgina *(Nipote di un noto Patriota e Martire Etiope)*
Matteo Lollobrigida *(Comitato Antifascista di Affile)*
Carla Di Veroli *(Staff del Sindaco di Roma)*
On. Monica Gregori *(Camera dei Deputati)*
Ernesto Nassi *(Consigliere provinciale ANPI)*

Contatti e-mail:
ghebredesta@yahoo.it; comunita.etiopica@yahoo.it

ROMA
CAPITALE

Flyer announcing a meeting in Rome on the Fascist Italian aggression (Feb. 22, 2014)292

(d) The Lazio Regional Council has issued a resolution demanding that the Affile Town Council remove the name Graziani from the mausoleum within 15 days failing which the funds provided for the construction of the mausoleum would have to be refunded and additional action would be taken (for more details, please refer to www.globalallianceforethiopia.org).

However, at the time of writing this book, it was reported that the mayor of Affile has appealed both the indictment as well as the budget withdrawal. Therefore, the Alliance decided to proceed with its international campaign for the removal of the mausoleum.

It is also important to recall here that Italy's Deputy Foreign Minister had completely denied the existence if the Grazian Mausoleum, in an interview with The Reporter, during his visit to Ethiopia. The Alliance's letter to the Italian Foreign Minister seeking a clarification for such an obvious misrepresentation remains unanswered.

It can be concluded that although GAJEC has exerted a substantial effort, despite its limited capacity and based on voluntary part-time individual initiatives, the tangible outcomes still leave a lot to be desired. What has been achieved is the fact that some degree of awareness and recognition of the justice that is still owed to Ethiopia. The struggle for the achievement of concrete results in terms of adequate reparations, restitution of Ethiopian properties, a Vatican apology to the Ethiopian people, the removal of the Graziani monument as well as the inclusion of the Fascist war crimes in the United Nations' historic annals shall continue.

Annex 1

European Parliament
Committee on Petitions
The Secretariat
Rue Wiertz
B-1047 Brussels

Petition against the Resurgence of Fascism and Racism in Italy

Petitioners:

Muluwork Ayele Belay, presidente
Associazione Della Comunità Etiopica in Italia
Via Grosseto, 5 00176 Roma

Kidane Alemayehu
Global Alliance for Justice: The Ethiopian Cause,
4002 Blacksmith Drive, Garland, TX 75044, USA

Racism and xenophobia are direct violations of the principles of liberty, democracy, respect for human rights and fundamental freedoms and the rule of law, principles upon which the European Union is founded and which are common to the Member States. (EU Council Framework Decision 2008/913/JHA of 28 November 2008)

On August 11, 2012, a ceremony was held in the presence of Italian dignitaries and a Vatican representative during which a memorial was opened draped in the Italian flag to "honor" Rodolfo Graziani, one of the most heinous figures of the Second World War. This event occurred at the "Rodolfo Graziani Park and Memorial" in the little town of Affile, 50 miles east of Rome.

Rodolfo Graziani was a major war criminal, imperialist, and fascist. He promoted racial inequality and hatred throughout Europe and Africa, first as the Military Governor of Libya and Ethiopia and later as the Minister of defence of the Republic of Salò. Graziani remained loyal to Mussolini until the end of that regime in 1945. In 1948, a military tribunal sentenced Graziani to 19 years' jail, as punishment for his collaboration with the Nazis; but he was released after serving only a few months of the sentence. Now a subdivision the Italian government honoured him with a mausoleum and memorial park, built at taxpayers' expense, in a village south of Rome

In 1937, Rodolfo Graziani directed a three day massacre of over 30,000 unarmed civilians in the capital of Ethiopia upon the orders of Benito Mussolini. Over 440 Christian monks were singled out and murdered. People were dismembered and soldiers took photos of the hangings, beheadings and torture proudly alongside their dead victims. The "Graziani Massacre" is well known to every Ethiopian and virtually and disgracefully unknown to the rest of the world. Graziani, prior to arriving in Ethiopia, was named "The Butcher of Libya." In Libya, Graziani presided over concentration camps, used chemical weapons and murdered thousands of innocents for Fascism.

In Ethiopia, one million Ethiopians perished as a result of the genocidal Fascist occupation. 2,000 churches as well as 525,000 homes were destroyed. The poison gas sprayed by numerous Fascists air planes also destroyed 14 million animals and the environment. Graziani later came to be forever known as the "Butcher of Ethiopia".

Italy's own Law N° 205/1993 prohibits the dissemination of ideas based on superiority or racial and ethnic discrimination.

1. A formal inquiry was initiated in the Italian Parliament inquiring as to who gave the authority to use public money to build the monument.

2. A lawsuit has been filed by a citizen of Italy calling for the dismantlement of the Graziani monument and the conviction under the law of the mayor of the small town of Affile who approved the opening of the Graziani monument in his town only 1,562 people. This lawsuit also names as defendants regional government officials who approved the money to build and open the monument. The lawsuit states that under the Italian constitution as well as its criminal laws, it is unlawful to build a monument in honour of a Fascist.

3. The President of the province of Rome, Nicola Zingaretti, has denounced the building and opening of the Graziani monument. He has promised to dismantle it and is now running for Governor of Lazio, the region where the monument was erected. Presently, Mr. Zingaretti is delegate to the European Union from Italy as well.

4. Two public demonstrations in the town of Affile and one in the capital of Rome have taken place to denounce the Graziani monument. The group includes Ethiopians in Italy as well as veterans who fought against Mussolini and Graziani in Italy.

5. The Graziani monument has been forced to close on several occasions due to opponents writing on the walls denouncing its construction and urging all to remember the victims of Fascism and not to honour a war criminal. One recent artist posted hanging cardboard figures around the Graziani monument with each figure detailing the crimes against Ethiopians, Libyans and fellow Italians committed by Graziani.

6. In Bologna, a town in northern Italy, a public toilet was satirically "converted" into the Graziani monument meaning that the only worthwhile dedication to this war criminal is for using it as a toilet.

7. Many major Italian publications online and in print have denounced the building of the Graziani monument.

8. The largest Jewish organization in Italy has denounced the building of the Graziani monument and has called on the government to dismantle it.

9. Here in America, a gathering of Italians during late January and early February of 2013 in New York City will remember all victims of Italian Fascism with a special panel discussion on January 31 specifically focused on the Graziani monument. Leading Italian journalists will join an Ethiopian scholar on that panel.

10. Also in America, activists of Italian heritage have teamed up with Ethiopians, Jews and all people who seek justice to denounce the Graziani monument and have it dismantled. One of those Italian-Americans is Nicola Antonio DeMarco, J.D of New York who works with the Global Alliance for Justice, the Ethiopian Cause. He previously served with Dr. Richard Pankhurst on the Axum Obelisk Return Committee. On February 19, 2013, the 76th anniversary of the Graziani massacre, Italians will join Ethiopians and people of good will in front of the Italian mission to the United Nations in New York City to denounce the opening of the Graziani monument. Thirty other cities worldwide will hold similar demonstrations.

11. The Ethiopian Community in Italy, headed by Ms. Muluwork Ayele has been active in denouncing the Graziani monument. She has also met with Jewish descendents of victims of Fascism in Italy to discuss their common goal to dismantle the Graziani monument. Ms. Ayele communicates daily with Italian-American activists as well updating all on the latest.

12. After the Graziani monument was opened, the entire regional government of Lazio where the small town of Affile lies, was forced to resign due to a massive corruption scandal. The former governor, Polvernini, who was also part of that mass resignation later, claimed she was against the authorization of public money to build the Graziani monument and that if she could have

done anything to stop its opening, she would have. Very few people believe her story but even in her lying we can see that there is no public official in Italy, except the mayor of Affile, willing to defend using over 130,000 Euros to build a monument to a convicted war criminal and Fascist.

13. Associations including the Anti-Fascist Committee of Affile (comitato affile antifascista) ANED (Italian Association of Deportees), ANPI (Association of Resistance Partisans) and UCEI (Union of the Italian Jewish Communities) have made formal requests to remove the monument.

14. Anti fascist demonstrations are scheduled to continue in America, the Caribbean, Africa, Asia and Europe to protest the Graziani Memorial.

Despite our demand the President of Italy and its Prime Minster refuse to act to close this disgraceful xenophobic and racist monument to one of the leading fascists and imperialists of the 20th Century.

Italy must also fulfil its obligations to restore all looted Ethiopian properties, specifically the Italian government has refused several reasonable request to account for the The Ethiopian Aeroplane "Tsehai" commonly known as the "The Aeroplane of the Negus" and its associated records. The Tsehai is the property of the Ethiopian Crown and was looted from Ethiopia circa 1937 by Italian forces during the occupation of that country and subsequently came into the possession of the Italian National Air Force Museum.

Pursuant to Article 37 of the Italian Peace Treaty of 1947, this property ought to have been restored to the Ethiopian Crown but was overlooked by both Ethiopian and Italian authorities. The Crown however has never relinquished its claim to this property which we have learned is now in storage at the Museo Storico di Vigna di Valle.

The airplane in question is not only the property of the Ethiopian Crown but holds historical and cultural significance to Ethiopia and for all Africans as it was the first airplane assembled in Africa by an independent African state.

Our repeated requests to the Italian government have gone unheeded.

Finally several ancient Ethiopian manuscripts were deposited with the Vatican Library for safekeeping by Enrico Cerulli, a scholar but also a former fascist governor in Ethiopia. These manuscripts were looted by Cerulli during the Italian occupation thus he could not have obtained legal title to them. The Vatican Library catalogue lists these items thusly: Osvaldo Raineri, "Enrico Cerulli: Inventario dei Manoscritti CerulliEtiopici," (Studi e Testi, no. 420) Citta del Vaticano, Biblioteca Apostolica Vaticana, 2004.

The Vatican Library has refused our requests for an accounting of these cultural artefacts.

We call upon the European Parliament to denounce the resurgence of fascism, xenophobia and racism in Italy and to request that Italy takes measures to close down the Graziani memorial and return Ethiopian cultural property from the Museo Storico di Vigna di Valle and assist with the resolution of the stolen artefacts at the Vatican Library.

DATE: 14-02-2013

Dr. Jonathan Levy
Legal Representative for Petitioners

Global Alliance for Justice

The Ethiopian Cause

Annex 2

PARLAMENTO EUROPEO   EVROPSKÝ PARLAMENT   EUROPA-PARLAMENTET
EUROPÄISCHES PARLAMENT   EUROOPA PARLAMENT   ΕΥΡΩΠΑΪΚΟ ΚΟΙΝΟΒΟΥΛΙΟ   EUROPEAN PARLIAMENT
PARLEMENT EUROPÉEN   PARLAMENTO EUROPEO   EIROPAS PARLAMENTS
EUROPOS PARLAMENTAS   EURÓPAI PARLAMENT   IL-PARLAMENT EWROPEW   EUROPEES PARLEMENT
PARLAMENT EUROPEJSKI   PARLAMENTO EUROPEU   EURÓPSKY PARLAMENT
EVROPSKI PARLAMENT   EUROOPAN PARLAMENTTI   EUROPAPARLAMENTET

Directorate-General for the Presidency
Directorate for Plenary Sittings
Reception and Referral of
Official Documents Unit

Luxembourg,

104229   27.03.2013

Mr Jonathan Levy
Office Unit 7810
P.O. Box 6945
LONDON
W1A 6US
ROYAUME-UNI

Dear Sir,

I am writing on behalf of the Secretary-General to thank you for your petition sent by e-mail of 15.02.2013.

Your petition has been entered in the general register under number 0265/2013; I should be grateful if you would mention this number in any further correspondence.

It has been forwarded to the Committee on Petitions, which will first decide whether it is admissible; it is considered admissible if it comes within the European Union's fields of activity. The substance of your petition will be considered only if this is the case.

You will receive written notice directly from the Committee on Petitions to inform you whether your petition is admissible.

However, you should note that, because of the large number of petitions received, the procedure for consideration of a petition can take a relatively long time.

For any correspondence on this case, would you make direct contact with the Committee on Petitions secretariat, European Parliament, Rue Wiertz, B-1047 Brussels (fax no 0032/22846844).

Yours sincerely,

Gabriel SANCHEZ RODRIGUEZ

Head of Unit

Annex 3

October 26, 2013

OPEN LETTER:

To His Holiness Pope Francis I
From: Kidane Alemayehu
Subject: **Application of Justice to Fascist Rodolfo Graziani Similar to Nazi Erich Priebke**

Your Holiness,

Please permit me, Your Holiness, to express my respectful regards and to submit this humble appeal for justice for your consideration. I hope and pray that Your Holiness will grace me with your kind response unlike the Vatican's stunning silence concerning my previous letter dated August 18, 2005 to His Holiness Pope Benedict XVI and the other one to Your Holiness dated February 14, 2013.

I have the honour to refer here to the AP (Associated Press) report dated October 14, 2013 in the various media concerning Your Holiness' decision to forbid a church funeral in the city of Rome for the recently deceased Nazi war criminal, Erich Priebke. It is interesting to note that according to the same AP report, the Foreign Minister of Argentina, Mr. Hector Timerman has also decided that Priebke's remains would not be allowed to be buried in the latter's adopted homeland, Argentina's territory. The report has also stated that Rome's Mayor and Chief of Police have forbidden the Nazi SS criminal, Erich Priebke's funeral from taking place in Rome.

It is well known that Erich Priebke was a former SS who participated in the massacre of 335 civilians in Italy.

The Vatican's decision not to allow a church funeral for the Nazi criminal indicates that it has a clear policy of justice with regard to former war criminals. I, therefore, humbly and respectfully applaud Your Holiness' directive on the issue.

I should, however, bring to Your Holiness' kind attention that a worse war criminal has been honoured, **in the presence of a Vatican representative**, with a mausoleum inaugurated, in his name, in Italy, at a town called Affile. I am referring here to the "Butcher of Ethiopia", Rodolfo Graziani, who, as I feel sure, Your Holiness is aware was responsible for the massacre of one million Ethiopians of whom 30,000 were murdered within three days in the city of Addis Ababa in 1937. It is well known that Graziani used mustard poison gas and other arms as well as the use of hanging some patriots while cutting others' heads off. Among the numerous victims of the Fascist war crimes were Abune Petros and Abune Michael, both of whom were bishops of the Ethiopian Orthodox Tewahedo Church as well as over 400 monks and nuns at the Debre Libanos Monastery in Ethiopia. The Fascist army is also responsible for the destruction of 2,000 churches, 525,000 homes and 14 million animals in Ethiopia. Mention should also be made of the fact that huge quantities of Ethiopian properties were looted from Ethiopia including over 500 documents currently in the possession of the Vatican.

The BBC report of August 15, 2012 entitled: "Italy memorial to Fascist Hero Graziani sparks row" states:

> "The mayor of the village of Affile attended the opening ceremony on Saturday, together with a representative from the Vatican."…
>
> "Graziani was honoured with a mausoleum and memorial park, built at taxpayer's expense, in a village south of Rome." (Affile)…
>
> "He (Graziani) was a notorious as Benito Mussolini's military commander in colonial wars in Ethiopia and Libya where he carried out massacres and used chemical weapons."

It is obvious that if the Vatican would not allow a church funeral in the city of Rome for a Nazi war criminal who was responsible for the massacre of 335 people, the Holy See should apply the same principle of justice by not being party to an action that honoured a worse Fascist, namely, Rodolfo Graziani who committed a much more devastating war crime on humanity in Ethiopia.

I, therefore, submit this fervent appeal to Your Holiness so that the Vatican would express a consistent policy against war criminals be they Nazis or Fascists by calling on the Italian Government for the removal of the Graziani monument or renaming it to a true anti-Fascist patriot. I also take this opportunity to call on Your Holiness to facilitate the Vatican's apology to the Ethiopian people for its complicity with the Fascists in terms of the Lateran

Fascist atrocity in Ethiopia

A Vatican priest blessing the Fascist Army

Treaty between Mussolini and the Vatican as well as the blessing of the Fascist army by the Vatican. Since the Vatican has apologized repeatedly to the Jewish people for no other reason than for its silence during the Nazi holocaust, there is no reason why the Vatican should not perform its Christian duty of apologizing to the Ethiopian people for its unbridled support of the Fascist invasion and war crimes in Ethiopia.

The restitution of Ethiopian properties currently in the Vatican's possession to the rightful owners i.e. Ethiopians is another important Christian obligation required from the Vatican.

I also take this privilege to call, by copy of this appeal, upon the United Nations to include the Fascist war crimes in Ethiopia in its historic annals as well as the Italian Government to render adequate reparations for the Fascist war crimes in Ethiopia, return the properties looted from Ethiopia as well as to remove the mausoleum installed at Affile for the Fascist war criminal, Rodolfo Graziani.

With my utmost respect,

Kidane Alemayehu
Executive Director

CC: Prime Minister Hailemariam Dessalegn, Ethiopia; and Chairman of the African Union
CC: Prime Minister Enrico Letta, Italy
CC: President Barack Obama, USA
CC: Secretary-General Ban Ki-moon, United Nations
CC: Commissioner Nils Muiznieks, Human Rights, Council of Europe
CC: Governor Nicola Zingaretti, Lazio Region, Italy

Annex 4

Global Alliance for Justice:
The Ethiopian Cause

4002 Blacksmith Drive, Garland, TX 75044, U.S.A.

February 7, 2013

Al Presidente della Repubblica Italiana
On.le Dott. Giorgio Napolitano
Palazzo del Quirinale
00187 Roma
Italy

H.E. Mr. Mario Monti
President of the Council of Ministers
Piazza Colonna, 370
00187 Rome
Italy

Your Excellencies:

The Global Alliance for Justice – The Ethiopian Cause presents its compliments to the Honorable President Giorgio Napolitano, and the Honorable Prime Minister Mario Monti of Italy.

Our Alliance recalls, with deep appreciation, the long and historic relations between our two nations, Ethiopia and Italy, and wishes to draw Your Excellencies' kind attention to the recent action by the Italian Government of establishing a memorial and an adjoining "park" for the notorious Fascist war criminal and genocidist, Rodolfo Graziani.

As we have previously written to you in September of 2012, Your Excellencies are aware that on August 11, 2012, a ceremony was held in the presence of a Vatican representative during which a memorial was opened draped in the Italian flag to "honor" Rodolfo Graziani, one of the most heinous figures of the Second World War.

Global Alliance for Justice: The Ethiopian Cause,
4002 Blacksmith Drive, Garland, TX 75044, U.S.A.

Italy has long been a supporter of the victims of Nazism and Fascism thus this incredible insult to the memory of over 1 million Ehtiopian victims of genocide is incomprehensible. Even more appalling is the lack of official action and condemnation of the Graziani memorial. We, therefore, demand, in the name of justice and respect for human rights and humanity, that the Italian government dismantle this outrageous memorial and adjoining "park" immediately.

In 1937, Rodolfo Graziani directed a three day massacre of over 30,000 unarmed civilians in the capital of Ethiopia upon the orders of Benito Mussolini. Over 440 Christian monks were singled out and murdered. People were dismembered and soldiers took photos of the hangings, beheadings and torture proudly alongside their dead victims. The "Graziani Massacre" is well known to every Ethiopian and virtually and disgracefully unknown to the rest of the world. Graziani, prior to arriving in Ethiopia, was named "The Butcher of Libya." In Libya, Graziani presided over concentration camps, used chemical weapons and murdered thousands of innocents for Fascism.

In Ethiopia, one million Ethiopians perished as a result of the genocidal Fascist occupation. 2,000 churches as well as 525,000 homes were destroyed. The poison gas sprayed by numerous Fascists air planes also destroyed 14 million animals and the environment. Gaziani later came to be forever known as the "Butcher of Ethiopia".

Humanity will never forget the victims of genocide under Fascism including those tortured and lynched in the Graziani Massacre.

Italy has achieved a great deal since the defeat of Fascism, including making enduring peace efforts with former enemies like Ethiopia. Former Italian President Oscar Scalfaro's 1997 visit to Ethiopia is an example. That year, President Scalfaro formally apologized to the Ethiopian people for the invasion and promised meaningful cooperation including the return of looted artifacts (some of irreplaceable national significance) to Ethiopia. While better trade relations and foreign assistance has healed some of the wounds of war, the death and destruction at the hands of Mussolini's forces in Ethiopia during 1936-41 remain largely unaddressed.

Global Alliance for Justice: The Ethiopian Cause,
4002 Blacksmith Drive, Garland, TX 75044, U.S.A.

Today, Italy must immediately act to halt a handful of right-wing extremists from ruining Italy's international reputation and credibility. No park or memorial should be named in honor of Rodolfo Graziani and those who perpetuate it should be stopped from doing so. If someone were to paint a portrait of Mussolini on the side of the Coliseum, wouldn't it be a national imperative to reverse that? We expect such action now to reverse the opening of the "Rodolfo Graziani Park and Memorial" which occurred on August 11, 2012 in the little town of Affile, 50 miles east of Rome.

Since its opening on August 11 of this year, thousands of Italians have voiced their opposition to the Graziani monument. Although the Italian central government must and can do more to close the Graziani monument, here are some of the significant ways Italians have been opposing the Graziani monument:

1. A formal Parliamentary inquiry was initiated in the Italian Parliament inquiring as to who gave the authority to use public money to build the monument.

2. A lawsuit has been filed by a citizen of Italy calling for the dismantlement of the Graziani monument and the conviction under the law of the mayor of the small town of Affile who approved the opening of the Graziani monument in his town only 1,562 people. This lawsuit also names as defendants regional government officials who approved the money to build and open the monument. The lawsuit states that under the Italian constitution as well as its criminal laws, it is unlawful to build a monument in honor of a Fascist.

3. The President of the province of Rome, Nicola Zingaretti, has denounced the building and opening of the Graziani monument. He has promised to dismantle it and is now running for Governor of Lazio, the region where the monument was erected. Presently, Mr. Zingaretti is delegate to the European Union from Italy as well.

Global Alliance for Justice: The Ethiopian Cause,
4002 Blacksmith Drive, Garland, TX 75044, U.S.A.

4. Two public demonstrations in the town of Affile and one in the capital of Rome have taken place to denounce the Graziani monument. The group includes Ethiopians in Italy as well as veterans who fought against Musssolini and Graziani in Italy.

5. The Graziani monument has been forced to close on several occasions due to opponents writing on the walls denouncing its construction and urging all to remember the victims of Fascism and not to honor a war criminal. One recent artist posted hanging cardboard figures around the Graziani monument with each figure detailing the crimes against Ethiopians, Libyans and fellow Italians committed by Graziani.

6. In Bologna, a town in northern Italy, a public toilet was satirically "converted" into the Graziani monument meaning that the only worthwhile dedication to this war criminal is for using it as a toilet.

7. Many major Italian publications online and in print have denounced the building of the Graziani monument.

8. The largest Jewish organization in Italy has denounced the building

of the Graziani monument and has called on the government to dismantle it.

9. Here in America, a gathering of Italians during late January and early February of 2013 in New York City will remember all victims of Italian Fascism with a special panel discussion on January 31 specifically focused on the Graziani monument. Leading Italian journalists will join an Ethiopian scholar on that panel.

10. Also in America, activists of Italian heritage have teamed up with Ethiopians, Jews and all people who seek justice to denounce the Graziani monument and have it dismantled. One of those Italian-Americans is Nicola Antonio DeMarco, J.D of New York who works with the Global Alliance for Justice, the Ethiopian Cause. He previously served with Dr. Richard Pankhurst on the Axum Obelisk Return Committee. On February 19, 2013, the 76th anniversary of the Graziani massacre, Italians will join Ethiopians and people of good will in front of the Italian mission to the United Nations in New York City to denounce the opening of the Graziani monument. Thirty other cities worldwide will hold similar demonstrations.

11. The Ethiopian Community in Italy, headed by Ms. Muluwork Ayele has been active in denouncing the Graziani monument. She has also met with Jewish descendents of victims of Fascism in Italy to discuss their common goal to dismantle the Graziani monument. Ms. Ayele communicates daily with Italian-American activists as well updating all on the latest.

12. After the Graziani monument was opened, the entire regional government of Lazio where the small town of Affile lies, was forced to resign due to a massive corruption scandal. The former governor, Polvernini, who was also part of that mass resignation later claimed she was against the authorization of public money to build the Graziani monument and that if she could have done anything to stop its opening, she would have. Very few people believe her story but even in her lying we can see that there is no public official in Italy, except the mayor of Affile, willing to defend using over 130,000 Euros to build a monument to a convicted war criminal and Fascist.

13. Associations including ANED (Italian Association of Deportees), ANPI (Association of Resistance Partisans) and UCEI (Union of the Italian Jewish Communities) have made formal requests to remove the monument.

That town of Affile has a population of only 1,562 people while the nation of Italy has over 60,000,000! A small mountain village does not represent the sentiments of the entire nation. So, when will the President of Italy and its Prime Minster act to close this disgraceful and anti-Italian monument to an enemy of the nation and an enemy of humanity?

Italy must also fulfill its obligations to restore all looted Ethiopian properties and pay adequate reparations to Ethiopia.

Ethiopians and Italians around the world join the international community in proclaiming:"Never Again!" to genocide and we expect immediate action by the Italian government to reverse this disgraceful attempt to celebrate hatred and racism which violates Italy's own Law N° 205/1993 prohibiting the dissemination of ideas based on superiority or racial and ethnic discrimination.

Sincerely,

Kidane Alemayehu
Global Alliance for Justice: The Ethiopian Cause

cc:

Ban Ki-moon, UN Secretary General
Nkosazana Dlamini-Zuma, Chairperson of the African Union Commission
Martin Schultz, President of the European Parliament
Thorbjørn Jagland, Secretary General of the Council of Europe

Annex 5

March 23, 2014

Ufficio Relazioni con il Pubblico
The Honorable Minister of Foreign Affairs, Federica Mogherini
Ministero Affari Esteri
Piazzale della Farnesina, 00135 Roma
ITALY

Your Excellency:

The Global Alliance for Justice – The Ethiopian Cause presents its compliments to the Honorable Foreign Minister of Italy, Federica Mogherini.

Our Alliance recalls, with deep appreciation, the long and historic relations between our two nations, Ethiopia and Italy, and wishes to draw Your Excellency's kind attention to the recent action by elements within the Italian Local Government of establishing a memorial and an adjoining "park" for the notorious Fascist war criminal and genocidist, Rodolfo Graziani.

Your Excellency is aware that on August 11, 2012, a ceremony was held in the presence of a Vatican representative during which a memorial was opened draped in the Italian flag to "honor" Rodolfo Graziani, one of the most heinous figures of the Second World War.

Therefore, we are extremely confused by statements to the Ethiopian press by Deputy Foreign Minister Lapo Pistelli on the occasion of the 22nd Ordinary Session of African heads of state and government summit meeting in the Addis Ababa headquarters of the African Union as reported herein:

http://www.thereporterethiopia.com/index.php/interview/item/1593

Mr. Pistelli is reported as stating in response to these questions:

A few months ago there was a movement objecting to the erection of a monument and a mausoleum to commemorate the former Italian viceroy in Ethiopia during the Italian Occupation, Marshal Rodolfo Graziani. What do you say about it?

Global Alliance for Justice: The Ethiopian Cause,
4002 Blacksmith Drive, Garland, TX 75044, U.S.A.

"For us it is a very old and buried story. It started some years ago. It was not an initiative by the Italian government; now it is over. For us, the file is completely closed. There is no monument at all: no new initiative in that regard. There is also an inquiry from the judiciary in Italy to understand whether some other aspects of the matters need to be explored."

So are you saying there is no monument erected to commemorate Graziani?
"No, not at all."

Mr. Pistelli seemed to indicate that there never was a monument to Rodolfo Graziani erected in Affile. Whether it was done with government authorization or not, the truth is that in August of 2012, just such a monument was erected.

Can you please clarify to us what Mr. Pistelli actually meant to say? Was this report due to translation problems or an incomplete record? Please give us the correct and official position of the Foreign Ministry on this topic.

In 1937, Rodolfo Graziani directed a three day massacre of over 30,000 unarmed civilians in the capital of Ethiopia upon the orders of Benito Mussolini. Over 440 Christian monks were singled out and murdered at the Debre Libanos monastery. People were dismembered and soldiers took photos of the hangings, beheadings and torture proudly alongside their dead victims. The "Graziani Massacre" is well known to every Ethiopian and virtually and disgracefully unknown to the rest of the world. Graziani, prior to arriving in Ethiopia, was named "The Butcher of Libya." In Libya, Graziani presided over concentration camps, used chemical weapons and murdered thousands of innocents for Fascism.

In Ethiopia, one million Ethiopians perished as a result of the genocidal Fascist occupation. 2,000 churches as well as 525,000 homes were destroyed. The poison gas sprayed by numerous Fascists air planes also destroyed 14 million animals and the environment. Gaziani later came to be forever known as the "Butcher of Ethiopia."

Humanity will never forget the victims of genocide under Fascism including those tortured and lynched in the Graziani Massacre.

Sincerely,

Kidane Alemayehu
Global Alliance for Justice: The Ethiopian Cause

Graziani mausoleum being inaugurated in the presence of a Vatican representative

http://www.nationalturk.com/en/why-italians-honored-a-fascist-butcher-general-rodolfo-graziani-italy-news-24058

C:\Users\Kidane\Documents\Vatican Apology\BBC News - Italy memorial to Fascist hero Graziani sparks row.mht

Annex 6

A Special Appeal for Justice and Human Rights Long Delayed to:

<u>ALL SUPPORTERS OF HUMAN RIGHTS</u>
And to the attention of:
Presidente della Repubblica Italiana, Giorgio Napolitano
His Holiness, Pope Francis
UN General Secretary, Ban Ki-moon
President of the European Commission, José Manuel Barroso
African Union Chairperson, Mohamed Ould Abdel Aziz

The Global Alliance for Justice: The Ethiopian Cause needs your help and support. The Global Alliance for Justice – The Ethiopian Cause advocates for the recognition of the Ethiopian Genocide and is chaired by His Imperial Highness Prince Ermias Sahle-

Selassie Haile Selassie, the grandson of Emperor Haile-Selassie I who along with Ethiopian patriots liberated the country from the Italians.

During the Italian war on Ethiopia 1936-1941, the Italian fascists carried out a systematic mass extermination campaign in Ethiopia with poison gas sprayed from airplanes and other horrific atrocities that claimed the lives of no less than 1,000,000 Ethiopian men, women and children, including 30,000 massacred in only three days in Addis Ababa as well as the reprisal killings of the entire monastic community at the historic Debre Libanos Monastery. In addition, 2,000 churches and 525,000 homes were destroyed by the Italian Fascists.

Unfortunately, it is also a historic fact that representatives of the Catholic Church supported, participated in and even encouraged these brazen acts of genocide against Orthodox Christian Ethiopians who were somehow viewed under the dogma of the time as less civilized and not deserving of respect as fellow Christians.

Today we fight on for international recognition of the Ethiopian Genocide, restitution, and against the resurgence of fascist ideology.

Some of our ongoing projects include:

1. Recognition that 1 million Ethiopians were among the first victims of Fascist Genocide.
2. Reparations by Italy for the huge losses incurred by Ethiopia including survivors and their heirs; Italy has never paid a penny in restitution to the victims of genocide.
3. Return of looted cultural property, including priceless manuscripts,

from Italy and the Vatican Library.

4. Dismantlement of the Graziani Park and Memorial which glorifies the war criminal Rodolfo Graziani who directed a three day massacre of over 30,000 unarmed civilians in the capital of Ethiopia upon the orders of Benito Mussolini

5. Apologies to the people of Ethiopia from the Pope and President of Italy.

All of the above projects are underway and include demonstrations, legal claims, petitions, education, research and other activities.

The Global Alliance is a nonprofit entity based in the United States. It is entirely self supporting and exists only through the direct services of its volunteers and donations. We are making a special appeal on the 70th anniversary of the end of the Second World War to honor the few remaining survivors of Fascist Genocide in Ethiopia.

We appeal to all people who believe in human rights and justice to please help us in any way possible by signing our petition (please see www.globalallianceforethiopia.org); by joining our demonstrations/public meetings/prayers; and by setting up a local chapter, writing letters, and providing material and moral support.

Sincerely,

Kidane Alemayehu
Executive Director

Annex 7

www.globalallianceforethiopia.org
4002 Blacksmith Drive, Garland, TX 75044, USA

Annex 7

Annex 7

www.globalallianceforethiopia.org
4002 Blacksmith Drive, Garland, TX 75044, USA

OPEN LETTER

September 20, 2010.

To: H.E. Mr. David Cameron,
    The Right Honourable Prime Minister
                &
    H.E. Mr. Nick Clegg
    The Right Honourable Dep. Prime Minister
    of the United Kingdom, Great Britain and
    Northern Ireland.

Your Excellencies,

Subject: <u>Vatican Apology for Its Complicity with the Fascist Genocide in Ethiopia</u>

A Vatican Clergy Blessing the Fascist Army

Please allow us, first of all, to express our humble compliments to Your Excellencies and your
government for the successful official visit by Pope Benedict XVI to the United Kingdom. It is also with

great satisfaction that I note His Holiness' official apology for the abuse of children perpetrated by some clergy within the Catholic Church.

We feel sure that Your Excellencies are aware of the historic fact that Italian Fascists had committed the war crime of genocide during 1935-41 in Ethiopia where hundreds of thousands of people were massacred including 30,000 people murdered in only three days in Addis Ababa. Among the numerous people killed by the Fascists were two Bishops: Abune Petros, and Abune Michael plus all but one of the monks and all the deacons at our famous monastery at Debre Libanos. In addition, 2,000 churches, 525,000 homes as well as 14 million animals were destroyed. Large numbers of airplanes were used to spray poison gas in urban as well as rural areas.

It is also a historic fact that the Vatican, under the leadership of Pope Pius XI and Pope Pius XII, was complicit in the war crime committed by the Fascists in Ethiopia. However, whereas the Vatican has apologized repeatedly to the Jews for having remained silent during the Nazi holocaust, it has so far refrained from performing the same Christian duty to Ethiopians despite repeated appeals by concerned people of many nationalities. For more details, Your Excellencies may view the international petition that has been signed by over 1,900 people from over 40 countries (www.globalallianceforethiopia.org) appealing to the international community to call upon the Vatican to apologize to the Ethiopian people for its complicity with the Fascists.

Your Excellencies are aware that there is no statute of limitation for the crime of genocide. However, the cry for justice in the case of Ethiopia remains unheeded. The Vatican continues to be completely silent.

We are, therefore, submitting this open letter to Your Excellencies to use your good offices in exerting the maximum possible influence so that, with the help of the Almighty, the Vatican will finally recognize its accountability for the murder of the hundreds of thousands of Africans and express its public apology to the Ethiopian people.

Yours respectfully,

Kidane Alemayehu
For/Global Alliance for Justice –The Ethiopian Cause.

Annex 8

ll'Onorevole Presidente della Regione Lazio Nicola Zingaretti
Oggetto: Appello e richiesta di abbattimento del monumento in onore del Gen, Rodolfo Graziani ad Affile.

16-04-2013

Onorevole Sig. Nicola Zingaretti,

Le giungano i nostri più cordiali auguri per la recente elezione alla Presidenza della Regione Lazio ed i nostri auspici affinché possa realizzare ogni Suo buon proposito a beneficio di tutti i cittadini laziali.

Le scriviamo confidando nella Sua sensibilità e nelle Sue autorevoli e condivisibili dichiarazioni rispetto ad una triste vicenda che molto ci sta a cuore e che, al tempo stesso, ci indigna profondamente.

L'episodio in questione risulta deplorabile per le coscienze di ogni società civile e per tutta la Comunità internazionale, innanzitutto perché estremamente offensivo nei confronti di milioni di vittime e dei loro familiari, causate dalle guerre e dalle stragi nazifasciste.

È questo il caso del Comune di Affile, dove il suo primo cittadino, Ercole Viri, ha progettato, realizzato ed inaugurato, nell'agosto dello scorso anno, un "luogo di culto" al Generale Graziani, avendo ottenuto l'approvazione e l'erogazione di un finanziamento di denaro pubblico dalla Regione Lazio.

Il Generale Graziani fu uno dei più spietati criminali di guerra dell'Italia fascista. Le atrocità di cui si è reso responsabile durante tutto il secondo conflitto mondiale, in particolare in Etiopia ed in Libia, sono state largamente documentate dagli storici, dalle testimonianze degli aggrediti e da molti reduci italiani, nonché dalle evidenze e dai documenti reperiti dai ricercatori. Il Graziani, tra l'altro, mai dimostrò pentimento o dubbio alcuno rispetto a queste sue abominazioni, né davanti a Dio, né davanti agli uomini. Né fu mai condannato per quei crimini da alcun tribunale internazionale.

A tal riguardo, fra i numerosissimi atti di spietatezza inaudita, citerò proprio alcune delle parole usate nelle dichiarazioni del Generale rispetto alla strage da lui ordinata di tutti i monaci e i chierici di Debre Libanos, la città conventuale per eccellenza della Chiesa Ortodossa d'Etiopia, ove più di 1.200 ecclesiastici e chierici innocenti, alcuni erano ancora fanciulli, furono trucidati senza pietà.

Graziani dopo l'eccidio non ha un solo ripensamento, né dubbi; l'assassinio dei monaci e dei chierici è per il viceré italiano: **"Un romano esempio di pronto e inflessibile rigore …. È stato sicuramente opportuno e salutare …. Non è millanteria la mia rivendicare la completa responsabilità della tremenda lezione data al clero intero dell'Etiopia con la**

chiusura del convento di Debre Libanos".

Per quanto ci riguarda, come cittadini dell'Etiopia ed insieme ai nostri Padri, ai nostri Patrioti combattenti ed a tutti i Figli d'Etiopia, abbiamo sconfitto quelle forze della trasgressione, dell'aggressione, dell'oppressione e della menzogna già a suo tempo, non solo sconfiggendole militarmente, ma anche con gesti ed atti onorevoli di misericordia e di perdono: non ricambiando il male subito con il male né con la vendetta.

A tal riguardo vorremmo ricordare al mondo e a tutte le persone di buona volontà che: nonostante gli atti atroci e disumani compiuti dagli italiani, la lunga serie di aggressioni, la spietata guerra da questi condotta anche con l'impiego sistematico delle armi chimiche, la moltitudine delle esecuzioni sommarie e tutte le nefandezze dei generali e dell'esercito dell'Italia fascista.

Nonostante ciò, di fronte a questa becera, disonesta, anacronistica e disumana iniziativa, negatrice dell'olocausto e del genocidio Etiopico, dissacrante ed offensiva nei confronti dei nostri martiri e di tutte le persone di buona volontà, voluta dal Sindaco di Affile e dai suoi sostenitori e condotta a termine nell'indifferenza e nel nefasto silenzio dei maggiori responsabili fra le Autorità istituzionali e governative italiane, rimaniamo sgomenti e Le esprimiamo tutto il nostro sdegno e le seguenti riflessioni:

Non siamo forse in presenza, con questo atto concreto e spregevole, di quel reato definito apologia del fascismo e quindi perseguibile per legge?

È esempio di civiltà, di umanità e di progresso recare offesa a centinaia di migliaia di vittime, uomini, donne, civili, anziani, bambini ed ecclesiastici barbaramente uccisi, massacrati, avvelenati con i gas, torturati e giustiziati senza colpe, e ai loro cari, ed invece elogiare ed esaltare uno dei maggiori artefici e responsabili di tali crimini ed atrocità contro altri esseri umani?

È lecito plagiare e coinvolgere una Comunità di persone semplici ed oneste, incline al perdono, di spirito cristiano e caritatevole, come gli abitanti dei nostro piccoli comuni italiani, fra i quali Affile, con atti e pronunciamenti che onorano gli assassini e gettano fango su un'intera innocente cittadinanza?

Che tipo di generazioni di giovani, gli italiani del futuro, questo tipo di "educazione" produce e quali danni contaminanti può costituire il suo esempio su tutto il territorio nazionale?

Siamo certi che, oltre ai membri delle nostre organizzazioni, ogni Essere umano di buona volontà ha chiare nella mente le risposte a questi drammatici interrogativi.

Ricordo che il martirio al quale tutto il popolo Etiope fu sottoposto da parte di Graziani, Badoglio, del loro capo il Duce, degli ufficiali e dei soldati giunti in Etiopia con l'intento di conquistare e sottomettere con qualsiasi mezzo, compreso lo sterminio delle sue genti, la nostra Patria e la nostra Terra di civiltà millenaria, ci è costato più di un milione di vittime e la devastazione del nostro Paese, l'Etiopia.

Illustrissimo Signor Presidente, La invitiamo ad intervenire in questa questione che vede coinvolto e, per certi versi, offuscato l'onore della nostra Patria Italiana e che reca un danno notevole nell'immagine e nella sostanza a questo nostro Paese, non fosse altro che per la mancata vigilanza e la mancanza di provvedimenti da parte delle nostre Istituzioni democratiche in relazione all'intera assurda vicenda.

Certi, inoltre, della sua conoscenza dei fatti storici accennati e della gravità anche morale di questi pur sporadici ma incivili accadimenti, facciamo affidamento a Lei, rispettabile Presidente, affinché un Suo autorevole intervento nelle funzioni da Lei esercitate, innanzitutto chiarisca e ribadisca i sani principi ai quali la nostra democrazia si ispira, esprimendo il suo saggio giudizio in merito a questa vicenda.

Di conseguenza Le chiediamo concretamente di attivarsi insieme agli altri competenti Uffici ed Autorità della Sua Istituzione Regionale affinché il "mausoleo" della vergogna venga demolito al più presto ed eventualmente, al suo posto, venga edificato un'opera che ricordi invece le vittime ed i perseguitati di quei territori e tutte le vittime del nazifascismo.

La informo inoltre che in seguito al becero episodio dell'inaugurazione di quel monumento è subito sorto un Comitato denominato "Affile Antifascista", sostenuto, oltre alle nostre Organizzazioni, da un folto gruppo di giovani di Affile, dall'ANPI, da diverse Organizzazioni territoriali democratiche ed antifasciste, fra i quali quella dei "Martiri delle Pratarelle", dalle Autorità dei Comuni limitrofi come Vicovaro, Genazzano, Subiaco etc.

Tutti questi soggetti, che hanno già organizzato diversi eventi pubblici di sensibilizzazione e che si continuano a riunire periodicamente, hanno già da tempo stabilito di impegnarsi a proprie spese a sostenere i costi ed i lavori per l'abbattimento di quell'ignobile monumento, senza chiedere finanziamenti alla Regione Lazio.

Il suddetto Comitato ed i suoi sostenitori hanno inoltre stabilito l'assoluta contrarietà ad ogni forma di riqualificazione di quell'opera infausta ed orribile, giudicandola indecente sia dal punto di vista simbolico che da quello architettonico.

Rispettabile Presidente, insieme al Comitato di cui sopra, fiduciosi della Sua condivisione con quanto sostenuto in questo appello, La invitiamo a andare ad Affile per verificare personalmente le affermazioni qui riportate.

In attesa di ricevere una Sua risposta e della Regione Lazio, Le giungano intanto i nostri più cordiali saluti e gli auguri di un buono e proficuo lavoro.

Kidane Alemayehu,
Alleanza Globale per la Giustizia
info@globalallianceforethiopia.com

Annex 9

Gajec's Registration with UN ECOSOC

The Global Alliance for Justice – The Ethiopian Cause Inc.

Organization's name :	The Global Alliance for Justice – The Ethiopian Cause Inc.
Organization's Acronym:	GAJEC

Headquarters address

Address:	4002 Blacksmith Drive Garland, Texas 75044 United States of America

Email:
info@globalallianceforethiopia.com
www.globalallianceforethiopia.org

Organization type:	Non-governmental organization
Languages:	- Amharic - English

Areas of expertise & Fields of activity:	**Economic and Social**: Human Rights International Law **Peace and Development in Africa**: Peace in Africa **Conflict Resolution in Africa**: Conflicts Resolution
Geographic scope:	International
Country / Geographical area of activity:	Ethiopia Holy See Italy United States of America
Mission Statement	Pursuant to the International Genocide Convention and the Declaration of Human Rights, and on behalf of the victims and survivors of the Ethiopian Genocide of 1935-1941, the Global Alliance for Justice seeks an apology from the Vatican along with acknowledgement, equity, justice, and fair compensation for the Ethiopian people from all concerned, and for the UN to rightfully include the genocide of the Ethiopian people in the annals of its historical genocide records and archives, in order that this long-ignored and untold story may be preserved, for a future world humanity
Year Established	2000
Year of Registration	2013
Organizational Structure	Non Profit Corporation - State of Texas, USA
Number and type of members:	No members per corporate structure
Affiliation with NGO networks:	Ethiopian cultural and religious organizations
Funding Structure	Donations and grants from domestic sources

Annex 10

HITLER FELICITATES POPE ON ANNIVERSARY

Pontiff, Pleased by Message, Has Cordial Reply Sent— In Excellent Spirits

VATICAN CITY, Feb. 12 (Æ).— Pope Pius and Chancellor Adolf Hitler exchanged cordial telegrams today, causing Vatican circles to hope for an improvement in the relations between Berlin and the Holy See, strained by conflict between the Nazi régime and the Catholic church in Germany.

Sources close to the Pope said he was highly satisfied with a solicitous message received from Hitler on the fifteenth anniversary of Pius's coronation. The Pontiff directed Cardinal Pacelli, Papal Secretary of State, to acknowledge the telegram.

The Pope today gave his blessing to studies in social security to be carried on by Catholic University at Washington, D. C., when he received the rector of the university, Mgr. Joseph Corrigan.

The Pontiff, almost free of the pain that has marked his long illness, granted his visitor a fifteen-minute audience. The rector outlined the university's plans for two new schools, one to be devoted to the study of social security and the other to exposition of the Catholic position in learning and culture.

The Pope was greatly interested and heartily approved the new development. Through Mgr. Corrigan he sent his apostolic blessing to the university, its faculty and the students.

Mgr. Corrigan said he found the Pope looking as well as when he saw him some years ago.

Tonight the Pope expressed his gratitude to the thirty-two Cardinals who participated in services in the Sistine Chapel observing the fifteenth anniversary of his coronation.

Earlier today the Pontiff had given his recognition of Italian sovereignty over Ethiopia by bestowing his apostolic benediction upon Victor Emmanuel as "King of Italy and Emperor of Ethiopia."

Although still confined to his wheeled divan, the Pope was in excellent spirits and read with joy many of the congratulatory telegrams that came today from all parts of the world.

PART 4

CONCLUSIONS

Conclusion

The main themes of this book are concerned with the objectives of a sustainable development, importance of unity for peace and progress and the achievement of justice.

The essence of my experience, initially in the service of the Ethiopian Government, and later, during 1972-2000, with the United Nations, in eight African countries (Lesotho, Tanzania, Uganda, Malawi, Botswana, Swaziland, Nigeria, and Gambia), and two countries in the Middle East (United Arab Emirates, and Qatar) was focused on the achievement of institutional development through an in depth and rigorous review of the mission, programs, objectives, plans, systems, activities, resource capacities, etc. and initiating pragmatic measures that would yield tangible benefits including self-reliance, an accelerated progress and development for the respective countries.

All the countries where I worked were facing severe capacity constraints in the formulation of their respective policies, objectives, plans, systems, and institutional arrangements. The United Nations projects in which I was involved were focused on alleviating these challenges. In some cases i.e. Malawi, Uganda, Botswana, Swaziland, Nigeria, Gambia, and Qatar, my service was for a short-term consultancy (1-2 months) and, therefore, the extent of my contribution was in terms of an in depth review and submission of reports containing the findings and recommendations. In the cases of Lesotho, Tanzania, and the United Arab Emirates, my assignments were for longer periods that had tangible impacts, the most effective of which occurred in Lesotho, and the United Arab Emirates, especially Dubai Municipality.

Among the most important institutional development impacts, those that, in my view, deserve mention are the actions taken by the Governments of

Lesotho and Dubai Municipality in terms of self-reliance by giving opportunities to local, educated youth who, in many instances, took over posts held by expatriates (foreigners) and were able to achieve an accelerated development.

The other major progress worthy of mention was the achievement of a paradigm shift with regard to services provided by the various governments. Instead of the previous attitude of treating the public requiring Government service in a condescending manner, a culture of treating them as respected customers was applied especially in Lesotho and Dubai Municipality. In this regard, Dubai Municipality deserves a special mention as it transformed its policy, objectives, plans, systems, activities, and institutional arrangements to be streamlined fully to promote and achieve the twin objectives of an accelerated development and an efficient service to the public. Among the pragmatic steps that the Municipality took was the fact that it established a Customer Service Center where services were provided to the public in a coordinated and effective manner. Another important action taken by the Municipality was to automate its operational systems to the extent that the public needing its services could have direct access on line. The Director General of Dubai Municipality informed me during my visit in December, 2011 that their aim was to continue extending the automated service to the point that the public would obtain it without having to come to the Municipality.

A related aspect that deserves appreciation is the fact that Dubai Municipality provides a 24-hour customer call service which receives requests/opinions from the public round the clock and takes prompt action as needed.

Another important development worth mentioning here was the issue of gender equality. Here again, Dubai Municipality deserves appreciation for giving opportunities to its female nationals. When the UN project commenced its operation at the Municipality in 1985, there were only 4 local female nationals, with university degrees. The then Director General of the Municipality, Mr. Qasim Sultan deserves the highest appreciation for virtually opening the Municipality's arms for the employment of numerous local, female nationals that resulted in many key posts being handled effectively by them. It was pleasing to note that once Dubai Municipality started giving employment opportunities to local females, other organizations followed suit. It eventually became commonplace to be served by female staff, an example of which is the Dubai airport.

Dubai Municipality and Lesotho were prime examples in one other respect, namely, that tangible impact could be achieved in terms of development through a rigorous effort in institutional progress. In the case of Lesotho, as a result of the institutional development effort undertaken at the Ministries of Transport and Communications, and Works and Housing, in collaboration with the Department of Planning, it was possible to initiate numerous projects including the Lesotho Mountain Water Project which is today generating significant revenues for Lesotho; extensive rural roads and communications services; a new international airport; labor-intensive projects, etc. In the case of Dubai, one can see the evidence that, largely due to the Municipality's highly improved leadership capacity, the Emirate has effectively transformed itself from a small fishing village within a life span to an urban conglomerate competing with the best throughout the world. And all this has happened despite the Emirate's meager natural resources. If proof is needed that good leadership could have a huge positive effect to the extent of mobilizing the required resources and the achievement of a fast and comprehensive socio-economic development, the Dubai Municipality is a case that certainly deserves a close scrutiny and emulation.

It is sad to note that if there is one region that is blessed with huge natural resources including an abundant fertile land, vast water resources, excellent climate, and minerals, but remains a region of poverty and destabilization mainly as a result of poor leadership and the consequent undiminished tension and underdevelopment, it is the Horn of Africa. It is hoped that a new generation will emerge with the wisdom of generating unity and development strategies that would finally enable the region's poor people to escape their desperate predicament. In particular, it is hoped that the Horn of Africa would generate leaders that would facilitate the formation of a confederation or, even better, a federation among Djibouti, Eritrea, Ethiopia, and Somalia so that peace and stability would prevail for the achievement of an accelerated development by overcoming the current dangerous turmoil in Ethiopia and Somalia as well as the disjointed efforts of the civic and political opposition groups.

The Red Sea has so far been used merely as a lane for transportation of goods. The adjacent countries, in the most, see each other as adversaries and competitors. It is time that a fundamental change takes place from such a negative attitude to one of collaboration for significant mutual advantages by establishing a Red Sea Cooperative Council comprising Djibouti, Egypt, Eritrea, Ethiopia, Israel, Jordan, Saudi Arabia, Somalia, Sudan and Yemen.

The war crimes perpetrated by Fascist Italy against Ethiopia have not been dealt with in a manner that meets the norms of international justice. If there is a case of a "justice delayed is justice denied", it is the tragic situation being confronted by Ethiopia. The war crimes that included the massacre of one million people with the use of internationally forbidden chemical weapons, the destruction of 2,000 churches and 525,000 homes, etc. are still awaiting the justice that is owed to Ethiopia for over three quarters of a century. Vast numbers and quantities of looted properties are still in the custody of the Vatican and the Italian Governments and need to be returned to the legal owners: the Ethiopian people. Above all, the complicity between Pope Pius XI and Mussolini is an issue that continues to loom large in the pursuit of justice for Ethiopia. The Vatican has apologized to the Jewish people for its silence during the Nazi holocaust but has reneged from its Christian duty to apologize to the Ethiopian people. On the contrary, as if to add insult to injury, the Vatican has participated in the inauguration of a monument for the Fascist criminal, "Butcher of Ethiopia", Rodolfo Graziani, at an Italian city called Affile.

It is suggested that the main aspects of this book are of fundamental interest to all those who are concerned with peace, unity, development, and justice. It is, therefore, hoped that others will be encouraged to explore the issues further and enhance the general knowledge.

Notes

Chapter 1:
1   At Dr. Kiderlen's farewell party, Lesotho's Minister of Works made some glowing remarks about him. Dr. Kiderlen came to where I was standing and asked if I took note of the Minister's statement. He seemed taken aback when I told him that I had written the speech! I suppose that it finally dawned on him that he was being removed with grace.

2   Alemayehu, Kidane, "Preliminary Report", July, 1976

3   Ibid, p.13

4   World Bank, "Project Performance Assessment Report, Lesotho Highlands Water Project, Phase 1B", April 6, 2010

Chapter 2
1   CDA, "CAPITAL DEVELOPMENT PROGRAMME PROFILE", 2008,

2   UN Project URT/77/163, (Alemayehu, Kidane), "Report on Proposed Functions of the Minister of State's Office, (President's Office)", 1981.

3   Ibid, p. 1

Chapter 3
1   United Nations Centre for Human Settlements/HABITAT, "Manpower Plan and Development Strategy for The Human Settlement Sector in Uganda"; November 1981; pp. 1-67+attachments.

2   Ibid, pp. 15-16

3   Op.cit. p. 24

4   Op.cit. pp. 30/31

5   Ministry of Education, "The Reconstruction and Rehabilitation of Formal Education in Uganda", 1980

6   Ministry of Planning and Economic Development, High level manpower survey, 1967 and Analysis of Requirements 1967-81

7   UNESCO, Technical and Technological Manpower Survey (serial No. 868/BMS.RD/APS, October 1968

8   Ministry of Public Service and Cabinet Affairs, June 1979

9   James, John R., "Proposed UNDP/UNCHS Co-operation with the Government of Republic of Uganda for the Training of Manpower in Physical Planning", February, 1980

10   United Nations Centre for Human Settlements/HABITAT, "Manpower Plan and Development Strategy for the Human Settlements Sector in Uganda", November, 1981

11   Ibid, "Table 7", pp 54 (1-6)

12   Schuler, Feronard (UNDP Resident Representative a.i. in Uganda) letter to Dr. A. Ramachaurdran, Executive Director of UNCHS, November 16, 1981.

Chapter 4

Chapter 5

1   www.resimsakla.com

2   Daniel Biau, June 2013

3   Qassim Sultan, "The Years of Construction & Transformation"

4   Government of Dubai Statistics Center, "Population Bulletin Emirate of Dubai 2010", p.1

5   www.dubainight.com

6   Dubai Municipality, Organization Chart, 1986

7   Qassim Sultan, "The Yeas of Construction & Transportation, p. 353

8   Ibid., p. 35

9   Ibid., p.40

10   Dubai Municipality

Chapter 6

1   Mesfin Wolde-Mariam, "The Horn of Africa: Conflict and Poverty", 1999, pp.68-69

2   German Foreign Policy Strategy on the Horn of Africa, website update, January 2004

3   For a more comprehensive study and analysis of the cultural traits of the people in the Horn of Africa using objective criteria, please see Donald Levine's "Greater Ethiopia", pp 47-64.

4   Pankhurst , Richard, "The Ethiopian Borderlands", p.1

5   Naville, E. "The Tomb of Hatshopsitu, Her Life and Monuments", 1906, p.26 (cited by Sergew Hable Sellassie op.cit., p.21

6   Sergew Hable Sellassie, "Ancient and Medieval Ethiopian History to 1270", 1972, p.25

7   Sergew Hable Sellassie, "Ancient and Medieval Ethiopian History to 1270", 1972, p.22

8   Ibid. p.64

9   Ibid. p.80 (cited from H. von Wissman, "Himyar", p.191

10 Ibid. p.121

11 Miles, S.B., "The Countries and Tribes of the Persian Gulf", p.24

12 Levine, Donald N., "Greater Ethiopia", 1974, p.7

13 Kendie, Daniel, "The Five Dimensions of The Eritrean Conflict, 1941-2004", p. 5

14 Ibid. p.7

15 Sergew Hable Sellassie, "Ancient and Medieval Ethiopian History to 1270", 1972, p.128-137

16 Miles, S.B., "The Countries and Tribes of the Persian Gulf", p.24

17 Ibid. pp.135-154

18 Ibid. pp.155-157

19 Ibid. p181

20 Ibid. pp.182-186

21 Ibid. p.195

22 Ibid. p.141

23 The Holy Bible, New Testament, The Acts, Chapter 8:26-40

24 Op.cit. p.239

25 Taddesse Tamrat, "Church and State in Ethiopia, 1270-1527", 1972

26 Ibid. p. 255

27 Ibid. p. 262

28 Rubenson, Sven, "The Survival of Ethiopian Independence", 1976, p.311, citing Donia, "Ismail"

29 Ibid. p.324

30 Ibid. p.356

31 Ibid. p.362; Source: Giglio, "Ethiopia-Mar Rosso", Vol. I, pp335-54, 369-83

32 Ibid. p.231: cited from Lejean, Theodore II, p.160

33 Tampa Declaration, 2002 (from the Institute on Black Life, University of South Florida website)

34 Mesfin Wolde-Mariam, "Yekehedet Qulqulet", EC 1996, pp 120 and 171

35 Daniel Kendie, "Problems and Prospects for a Horn of Africa Confederation", 2002

36 Lefebvre, Jeffery A., "Arms for the Horn," 1991, p.270

37 Ibid. p.274

38 Mesfin Wolde-Mariam, "The Horn of Africa-Conflict and Poverty", 1999, p.84

39 Ibid. pp.95-96

40 Ibid. p.79

41 Kidane, Alemayehu,"Turn from the Brink-an Opportunity for Eritrea, Ethiopia and the International Community", 2001

42 Cited by Lefebvre, Jeffrey A., "Arms for the Horn", 1991, p.3

43 Tesfatsion Medhanie, "Ethiopia, Eritrea and Confederal Union", 1993

Chapter 7

Chapter 8

Chapter 9

1 Tekletsadeq Mekuria, "Atse Minelik Enna YeEthiopia Adnnet" (in Amharic), p. 54

2 Pankhurst, Richard, "Sylvia Pankhurst, Counsel for Ethiopia", p. 13

3. Wikpedia:

4 Kali-Nyah, Imani, "Italy's War Crimes in Ethiopia 1935-1941", p. 112"

5 Gnogno, Paulos, "Ye Ethiopianna Ye Italia Tornet", (in Amharic; English translation: The Italo-Ethiopian War), p.225

6 Emperor Haile Selassie I, Hiywotenna Ye Ethiopia Ermeja" (in Amharic; English translation: My Life and Ethiopian's Progress), 1929 EC, (Ethiopian Calendar) p. 255

7 Ibid, p. 244

8 Sbacchi, Alberto, "Ethiopia Under Mussolini-Fascism and the Colonia Experience", p.47

9 Ibid, p. 52

10 Campbell, Ian, "III-Gotten Gains", p. 164

11 Beyene Mogus and Sosenna Demesse," "Mot Yalgetaw Guzo") (Amharic) translation: (A Journey not Thwarted by Death); 2012, p. 56"

12 Alemayehu, Kidane, "Sylvia Pankhurst, Englizawituwa yeEthiopia

Jegna' in Amharic, 20 (translation: Sylvia Pankhurst, the British Ethiopian heroine)

13 Pankhurst, Richard, "Sylvia Pankhurst, Consul for Ethiopia', 2003

14 Arahartley, "African-American Participation in the Italo-Ethiopian War", 2012

15 Negussay Ayele, "African-Americans and Ethiopia on the Eve of the Fascist Invasion"

16 Campbell, Ian, "The Plot to Kill Graziani", p. 273

17   www.globalallianceforethiopia.org

18 Mockler Anthon, "Haile Selassie's War", p. 34

19 Campbell, Ian, "The Plot to Kill Graziani", p. 165

20 Op. cit. pp200-380

Chapter 10

1   Manhattan, Avro, "The Vatican in World Policies", 1947;

2   Gardini, T.L., "Towards the New Italy";

3   Tuling, "The Pope in Politics";

4   Salvemini, Gaetano, "Il Vatican eil Fasismo"

5   Corriere della Sera, January 10, 1938;

6   Manchester Guardian, February 12, 1929;

7   Sbacchi, Alberto, "Ethiopia Under Mussolini", p. 123;

8   Ibid, p.124;

9   New York Times, February 1937;

10   Retta, Zewdie, "YeQedamawi Haile Selassie Mengist", 2012;

11   G/Amanuel, Mikre-Sellassie, "Church and Missions in Ethiopia During The Italian Occupation" 2014, p. 148.

12   G/Ammanuel, Kesis; Dr. Mikre-Sellassie, "Church and Mission in Ethiopia During The Italian Occupation", 2014, p. 149.